TRISTRAM RILEY-SMITH worked as a journalist before going to Cambridge University, where he completed a PhD in social anthropology. In 2002, he took up a three-year posting to the British Embassy in Washington, DC, and has spent much of the first decade of the twenty-first century gathering and analysing material for *The Cracked Bell*. He has lectured on the anthropology of art at the Smithsonian Institution and contributed to *A Dictionary of Classical Reference in English Poetry*, *Travellers' Dictionary of Quotations* and Macmillan's *Encyclopaedia of Art*. He is a Fellow of the Royal Society of Arts and a member of the British-American Pilgrims Society. He is married with three sons.

Gaby & David,
with love & warmest regards

THE CRACKED BELL

Tristram
3. i. 10

TRISTRAM RILEY-SMITH

Constable • London

Constable & Robinson Ltd
3 The Lanchesters
162 Fulham Palace Road
London W6 9ER
www.constablerobinson.com

First published in the UK by Constable,
an imprint of Constable & Robinson Ltd, 2010

A copy of the British Library Cataloguing in
Publication Data is available from the British Library

ISBN: 978-1-84901-104-4

Typeset by TW Typesetting, Plymouth, Devon
Printed and bound in the EU

'. . . so far as my knowledge goes the United States stands out as preeminently the "Land of Contrasts" – the land of stark, staring, and stimulating inconsistency; at once the home of enlightenment and the happy hunting ground of the charlatan and the quack; a land in which nothing happens but the unexpected; the home of Hyperion, but no less the haunt of the satyr; always the land of promise, but not invariably the land of performance; a land which may be bounded by the aurora borealis, but which has also undeniable acquaintance with the flames of the bottomless pit; a land which is laved at once by the rivers of Paradise and the leaden waters of Acheron'.

James Fullarton Muirhead, *The Land of Contrasts:*
A Briton's View of His American Kin,
Boston: Lamson, Wolffe and Co., 1898

'"Why do you speak of certain reversals – machinery connected wrong, for instance, as being *ass backwards*? I can't understand that. Ass usually *is* backwards, right? You ought to be saying *ass forwards*, if backwards is what you mean."

"Uh," sez Slothrop.

"This is only one of many American Mysteries," Säure sighs, "I wish somebody could clear up for me."'

Thomas Pynchon, *Gravity's Rainbow*,
New York: Viking Press, 1973

Contents

Acknowledgements

The number of people who have contributed to the making of *The Cracked Bell* is legion. Many were nameless voices encountered along the American Way; many others have chosen to remain incognito, but they know – I hope – how much I have appreciated their contribution. I owe a particular debt to Graham Baker, who not only started the process off in January 2002 by pointing me to Geoffrey Gorer's work, but also provided encouragement and criticism as each draft chapter emerged. I am grateful to two British ambassadors, Christopher Meyer and David Manning, for tolerating my presence in their embassy, and through them I extend my thanks to all their staff – and my former colleagues – in Massachusetts Avenue; a particular salute has to be directed towards Anthony Dymock for his expert comments on 'The Cicada's Wing'.

I am honoured to have received guidance from three of Cambridge University's distinguished professors: John Bell (Law), John Dunn (Political Theory) and my old mentor and friend Alan Macfarlane (Social Anthropology). I am fortunate to have a fourth Cambridge professor 'on the books': Jonathan Riley-Smith (Ecclesiastical History) is a brother who represents a large and inspirational clan that has shaped and influenced my journey through life. I am aware of one long-dead member of this family whose spirit will be looking critically at my efforts: Evelyn Hertslet travelled across the United States in the middle of the nineteenth century, capturing her experiences in *Ranch Life in California* (1886). If Evelyn is a distant presence, the memory of my brother Prosper has been with me throughout this endeavour: we watched, together, those television images of the twin towers falling in 2001; he died a few days later. Through the enduring loss that I feel for Prosper's premature death, I share something of the grief experienced by tens of thousands of people who lost loved ones on 9/11. *Requiescat in pace.*

Others who have contributed invaluable advice as the book has gone through its embryonic phases are, in alphabetical order: James Bennett, Matthew Cotton, Simon Fitall, Harriet Getzels, David Giles, Gaby Grosvenor, Tom Harrison, Anthony Hayward, Richard Hewlings, General Frank Libutti, Ambassador James R. and Sally Lilley, Lawrence Lindsey, Leander and Stephanie McCormick-Goodhart, Sarah Macfarlane, Marfie Mair, Edmund and Sally Rowley-Williams, Irwin and Cita Stelzer, Cole Swensen and Andrew Wylie. I am especially grateful to my publisher, Nick Robinson, my commissioning editor, Andreas Campomar, and my copy-editor, Howard Watson.

It is my immediate family which has borne the greatest burden and provided the greatest support over the last ten years. This book is dedicated to them: the three boys – Oliver, Benedict and Piers – and my beloved wife Louisa.

The American Crisis and the American Dream

'These are the times that try men's souls.'

With this lament, Thomas Paine began the series of revolutionary tracts known as *The American Crisis*. There is something in the cadence and phrasing of his first article that is reminiscent of Shakespeare's *Henry V*, when young King Hal rallies his troops before Agincourt. It is fitting, then, that George Washington had Paine's words read out to his dispirited troops before they embarked on a dangerous mission across the Delaware River in December 1776.

It is fitting, too, that Barack Obama drew on this text in January 2009 when he was inaugurated as the forty-fourth President of the United States. His address was sombre and portentous. The nation was at war and the economy was weakened. Homes were lost. Jobs were shed. There had been, he said, a sapping of confidence in the country. Obama then referred to the darkest days of the American Revolution by quoting directly from a passage in *The American Crisis*: 'Let it be told to the future world, that in the depth of winter, when nothing but hope and virtue could survive, that the city and the country, alarmed at one common danger, came forth to meet and to repulse it.'

Truly these have been times to try men's souls. Obama took office at the end of a tormented decade for the United States.

First and foremost, there was the terrorist atrocity of '9/11': the death and destruction caused by eighteen men (armed with nothing more than box-cutters) crashing jet-liners into those iconic buildings was grim enough, but the magnitude of the attack was amplified by the damage done to America's sense of invulnerability. Smaller terrorist incidents, including the anthrax attack against Congress and the scourge of the Washington sniper, seemed to provide evidence of malign intent directed against the representatives of the republic.

Then there were the natural disasters – tornadoes, wild-fires, hurricanes and the first flu pandemic in forty years. In 2009, H1N1 – or 'Mexican Swine Flu' – briefly fuelled a bout of xenophobic angst about the northward flow of Hispanic immigrants. However, Hurricane Katrina had already revealed deeper flaws in the country's social fabric. The physical devastation wreaked on New Orleans and its environs was dwarfed by the psychological fall-out: the whole country experienced a sense of ignominy both at its inability to act expeditiously and at the desperate suffering of the have-nots in the richest country on the planet.

A third blow to the United States' self-esteem came in 2008, when the nation experienced a financial super-crisis arising from excessive levels of personal and public debt. Credit markets seized up, liquidity froze, banks crashed and, with a recession threatening to turn into a depression, the world's greatest champion of Free Market Capitalism saw major financial institutions become effectively nationalized.

It is not surprising, then, that the raw and penetrating glare from these thunderbolts has revealed fractures and stress-lines in the social fabric of the nation. This has led one writer, Juan Enriquez, to describe his country as the 'Untied States of America', and Barack Obama himself has expressed concern about the conflicted nature of society: '... if we don't change course soon, we may be the first generation in a very long time that leaves behind a weaker and more fractured America than the one we inherited'.

This book – *The Cracked Bell* – is essentially a survey of the gap between the American Crisis and the American Dream. It began as a dispassionate attempt to review the state of America at the advent of the twenty-first century, employing the tools and techniques of social anthropology. It has found a country suffering from an array of conflicted conditions, where questions about the essence of the American Way – profound questions about identity, security, power and opportunity – reveal rich and confusing patterns of paradox.

In one sense, this revelation does little more than confirm Kant's memorable dictum that 'out of the crooked timber of humanity no straight thing was ever made'. However, American culture appears to offer the anthropologist exceptional levels of contrast. Michael Kammen has produced a history of this phenomenon in *People of Paradox* – a book that teems with terms like 'dualism', 'biformity', 'contradictory tendencies', 'the perplexity of unstable pluralism' and 'syzygy' (a word beloved of *Scrabble* players, meaning a paradoxical coupling of opposites).

There are many different explanations for this cultural dissonance, but as I encountered and explored the varieties of American paradox in greater detail I discovered a common denominator: the ideal of freedom. The US seems to be suffering from the afflictions of liberty – a condition emblemized for me by the fractured Liberty Bell in Philadelphia's Independence National Historical Park.

'The old cracked Bell still proclaims Liberty,' the US Park Service asserts in its visitors' guide. Legend has it that the bronze behemoth – weighing in at over a ton – was rung when the Declaration of Independence was read out in 'Liberty Hall'; and it bears an inscription, from the Book of Leviticus, that seems to offer both a mission and a promise for the citizens of the United States: 'Proclaim liberty throughout all the land unto all the inhabitants thereof.'

The bell was commissioned from London's Whitechapel Bell Foundry by the Pennsylvania Provincial Assembly and it first fractured soon after its delivery in 1752. Local artisans melted it down and cast a new bell that gave sound service for almost a century. However, as Philadelphia's *Public Ledger* reported, it was damaged beyond repair on 23 February 1846, when rung in honour of George Washington's birthday:

> This venerable relic of the Revolution rang its last clear note on Monday last and now hangs in the great city steeple irreparably cracked and forever dumb . . . It gave out clear notes and loud, and appeared to be in excellent condition until noon when it received a sort of compound fracture in a zigzag direction through one of its sides.

The crack is as renowned as the bell itself and it is commonplace for images of the 'relic' to be reproduced with the fracture prominently displayed (like a signature on its side, running from lip to crown). It has been a favourite emblem for the US Postal Service over the years, appearing most recently on the 'Forever Stamp' (issued in 2007) that is valid for first-class delivery indefinitely. It also featured on over 500 million 'Franklin Halfs' that circulated as common currency for many years, until a new 50 cent coin was minted in memory of John F. Kennedy in 1963.

I keep a Franklin Half nearby as I write these words. The image of the Liberty Bell – with that deep fault in its side – acts as a Rosetta Stone for me, making sense of those riddles and conundrums encountered in the course of my research. It reminds me that America, early in its prehistory, imported an English ideal of freedom that was tempered and contained by the moral sensibility of the Scottish Enlightenment (aptly symbolized by the fact that the ship that lifted the bell across the Atlantic was called *Hibernia*). However, in the pressured atmosphere of America's 'Liberty Hall', this ideal has been inflated and distorted by a radical form of individualism: it is cracked, like the Liberty Bell, and is now undermining and afflicting the very society that it was intended to underpin.

This conclusion has taken me by surprise. Like most Britons, I have developed a Pavlovian response to the word 'freedom' and spring unthinkingly to its defence. But in *The Cracked Bell* I find myself challenging the place of freedom in a society that attaches the highest premium to this ideal. I argue that there is something almost pathological about a national narrative that is intoxicated by the spirit of freedom while failing to pay sufficient attention to its meaning. And so this attempt at a measured, objective survey has ended with the butchery of a 'sacred cow'.

A corrective is needed at this point, lest I leave the impression that *The Cracked Bell* is a lamentation, or jeremiad, for the twenty-first century. (The jeremiad is little-known today, but some claim that the art-form represents America's greatest contribution to English letters. This product of Colonial New England was characterized by beefy prophecies of social collapse, filled with bitter regret about the moral state of the nation and further seasoned with the hot mustard of puritanical vituperation.) I am no Jeremiah, and a very different vision instigated *The Cracked Bell*. Inspiration, in fact, came from reading *The Americans* by Geoffrey Gorer, first published in 1948. This ethnographic monograph belongs to a genre of European literature that has mapped the cultural topography of North America over the centuries. A feature of the genus – represented by the work of such different writers as Jacques Maritain, Alexis de Tocqueville, J. Hector St John de Crèvecoeur, Captain John Smith of Jamestown and Thomas Harriot – is a focus on the present (not the past), with the author immersing himself into his subject-matter.

Gorer's endeavour appealed to me as a graduate of the Cambridge School of Social Anthropology, but, in truth, the inspiration was more personal than purely academic. There were several elements in Gorer's life-story that appeared to be linked to my own. Here was a Briton who had preceded his assignment in the United States with anthropological research among the Tantric Buddhist Lepchas of Sikkim and whose study of American character was made possible by a wartime posting to the British Embassy in Washington, DC. I, too, had worked as an anthropologist in the Himalayas, studying the Tantric Buddhist Newars of Nepal, and, in 2002, I took up a post in the

British Embassy in Washington, DC, at a time of heightened tension and conflict, when the capital city felt and behaved as if it was on a wartime footing.

As these links in the chain were revealed, I felt inspired and compelled to follow Gorer's example in applying the lens of the anthropologist to reveal contemporary American culture. My path would inevitably deviate from his: I did not, for instance, adhere to the socio-psychological approach that he had learned from Margaret Mead, the American cultural anthropologist. Nor did I share his unbending belief that the future peace and prosperity of the world depended upon the mutual understanding and fruitful collaboration of the English and American peoples and governments.

Nevertheless, I sympathize with Gorer's commitment to helping the world comprehend the United States. He wrote: 'Mutual understanding cannot endure if it is founded on delusions and falsifications; it must be based on the acceptance of our widely differing characters and ways of looking at and interpreting the world.' There may be something impertinent about trying to encompass a society of over 300 million people occupying 3.5 million square miles within the covers of a single volume, but it remains my aspiration that the panoramic, synoptic scan presented in *The Cracked Bell* provides the sort of opportunity for insight, reflection and understanding that Gorer achieved in his own work.

I would go further. With Obama's election to the presidency, this is an appropriate time for the citizens of the republic themselves to take stock. The president has described his mission as the promotion of the unity of hope over conflict and discord, in an effort to reclaim and reconstitute the American Dream. The appointment of this impassioned advocate for change coincides with a growing realization that the age of American hyper-power is drawing to a close. Little by little, the United States' global dominance of the world (economic, cultural and military) will wane through the course of the twenty-first century as China and India grow in strength. The US needs to consider not only how it makes the transition with dignity, but also what this means for 'the American Promise' (including the fragile relationship between freedom, justice and equality).

Each one of the seven chapters that follow is sufficiently self-standing that a reader wishing to contemplate the 'Cult of the New', say, or questions of war and peace could choose to go directly to 'The Lattice Constant' or 'The Cicada's Wing'. Only the eighth chapter, with its comparative analysis of the United States and the United Kingdom based on what has gone before, needs to be taken on a full stomach – once the seven American paradoxes have been reviewed. There is no great science to the order in which these paradoxes appear, but the question of identity – the riddle of 'e pluribus unum' – is so fundamental to the life of every American that this seems the obvious place to begin.

CHAPTER ONE

The Many and the One – On Identity

'We Are All Americans Now,' proclaimed the French newspaper, *Le Monde*, after the world watched terrorists fly jet-liners into the twin towers of New York's World Trade Center and into the Pentagon. A fourth attack was almost certainly destined for the Capitol (the heart of America's democracy).

That phrase captured the sentiment of millions around the world who – for a few weeks, at least – were overtaken by an overwhelming sense of solidarity with the American people. It also reflected the fact that, within Al-Qaeda's makeshift in-cinerators, the flesh, blood and bones of people originating from around the world, from every race and creed, were reduced to ashes.

Three arcane words, embossed into the alloy of America's one cent coin, took on a fresh significance that day: '*e pluribus unum*'. This Latin phrase, meaning 'Out of the Many, One', forms the motto of the US and its appearance on the humble penny suggests a truth as universal as the smallest denomination in the nation's mint.

It is uncertain, however, how many Americans understand the words. Some will recall that *The Wizard of Oz* refers to the United States as the 'The Land of *E Pluribus Unum*'. It is unlikely, though, that many stop to scrutinize these thirteen letters as they go about the rush of business – and Americans are almost always in a rush. It is telling that the National Endowment for the Humanities has funded an '*E Pluribus*

Unum Project' that aims to support students and teachers 'who wish to examine the attempt to make "one from many" in three critical decades of American life'. The project explains how John Adams, Thomas Jefferson and Benjamin Franklin devised this linguistic formula in response to tasking by the Continental Congress, the first national government of the United States; and they did so, if history is to be believed, on that most auspicious of days, 4 July 1776.

It may be a coincidence, but their composition chimes with a line from a Latin poem written almost 2,000 years earlier. In 'Moretum' ('The Salad'), the Roman poet Virgil records the humdrum life of a ploughman called Symilus and describes him preparing his morning meal – a compôte of garlic root, coriander seed, parsley, cheese and salt:

> Then everything he equally doth rub
> I' th' mingled juice. His hand in circles moves:
> Till by degrees they one by one lose
> Their proper powers,
> And out of many comes
> A single colour, not entirely green
> Because the milky fragments this forbid,
> Nor showing white as from the milk because
> That colour's altered by so many herbs.

The intent of Adams, Jefferson and Franklin was to form an epigram of thirteen letters that signified the unifying power of thirteen independent states operating together in a federal republic. However, over time their words have come to express a perceived blending of the peoples of the Old World into the citizens of the New, making a unified nation from a host of different countries and cultures. The *E Pluribus Unum* Project argues that, 'The challenge of seeking unity while respecting diversity has played a critical role in shaping our history, our literature, and our national character.'

This is a challenge indeed. Is it really possible to form a single American identity, and if so, is the USA succeeding in this task?

Arthur Schlesinger expressed his doubts in *The Disuniting of America*, where he sees a 'multiethnic dogma' that glorifies *pluribus* at the expense of *unum*, replacing assimilation with fragmentation and swapping integration for separatism.

It is true – even in a period that has seen Barack Obama elected president – that ethnic intolerance is endemic in the land. While the atrocities of 9/11 were clearly the manifestation of an external threat, it is far more common for Americans to wake to news of attacks motivated by racial hatred from within its borders. In January 2009, for instance, the FBI charged three young Staten Island men with Federal Hate Crime, looking for African-Americans to assault in retaliation for Obama's victory. This phenomenon is not confined to the hot blood of youth: in June 2009, an eighty-five-year-old white supremacist attacked two of his hate objects simultaneously, shooting dead a black guard at the Holocaust Museum in Washington, DC. The following examples, selected at random from the beginning and the end of our decade, illustrate the variety – if not the scale – of the phenomenon.

In April 2000, readers of the *Pittsburgh Post-Gazette* read about the arrest of Richard Scott Baumhammers, after a 'shooting rampage' that left five dead. The victims were Jewish, Vietnamese, Chinese, Indian and Korean. Baumhammers also set fire to the home of his Jewish neighbour and fired on two synagogues, painting swastikas and 'Jew' on the buildings. His parents – Latvian immigrants and successful dentists – were described as 'pillars of the community'. Baumhammers himself held a law degree and had practised law in Atlanta. However, when police searched his home they found a manifesto for the 'Free Market Party': this draft championed the rights of European Americans, complaining that they were outnumbered by minorities and immigrants. The Pittsburgh press lamented the fact that these killings followed another shooting rampage in nearby Wilkinsburg that had left three dead: the gunman (Ronald Taylor) was black, his victims were white, and police found handwritten references to 'white trash' that denounced Asians and Italians.

Ten years later, an attack in Binghamton, some 200 miles north of New York City, seemed to strike at the heart of the American Dream. Jiverly Voong was a Sino-Vietnamese who had migrated to the United States fourteen years earlier and become a citizen in 1995. He shot dead thirteen immigrants sitting a citizenship test in the local American Civic Center before turning the gun on himself. He had taken English classes at the Center but was reputedly teased at work for his poor grasp of the language. Binghamton (population 47,000) has a racial mix that is 83 per cent white, 8.5 per cent African-American, 4 per cent Latino, 3 per cent Asian and 0.25 per cent Native American. It is telling that a short list of 'Binghamton in Books' opens with *A History of the Binghamton Slovaks* (described as 'a chronicle of one of the city's largest ethnic populations'). The list of Voong's victims, in turn, shows the cross-section of people seeking to build a new life for themselves in the United States. In addition to two staff at the Center – Roberta King (a substitute teacher) and Maria Zobniw (a part-time caseworker, originally from Ukraine), they were: Almir Olimpio Alves (43) from Brazil; Layla Khalil (53) from Iraq; Parveen Ali (26) from northern Pakistan; Dolores Yigal (53) from the Philippines; Lan Ho (39) a migrant from Vietnam; Marc Henry and Maria Sonia Bernard (44 and 46) from Haiti; Jiang Ling (22), Hong Xiu 'Amy' Mao Marsland (35), Li Guo (47) and Hai Hong Zhong (54) from China.

Voong posted a letter (with a stamp bearing the image of the Liberty Bell) to a television station before embarking on his murderous mission. His words exhibit symptoms of paranoia and delusion as he rants against undercover policemen who are harassing him with messages left on his voicemail telling him to go back to his own country; and the letter concludes with one of the few fluent phrases he had mastered: 'And you have a nice day.'

American history is, of course, littered with examples of mob violence directed against racial minorities: Indians, blacks, Germans, Japanese, Jews and Hispanics have all suffered to a greater or lesser extent over the decades, but there are countless other symptoms of the racism inherent in America. There is, for example, something deeply emblematic about the nation's first television broadcast. In New York, in April 1927, viewers watched 'live' pictures of a popular vaudeville comic – A. Dolan (whose given name has disappeared in the mists of time) – who stood before the camera in a studio in Whippany, New Jersey, and told some Irish jokes before blacking himself up and entertaining his audience with 'darkie' gags.

There is also something significant about those plentiful examples of espionage against the state, enacted by individuals who feel a closer allegiance to a foreign government than to their own. There is a distinction to be drawn, here, with the ideological motivation that drew British spies – sickened by a hide-bound class system – to betray their country to the Soviet Union. In the United States, hyphenated-espionage has been perpetrated over the years by German-, Japanese-, Chinese-, Jewish- and Hispanic-Americans who have passed on secrets to Germany, Japan, China, Taiwan, Israel and Cuba.

What, then, are the realities of *e pluribus unum*? How do Americans perceive themselves – as Many or One? Can they claim to be, metaphorically, the Children of Symilus, or is the country like the array of tribes and barbarians that ultimately overthrew the empire that Symilus served?

From a distance there appears to be substantial uniformity to American society. Through the lens of TV and cinema screens, or through encounters with those few Americans who venture abroad, a common identity transcends any differences in ethnic, cultural or economic makeup. A universal American style is projected: an easy confidence; a positive can-do attitude; self-belief and tolerance; energy and humour. This has been defined by Samuel Huntington as an Anglo-Protestant identity, whose distinctive qualities include a shared sense of community, a strong work ethic, individualism, belief in the gospel of success and – often – a crusading moralism. It is remarkable that 80 per cent of US nationals say they are 'very proud' to be Americans, compared with similar sentiments expressed by only 45 per cent of Britons, 38 per cent of French and 18 per cent of Germans. This strong attachment to the nation seems to be affirmed by Organization for Economic Co-Operation and Development (OECD) statistics that show a tiny proportion of Americans living permanently abroad: 1,200,000 – less than 0.5 per cent of the national population. (This compares with over 9 per cent of British nationals.)

Marriage across the ethnic divide is one of the most prominent ways in which a common American identity is forged. Geoffrey Gorer paid homage to this distinctive sense of identity in the dedication placed at the front of *The Americans*. It is to 'Erling C. Olsen, Jr., half-Norwegian, half-Czech, good American, killed in Normandy, July 1944'. Americans have given mythical status to their first inter-racial union, between John Rolfe and Pocahontas in seventeenth-century Virginia, and it is commonplace to hear Americans describe the ethnic cocktail flowing through their veins. The old strictures that forced marriage to 'your own kind' – the world of Puerto Ricans and Italians in *West Side Story* (1957 stage musical; 1961 film) – have given way, at least in modern, middle-class America, to marriage across ethnic and religious boundaries. At weddings like that between Mike (three-quarters German, one-quarter Welsh, Lutheran) and Julia (English mother, Lithuanian father, Catholic) beside a wooded lake in Minnesota you can hear people rehearse their ancestry: Tony has a Swedish mother and a Ukrainian father; Keenan's mum is Russian, her dad a mix of Portuguese, Irish and French. Valerie, counting the countries of origin off on her fingers, says: 'Poland, Nova Scotia, British, then it gets complicated: France on one side; Colombia, Spain, and Mexico on the other.'

There is no better example, at the moment, of this racial integration than the story of the United States' forty-fourth President. Barack Obama has described family get-togethers over Christmas taking on the appearance of a United Nations (UN) General Assembly meeting:

As the child of a black man and a white woman, someone who was born in the racial melting pot of Hawaii, with a sister who's half Indonesian but who's usually mistaken for Mexican or Puerto Rican and a brother-in-law and niece of Chinese descent, with some blood relatives who resemble Margaret Thatcher and others who could pass for Bernie Mac, I've never had the option of restricting my loyalties on the basis of race, or measuring my worth on the basis of tribe.

He believes that part of America's genius lies in its ability to absorb newcomers, to forge a national identity out of the disparate lot that arrived on its shores.

There are, of course, other factors that contribute to a shared American identity. Some are deep and subtle, others more superficial. All seem to act, like the hand of Symilus in the mixing bowl, to merge diverse ingredients together.

Firstly – language. 'People have a duty to America to speak the language,' says Frank, born in Nazi Germany to a Jewish father and German mother who migrated to America to escape Hitler's regime. 'That is the price you pay, the coin you should pay, for moving here.' He worries about poor migrants from El Salvador who live in communities where no English is spoken or heard. He remembers how hard the German and Hungarian migrants of his childhood home – Brunswick, New Jersey – worked to conform to American standards of speech, behaviour and dress. He chuckles at the memory of his German-speaking cousins as they started producing Americanisms – parroting slang was a way of belonging.

Education is another mainspring. The principles were expressed – albeit in a blatant act of internal colonialism – by Thomas Jefferson Morgan, Commissioner for Indian Affairs, in 1888 when he rehearsed the fictional pleas of Indians begging to gain American identity through schooling:

Our only hope is in your civilization, which we cannot adopt unless you give us your Bible, your spelling book, your plow and your ax. Grant us these and teach us how to use them, and then we shall be like you.

That reference to the spelling book rings true, even today. There is a Cult of Spelling in the country, dating back to Benjamin Franklin's proposal for a public spelling contest in 1750. Spelling matches promote a standard pronunciation of words and, hence, a linguistic hegemony. They feature in Myla Goldberg's novel *Bee Season* (2001), about a Jewish girl from Pennsylvania with an extraordinary gift for spelling. The tradition is also celebrated in one of the most successful documentaries of all time: *Spellbound* (2003) follows the progress of eight children out of the 9,000,000 who participate each year in the National Spelling Bee Championship. Here we witness the principle of *e pluribus unum* harnessed and set to work: competitors include the daughter of a Mexican cow-hand who speaks no English (in fact, he is only ever seen lowing and hallooing at cattle); two children of middle-class migrants from India, now living in California and Florida; a black girl from the ghettoes of Washington, DC; a poor white girl from Pennsylvania; a farmer's son from Missouri; and a rich Jewish girl from Connecticut. This may be a far cry from the stories of Gold Rush pioneers resorting to knives over the spelling of *gneiss*, but the sentiment – and the social imperative – is the same.

For many first-generation Americans, progress through the educational system has provided a springboard for success as US citizens. Viet Dinh is an exemplar: in 1978, he was a ten-year-old refugee from Vietnam, washed up on a Malaysian beach. By 2002, he was assistant attorney general of the US, drafting the Patriot Act – the Justice Department's response to the terrorist attacks of 9/11. In between, he migrated to California, attended high school, became a leading law student at Harvard and worked as a clerk in the Supreme Court, before becoming professor of law at Georgetown University. Through the bamboo curtain of a strong Vietnamese accent you can hear him speak with pride at the honour of being an American.

Another formative American experience is the summer camp. This is an important rite of passage and many recall their initiation into the summer camp cabin with its own songs; ghost stories told around the fire; ordeals set by camp counsellors who imbue their young charges with American values; and the first kiss between young campers.

There are also the 'egg-white' festivals that bind the nation together. Giuseppe, an Italian barber who migrated to Washington, DC, from Abruzzo forty-four years ago, says that he still celebrates the old saints' days that meant so much to him in Italy. Yet he became an American, he said, by celebrating the Fourth of July and Thanksgiving. He prides himself on cutting the locks of Robert Mueller, director of the FBI; and now his sons have abandoned the sacred days of his forefathers and it is these American festivals that matter to them. Thanksgiving is of special significance, celebrating collaboration and commensality between the Pilgrim Fathers and the Native Americans. There is extraordinary power to the shared ritual of the nation's families consuming turkey together, regardless of whether the bird is free-range and oven-roasted or – as is the case of migrant communities throughout the country – the white meat comes pre-sliced and shrink-wrapped from the Wal-Mart sandwich counter, to be eaten by American-Chinese with stir-fried bamboo shoots, or by Mexican-Americans with black beans.

Then there is music and sport. Madeleine Albright, a Czech immigrant who became secretary of state in the Clinton administration, has described jazz as an embodiment of American diversity and freedom, becoming the symbol of democratic hope and opposition to communist tyranny during the Cold War. Different cities vie for bragging rights to be known as the nursery of jazz: the truth is less important here than the serial myth-making, since it sheds light on something that matters to Americans. New Orleans speaks of slaves gathering in Congo Square to dance to drumbeats from West African rites (where each spirit had his own, personalized, syncopated rhythm); of the brass bands accompanying Mardi Gras parades and funeral marches; of West African 'hollers' combining with gospel singing; and of the madams of licensed brothels in Storyville who summoned all of the above to entertain at their joints. Chicago and New York have their own versions of these myths, talking about the bars and clubs where white men could listen to black musicians in a tradition that goes back via Louis Armstrong, Sidney Bechet and Jelly Roll Morton to the 1890s.

Blues, rock and soul represent other examples of this phenomenon. The Smithsonian Museum of Rock 'n' Soul (housed in the Gibson Guitar Factory in Memphis) provides source material for the evolution of these musical forms, although it is difficult – again – to separate myth from reality. The roots appear embedded in the Mississippi Delta and the Tennessee hinterland between Nashville and Memphis, where a fusion took place between the Scots-Irish folkways of the Appalachians and the African musical traditions of the slaves, galvanized by the shared misery of sharecropping and the cotton fields. This world is evoked in the Coen brothers' film *O Brother, Where Art Thou?* (2000), but it is Elvis Presley – above all others – who personified this amalgam for those living through the emergence of rock 'n' roll in the 1950s. The reverence he receives from millions of Americans, the fondness for Elvis impersonators and those rumours of his life after death all owe something to his ability to transcend ethnic identity and represent the American ideal. His home, Graceland, has become a shrine receiving over 600,000 visitors a year.

Sport offers another engine of change. The great sporting triumvirate – American football, basketball and baseball – provide a forum for expressing national as well as local passion (the latter exemplified by the ecstasy of Bostonians when – in October 2004 – the Red Sox finally overcame 'The Curse of the Bambino', after eighty-six years, to win the World Series). The *Super Sunday* American football final programme dominates the league table of 'most watched TV broadcasts': only two programmes in the top twelve rankings are not linked to the Super Bowl: the *M*A*S*H Special* in 1983 and the drama of 23 February 1994, when figure-skater Nancy Kerrigan competed in the Winter Olympics against Tonya Harding (whose associates had arranged an attempt to disable Kerrigan a few weeks before). In 2009, a record number of viewers – close to 100 million – watched the Pittsburgh Steelers defeat the Arizona Cardinals.

The patriotism that accompanies these sporting events – a patriotism that gained a sharper edge in the years after 9/11 – is exemplified by the ritual associated with the Super Bowl Final. In 2003, for instance, Celine Dion was chosen to sing 'God Bless America' and the Dixie Chicks performed a close-harmony rendition of the 'Star-Spangled Banner'. Soldiers saluted and were saluted in turn by players who made their tribute to the men and women of the armed services. The accompanying advertisement for the leading sports channel ESPN showed Americans from white, black and Hispanic backgrounds, and from rich and poor, connecting with the game as if to say: 'This is emblematic of our united society. *E pluribus unum.*'

However, there comes a point, in the face of the promotion of united Americans, when willingness to suspend disbelief collapses. The reality is that in Walt Whitman's 'athletic democracy', race seems to matter as much as, if not more than, the race. This isn't new. In his introduction to *Democracy in America* (1835), Tocqueville promoted a forthcoming book by his friend and travel companion Gustave de Beaumont. *Marie*, also published in 1835, is an essay on 'slavery and the plight of the Negro' woven into a tale of forbidden love between a young Frenchman and a white American woman who has African blood; they experience prejudice and violence, and finally gain salvation among exiled Cherokee.

We need to test this question of race more fully. The place to start is with the original inhabitants of the continent: the 'Red' Indians.

Visitors to the UN Headquarters in Manhattan complete their tour in a shop where the goods represent each member state. The bronze spaniel bookends for Britain may be eccentric, but the choice of American Indian crafts for the US is breathtaking in its insensitivity. Woven baskets, dream-catchers and witch-doctor dolls in animal masks are not what America is about.

It is difficult to say when, precisely, the indigenous tribes of North America began to lose their grip on the territory, but according to Francis Drake's account, he accepted the surrender of sovereignty in 1579 from a tribe encountered near what is now San Francisco Bay. It seems more likely that Drake misread a ceremony to appease the Living Dead, since the Indians probably regarded the whey-faced figures appearing from the West on rich and elaborate barks as denizens of the afterlife. Over the next 300 years, the drive of Manifest Destiny and the impulse of what Herman Melville called 'the Metaphysics of Indian-Hating' led European invaders to repel, expel and exterminate those who had occupied the land for the previous ten millennia.

Images of this conflict persist today, even though they are softened by the light of nostalgia. For instance, in 2004 visitors to the Sergeant-at-Arms at the House of Representatives would have noticed – near the folded flag flown on the moon by Neil Armstrong – two canvases by Frederic Remington that depict cowboys defending themselves from Indian braves. This choice of imagery, matched by similar pictures in the corridors of the White House and elsewhere in Washington, suggests that those battles with the Indians loom large in the mythology of survival that sustains the Anglo-American establishment.

Elsewhere, feelings about the Indians still run deep. In Oklahoma, for example, there are some – especially among the poor white communities – who harbour deep prejudice and racial hatred. The state grew out of 'Indian Territory' – a large reservation holding forty-two tribes 'removed' from across America between 1817 and the 1880s in an exercise in mass deportation and ethnic cleansing one more readily associates with Joseph Stalin's treatment of the Crimean Tatars. In five officially endorsed 'Land Runs' that took place on specific days between 1889 and 1895, white settlers raced from a prescribed starting-line to stake their claims in land that was either 'unassigned' or formerly pledged to the Indians. These runs have acquired mythical status and are celebrated in *The Oklahoma Land Run Monument*, billed as 'the largest bronze sculpture in the history of the world', that is being produced by Paul Moore to a commission from the Oklahoma Centennial Commission.

The descendants of those tribes – who have been displaced twice – suffer excessive prejudice from the white community to this day. Bridget is quarter-Cherokee and discovered the depth of hatred for the Indian as a teenager thirty years ago. She was dating a boy whom she adored, but one evening, after they had driven out to a favourite trysting spot, he ordered her out of the car, shouting 'Gut-eater!' (a local term of abuse for an American Indian). 'You lied to me. You didn't tell me you were a gut-eater.' Bridget was so affected by this virulent rejection, that she became a teacher with the Bureau of Indian Affairs and dedicated herself to the schooling of Indian children. In the process, she discovered the harshness of an educational regime dating back to the General Allotment Act of 1887, designed to strip away a sense of identity from Indian children by transporting them to boarding schools hundreds of miles from their tribal homelands.

The American Indian has experienced centuries of oppression. Visitors to the National Museum of the American Indian discover that over 367 treaties were struck with Indian tribes, the last being signed in 1871, but all too often these were overturned with land-grabs by settlers supported by the federal government. For instance, a long-forgotten treaty with the West Cherokees in 1828 identified 'a permanent home . . . which shall under the most solemn guarantee of the United States be and remain theirs forever'. The American Indian is now fighting back through the law courts: as early as 1879, in fact, Standing Bear – chief of the Poncas – gained his liberty from military custody through the district court in Nebraska. He saluted the power of American law when he told his attorney: 'You have gone into court for us and I find that our wrongs have been righted there! Now I have no more use for the tomahawk. I want to lay it down forever.' Henry Buffalo has continued that struggle into the twenty-first century. This large, imposing, Indian attorney has solemn eyes and a neat ponytail of grey hair. He has managed to make a career for himself – in a way that no previous Indian would have been able to do – taking the United States to court over broken promises and winning back, for instance, the right that tribes had to hunt freely on land outside their reservations.

There are numerous examples of a renaissance among America's 2.4 million Indians. In California, for instance, Washoe Indians are challenging rock-climbers who clamber over Cave Rock by Lake Tahoe. This ancient site has a sacred power for the Indians which, they claim, is being drained away by Americans who believe they have a God-given right to 'recreate' themselves on federal land. In New Mexico, the Taos Pueblo once used violence to protect their interests and suffered grim retribution for the assassination of the American governor; now they are boxing clever in their bid to wrest Blue Lake away from the administrators of Kit Carson State Forest. They are using the Constitution to their advantage, arguing that they should have exclusive access to the space on the grounds of religious freedom: the Taos believe that they originated from this lake, and once a year they make the three-day journey to worship there.

In 2009 there were 564 Indian tribes who enjoyed official recognition; and another 220 or so were bidding for this status from the federal government. The sovereignty of large tracts of the country could be returned to the indigenous tribes, creating separate nations who would have a governmental relationship with the United States. Their populations are eligible to receive federal funds for housing, education and health, but they are exempt from state and local laws. Under these conditions, local economies can grow up that transcend the impoverished farmland to which so many tribes were confined. In some cases, they have discovered mineral wealth beneath the barren soil. Elsewhere, casinos have sprung up: Henry Buffalo welcomes this, saying it not only reflects a traditional Indian interest in gambling, but creates conditions where the Indian can rub shoulders as an equal (or even as an employer) with the local 'rednecks' who have too often regarded them as worthless and work-shy.

One Indian community has long enjoyed the privileges of tribal identity. Acoma Pueblo sits on a New Mexico mesa beyond a dusty plain that is filled with knuckles and fingers of ancient sandstone. It claims to be the oldest, continuously inhabited settlement in the States. There is an archaic quality to the path that climbs in deep silence to the tabletop sanctuary: steps and handholds are worn into the stone, overlooked by wind-carved anthropomorphic formations and guarded by huge boulders that appear to defy gravity as they balance on needles of rock. In this setting, the visitor begins to comprehend why the Indian feels himself to be at one with the land. 'When we die,' Orlando, the guide, explains, 'we are replanted – not buried – in the ground.' He leads you to the cemetery, which contains three layers of the dead, held in soil ceremonially carried from the valley below by the women of the Pueblo. The surrounding walls of this graveyard are topped with bullet-shaped clay heads, scored with harsh gashes for eyes and mouth: these are warriors guarding the dead. One wall is pierced with a hole, installed to allow the return of the spirits of eight children taken away by Spaniards over 300 years ago.

Orlando is an elder of the village, who enjoys talking about the ways of his people. Theirs is a matrilineal system, he says. Women propose to men, and property passes through the female line. The child of an Acoma woman is always an Acoma, and so the community contains children fathered by Spanish, Anglo and African-American men. Problems arise, Orlando said, if an Acoma man marries a woman from one of the patrilineal Indian tribes, such as the Sioux: because their children can claim neither an Acoma nor a Sioux identity. They are outcast.

The Acoma Pueblo retains its distinctive identity in other ways: their language, a form of Keresan, has been preserved; they till fields in the canyons in traditional style, growing 'three sisters' (corn, squash, beans) and 'two brothers' (tobacco and cotton); the women make pottery that is distinctively theirs, painted in black and white stripes, burnt umber and red, using designs passed down from generation to generation. The

Antelope clan dominates: the others (such as Pumpkin, Water, Eagle, Road-Runner and Salt) must seek the Antelopes' approval for any significant actions taken in the village.

Each clan has a *kiva* – a ritual chamber of the greatest importance, reached by a ladder that extends out of the flat roof to 'pierce the sky'. This is where the men gather. Orlando's *kiva* has a generator and satellite TV, and is packed out whenever football matches are on! Acoma's church is built over a *kiva*, Orlando said. It has thick adobe walls, beautiful proportions and a flat roof, with strong horizontal beams. It is filled with a symbolism that connects with the Indian tradition and – according to Orlando – subverts the Christian tradition. The altarpiece is dedicated to St Esteban, the village's patron saint, and bears images sacred to the Indians – sun, moon and stars.

So the oldest settlement in the US encapsulates a system of myths and values profoundly different from the American norm. Across the nation, there are native communities like Acoma asserting this alternative tradition. There is, today, a sense of these Indians rising to their feet, regaining their pride and asserting their ways. You experience this in Acoma and you experience it at the National Museum of the American Indian which opened on the National Mall in Washington, DC, in September 2004. Over 15 per cent of the $215 million cost came from Indian tribes, largely from casino profits. The building faces the Capitol and seems to project the tribal histories, with their tales of suppression, oppression and broken promises, directly into the heart of the legislature.

But the American Indian represents no more than 1 per cent of the US population. Their voice can hardly challenge the homogeneity of American identity. There is, however, another group whose voice is louder and whose sense of grievance against the majority is no less heartfelt.

Vitiligo is a rare skin disorder that has acquired, in recent years, troubling symbolic freight for those sensitive to the plight of African-Americans. It involves an attack by the body's immune system on cells responsible for skin pigmentation, causing dark skin to lose its colour. This condition gained notoriety after 1993, when Michael Jackson, the 'King of Pop' and one the most famous African-Americans in the world, blamed vitiligo for his transformation from a black to a white man. There has, of course, been speculation that Jackson suffered from a body dysmorphic disorder – a psychological condition where the sufferer hates his own appearance: the cover of his album *Bad* (1987), for instance, portrayed him not just with whitened skin but also straightened hair and a restructured nose that seemed to deny his African pedigree. Following Jackson's death in July 2009, questions remain as to why this extraordinary performer subjected his self-image to so many changes. Was he simply a victim of disease? Or was this a flight from blackness – a symptom of a deeper, social dis-ease? In this latter interpretation, Jackson's vitiligo becomes a metaphor for the endemic racism that has been attacking skin pigmentation in the American body politic ever since 160 million Africans (between the sixteenth and eighteenth centuries) were taken into captivity and transported across the Atlantic as slaves.

No one living in the US can fail to sense the reservoir of despair and loss that lies dammed up behind the country's 30 million African-Americans. Little instances, small pixels of experience, build a picture in the course of even a brief sojourn in the country. In a plantation outside New Orleans, for instance, you can read a nineteenth-century probate that lists slaves among the chattels: an old man in his eighties and a middle-aged slave with one arm were worth no more than $50; young nubile girls (good breeding stock) were worth $200 or more; sturdy men in their thirties were worth $500–$750; while skilled artisans such as bricklayers, carpenters and coach-builders were most valued at $1,000–$1,500 (equivalent to $28,000–$42,000 in 2009, based on the Consumer Price Index).

Racial segregation has made its mark – counter-intuitively – on many white, middle-aged, middle-class Americans, who are distressed by memories of the treatment of blacks. Bill, a senior figure in the Homeland Security Department, recalls, as a young boy in the early 1950s, being laughed at by the children in his town in Missouri for drinking at the local water fountain; he had gone to the tap marked 'Blacks Only'. Robert, a senior member of the Justice Department, conjures up the memory of climbing into a bus in Atlanta, aged seven, and running to the back where there were free seats; his older sister, aged twelve, beckoned him back and scolded him for running into the area reserved for blacks. John remembers when Washington was a Southern city with segregated cinemas where blacks sat in the circle up above. David Giles spent his childhood in Washington, DC, during the Second World War and recalls a bus ride across the Potomac which reached a hiatus as an old black lady was sent to the back of the bus as they moved from 'liberal' DC to segregated Virginia. Gail – the daughter of a former senator – remembers the cross burning in their smart Chicago suburb the day the first black man moved to their exclusive estate in the 1960s. Wade broods over another cross burning, when a black student became president of his year at Tennessee State University in the 1990s. Bob, posted to a law enforcement office in Jackson, Mississippi, in 2003, talks about a population that is 70 per cent black, but whose political establishment is dominated by whites.

Every city on the East Coast, and many in Middle America and the West, has suffered the problem of a smouldering, resentful, angry, impoverished black underclass. Baltimore, Chicago, Detroit, Hartford (Connecticut), St Louis and Washington, DC, gain – at different times – the title of 'Murder Capital of the USA', with an annual rate that hovers around 22 deaths per 100,000, with most deaths being black on black. (In 2005 the league table was led by Compton, California – an inner suburb of Los Angeles – with a shocking figure of 67.1 per 100,000.) FBI agents talk about the impact of crack cocaine in the 1980s. This mix of cocaine with baking powder provided a cheap, narcotic escape from a pitiful existence for the urban underclass, but it is highly addictive and has spawned both vigorous demand and violent crime. In the country that regards itself as the champion of the marketplace, this is free-market economics gone wild and Darwinian. This ghetto existence extends to US aircraft carriers:

the population numbers 5,000 on these battleships, of which 75 per cent are black, and it is said there are areas on the ships where no white officer would dare to tread. Drug-dealing and self-administration are rife here, with the Drug Enforcement Administration (DEA) running occasional undercover operations to catch the worst offenders.

Historically, the jobless rate for blacks has been more than twice that for whites. In 2007, over 8 per cent of African-Americans were unemployed (compared with 5.6 per cent of Hispanics, 4.1 per cent of whites and 3.2 per cent of Asians). There is no sign that this ratio is changing: by March 2009, black unemployment had climbed to 13 per cent. Seventeen per cent of black men have been in prison, compared with 8 per cent and 2.5 per cent of their Hispanic and white peers. The poverty of the black underclass is prevalent in the wealthiest cities. To this day, large tracts of Washington, DC, are regarded as 'no go' areas for the lawyers, politicians, administrators and diplomats who operate in and around the seat of government: you cross an invisible line and in an instant occupy a different universe, where litter-strewn roads are no longer maintained, where houses are boarded up and where you are an intruder. In Ward 8, drug abuse is rife, AIDS runs at levels equivalent to those in West African states and 83 per cent of pregnancies are carried by teenage unmarried girls.

In *The Audacity of Hope*, Barack Obama has described the West Side neighbourhood in Chicago, where the efforts of one man – Mac Alexander, founder of the Westside Business Improvement Association – have helped to create an oasis of wellbeing in what is otherwise a civic desert: 'the community's immune system has broken down almost entirely, weakened by drugs and gunfire and despair; that despite the best efforts of folks like Mac, a virus has taken hold, and a people is wasting away'.

Of course, the elevation of Barack Obama to the presidency demonstrates how mistaken it is to categorize, stigmatize or stereotype the black experience as that of an impoverished underclass. In 1991, over 13 per cent of households headed by an African-American had incomes of over $50,000; over the previous twenty years there had been gains of up to 470 per cent in the number of African-Americans in professions such as accounting, engineering, computer programming, law, medicine, journalism and management. Between 1990 and 2000, the number of African-Americans with incomes of over $100,000 increased 700 per cent (compared with an increase of 188 per cent for whites). The black middle class has grown fourfold and the black poverty rate has been cut in half in a generation. Howard University provides a centre of academic excellence dedicated to advancing African-Americans and there are role models (like Mac Alexander, Colin Powell and Condoleezza Rice) in every walk of life.

Particular credit should go to the National Association for the Advancement of Colored People (NAACP) which has fought to progress the interests of the black minority for one hundred years. Barack Obama joined in its centenary celebrations in July 2009. The NAACP emerged as a response to race riots in 1908 in Springfield, Illinois (home of Abraham Lincoln) and it has been agitating for African-American rights ever since, with some 400,000 members today. The campaigning continues. On 10 July 2007, for instance, the NAACP held a public burial for 'The N-word' during its annual convention, with two Percheron horses drawing a pine coffin with a bouquet of fake black roses.

The distinctive qualities of the African-American gospel tradition are renowned, and there are deep cultural streams running through the traditions of African-American worship. When they were liberated after the Civil War, many blacks adopted Baptism – connecting with a tradition which, like Catholicism, held special attraction to West African exiles. The regiment of saints could be related to the Yoruba and Dahomy spirits; and river cults feature in West African religious practice, involving a pilgrimage to sacred waters where – in a tradition that bears a striking resemblance to the rites of the 'Negro Baptist' church – worshippers will become possessed by a river god and throw themselves into the water. This recalls a hymn regularly sung with intensity and rhythm by gospel singers at their Sunday worship: 'Dipped in the Water'.

Voodoo is practised in many communities of the Deep South, but according to Paul Nevsky – a Parisian migrant to New Orleans who runs Le Monde Creole shop – a relatively small number of the practitioners are African-Americans. However, the African heritage is paramount in the voodoo ceremonies of the Haitian community in Maryland. The Haitians – who wrested power from their French masters in the eighteenth century – have sustained a religious tradition that is close to their African heritage. The 'White Ceremony' carries particular poignancy for the African diaspora: it involves a priest and priestess summoning cult spirits, led by Agbo, to return on a ship to the homeland. The rite begins in a shrine and proceeds to the shore (which, for those who are landlocked, can be represented by a small pond); here, a ship riding the waves is drawn on the ground with white flour, while members of the congregation become possessed by the spirits prior to their departure across the Atlantic.

Of course, black American identity takes particular pride in its tradition of resistance and struggle against repression. Isabella Van Wagener, for instance, was born into slavery in 1797 in Ulster County, NY. After gaining her freedom, she worked as a servant in New York City and began preaching on street corners with the evangelical missionary Elijah Pierson. Adopting the name 'Sojourner Truth', she left New York to obey a call to travel and preach; she added abolitionism and women's rights to her religious messages, travelling in the Midwest and drawing large crowds. In the Civil War she gathered supplies for black volunteer regiments and met with President Lincoln. After the war she worked for the freedmen's relief organization and encouraged migration to Kansas and Missouri. Her motto, 'sell the shadow to support the substance', derived from the photographs of herself that were sold to raise money for the cause. Her memory is sustained by the Sojourner Truth Institute, founded in 1999 in Battle Creek, Michigan.

Her grandson, James Caldwell, joined the Massachusetts 54th Regiment – the country's first volunteer black force, formed to fight in the Civil War with the Union soon after Lincoln's

Emancipation Declaration in January 1863. It suffered extensive casualties when it assaulted Fort Wagner near Charleston later that year: 50 per cent of its strength (600) were killed, wounded or missing. The dead were buried in a common grave. When it was suggested that their white commanding officer, Robert Gould Shaw, should be removed, his family refused; they suggested instead that a memorial should be dedicated to him and his men. The resulting sculpture – a tableau in bronze depicting Shaw and his troops marching into battle – is a masterpiece, one of the finest examples of nineteenth-century art in the United States. It was sculpted by Irish-born artist Augustus Saint-Gaudens, and was installed on Boston Common in 1897. A copy, originally produced by Saint-Gaudens to tour New England, stands in the National Gallery of Art, Washington, DC, and attracts large crowds to this day.

Black nationalism resurfaced in 1919, in response to white supremacist violence against black enfranchisement: Marcus Garvey's Universal Negro Improvement Association (continuing to this day in concert with the African Communities League) dominated the agenda with rhetoric full of pride in the black race and advocating a return to Africa. Garvey said memorably:

I asked, 'Where is the black man's Government? Where is his King and kingdom? Where is his President, his country, and his ambassador, his army, his navy, his men of big affairs?' I could not find them, and then I declared, 'I will help make them.'

Garvey's movement, with its connections to the Communist Party, was neutralized in the mid-1920s when he was deported to Jamaica. However, there have been other revolutionary movements which promote the idea of a national territory for African-Americans, either in Africa itself, or within the borders of the US, such as the Republic of New Africa, African People's Party and the Nation of Islam.

By the 1960s, black anger was evident in the extremist views of the Black Panthers and Malcolm X, and in the riots that flared up across the country when Martin Luther King was assassinated in 1967. The site of that killing, at the Lorraine Motel in Memphis, has become a place of pilgrimage for African-Americans. It is now home to the National Civil Rights Museum and is filled with displays that evoke the black struggle for independence, identity, dignity and respect. There are the stories of Rosa Parks, the tired black woman who refused to budge from her seat in the 'whites only' section of a bus; the young men at the Woolworth's cafe counter, who made their non-violent protest as white thugs taunted and eventually attacked them; James Meredith, escorted in 1961 by armed US Marshals as he dared to claim his place as the first black student at 'Ole Miss' (University of Mississippi in Oxford); Martin Luther King's imprisonment in Birmingham, Alabama; the march to Washington, DC, and King's great 'I have a dream' speech. These narratives are all the more powerful because the history is so recent, and it has been recorded on film and tape.

The town of Selma, Alabama, exemplified the worst forms of racial discrimination. It was the seat of Dallas County, with a majority of African-Americans – but only 1 per cent of registered voters in 1965 were black. Sheriff Jim Clark maintained the status quo through intimidation, discouragement and delay. Martin Luther King's Southern Christian Leadership Conference decided to focus national attention on this in 1964. They marched to the State Capitol of Montgomery suffering attacks from Ku Klux Klan and others; a number were killed (including white activists from the North).

On 6 August 1965, President Lyndon B. Johnson signed the Voting Rights Act. This initiated a new era in race relations in America. A visitor to the country is struck by the efforts of successive US governments to overcome the prejudice of the past and create a more equitable society, through positive discrimination if necessary. Progress is evident in the selection criteria at universities, the political establishment at both local and national level, and public employment policy. This was vividly expressed in 2004 in a photograph hanging on the wall of the Director's Conference Room of the Office of Personnel Management (OPM), a part of the President's executive office in Washington, DC. It shows a black girl looking down with pride at a US flag in her hands, standing in front of the faded blue clapperboard of a wooden shack. Paul Conway, the Chief of Staff, said, 'That is called *A Promise Kept*. The Director likes to draw people's attention to it. This symbolizes our nation's commitment to the African-American.' The OPM makes this promise a reality in its own employment strategy. What strikes the visitor, moving from the streets around Foggy Bottom that teem with the white middle classes, are the numbers of African-American employees going in and out through the large entrance as they take their mid-morning break.

However, these efforts to integrate can achieve the opposite result, reinforcing the reality of multiple American identities by creating new ghettoes. Just as Hispanics are the gardeners and Filipinas are the maids, just as Irish and Italians have come to dominate the police and fire services of New York and Boston, so African-Americans are establishing a preserve for themselves in certain occupations. The official statistics show that they made up 11 per cent of all workers in 2007, but accounted for 34 per cent of all nurses, 30 per cent of all security guards and bus drivers, and 24 per cent of corrections officers.

It is hardly surprising, then, that one still hears voices of resentment and resistance from within the black community. Rap musicians, like Sister Souljah, Paris, X-Clan, P.E. and Brand Nubian can be heard consciously promoting black nationalism. Others, like the Rev. Eugene Rivers III, argue for developing the concept of a black 'nation-within-a-nation'. The very name Nation of Islam challenges the concept of a single American state (echoing the American-Indian 'nations' that have sprung up across the country): its leader, Louis Farrakhan, argues that the United States owes reparation to the black people as an apology for slavery, just as the Germans have paid reparations to the Jews. You catch an echo of this in the title given to a book by Jayson Blair, where he defends his tenure at the *New York Times* which concluded with his dismissal for fraud and plagiarism: he calls it *Burning Down My Masters' House*.

The African-American poet Maya Angelou has asserted that in the face of hardship, hatred and intolerance, blacks have kept their spirit alive through laughter. However, it was a sense of pride, above all else, that Maya Angelou felt on 5 November 2008, when Barack Obama was elected President of the United States. She told Harry Smith on *CBS News*:

> I'm so proud. I'm filled – I can hardly talk without weeping. I'm so filled with pride for my country. What do you say? We are growing up! My God, I'm so grateful. I believe in the heart of every American there's the desire to belong to a great country. And look at it – not just powerful, not just might, not just things, not consumer goods. I mean, look at our souls, look at our hearts. We have elected a black man to talk for us, to speak for us. We, blacks, whites, Asians, Spanish-speaking, Native Americans, we have done it. Fat, thin, pretty, plain, gay, straight. We have done it! My Lord – I am an American, baby!'

In the spring of 2009, for the first time in the history of census-taking, African-Americans were expressing levels of satisfaction with race relations that matched the view of whites.

So far, this review of alternative identities has concentrated on the dispossessed. The Indians lost the struggle for natural resources. The Africans came to the Land of the Free in captivity. These communities represent no more than 1 per cent and 10 per cent of the population respectively and they are anomalous because they never threw themselves willingly into Symilus' mortar. In order to test the American archetype, we need to turn to those who came here in search of a new life: they were the ones ready to embrace a new identity.

This was the view of Frederick Jackson Turner – a young Wisconsin historian whose paper on 'The Significance of the Frontier in American History' (1893) formed the basis for the 'melting pot' theory of American identity. For Turner, the westward-moving frontier was a creative force supplying primitive conditions conducive to a rebirth. He described a 'composite nationality' being forged as old European ways were transformed into something new: 'In the crucible of the frontier the immigrants were Americanized, liberated and fused into a mixed race.' However, it is important here not to confuse myth and reality. Turner certainly believed that the 'frontier' turned incoming Europeans into Americans, but in other ways he was the reverse of a melting-pot theorist: his vision of incoming whites pouring westwards into rough and empty virgin land was not how it felt to the Mexicans, Native Americans, Canadians and others who were displaced in the process.

A similar melting-pot vision was articulated by future president Theodore Roosevelt, who published four volumes of *The Winning of the West* between 1889 and 1896; and in 1908, Israel Zangwill's play, *The Melting Pot*, was a box-office success and has continued to be regularly performed ever since. It ends with a happy variant of the Romeo and Juliet theme: the Russian Jew, David Quixano, watches the setting sun burnish the Statue of Liberty with his Christian inamorata, Vera, by his side. He tells her:

> It is the Fires of God round his Crucible. There she lies, the great Melting-Pot – Listen! Can't you hear the roaring and the bubbling? There gapes her mouth, the harbor where a thousand mammoth feeders come from the ends of the world to pour in their human freight.

He was referring, of course, to Ellis Island – now a national park. The Registration Room is a vast hall whose great arching windows look west to the organ-pipes and canyons of Manhattan, and east to the Statue of Liberty. Twelve million immigrants queued here in the nineteenth and early twentieth centuries, impelled by the two defining motors of migration – opportunity and security. Only two out of every hundred who knocked on America's Ellis Island door were turned away (on grounds of ill-health, a criminal record, or insanity). The rest cast off the past, represented by the heavy woollen garb of old Europe – the head-dresses, the shawls, the thick skirts – and donned modern American clothes supplied by the Immigration Aid Society. Then they stepped out into the New World.

However, there was no melting pot waiting for them. These new migrants were predominantly from two societies: German and Irish (33 per cent in each case). They were, furthermore, joining a country whose 'foundation stock' was far from homogeneous: there were French in Louisiana; Spanish in Florida, Texas, New Mexico and California; English on the Eastern Seaboard; and northern Britons on the western boundaries.

The newcomers experienced pressure to form 'mosaic' communities – precincts or regions dedicated to a particular migrant group, which retained substantial elements of the old culture. A change of costume was not going to be enough. German immigrants, for instance, were directed to German communities through guidebooks like the *Auswanderer-Ratgeber* by F.W. Bogen and through organizations like the German Settlement Society of Philadelphia, which founded the city of Hermann, Missouri – still renowned for its German architecture and wine. Other communities that have retained a Germanic identity include New Glarus, Wisconsin, with its Swiss architecture, cheese and annual William Tell festival, and Oldenburg, Indiana, which resembles a northern German town with street signs in German.

Across the United States, travellers will encounter these mosaic communities. A stroll into Boston's North End can transport you into Naples. There are the old grandmothers sitting outside on wooden chairs, exchanging small-talk in Italian with old men who wear the battered grey trilbies favoured by their compatriots in southern Italy. As the feast-day of the Madonna della Cava approaches, extravagant tinsel crowns are suspended across the streets like Christmas decorations and the heart of the precinct is closed off for the procession. A family sits eating at a large table in a restaurant celebrating a child's birthday or a First Communion: there is that distinctive backslap among the men that remains part of the body language of the Italian émigré: part bravura, part declaration of fraternity, part reflection of authority. This is Italy, not America.

And so it is across the country. Cultural shards form the basis of pluralist America. There are Chinatowns and Little Italys in most major cities. The Russians have moved into New Jersey. 'Czech-town' is found in Columbus, Ohio. There are Mexican enclaves in east Los Angeles, east San Jose and south El Paso. It is possible to identify Haitian, Ethiopian and Korean communities close to the country's capital. In Seattle, the airport shuttle gives out messages in Japanese and Chinese; Cambodians and Vietnamese live on Bainbridge Island; Scandinavians are in Ballard; and a community of some 60,000 Punjabis have established themselves in the suburbs. Mia, an Arab-American, said that Dearborn, Michigan, is like a Lebanese village: some 250,000 Arabs live in south-eastern Michigan, making it the second largest Arab community outside the Middle East. Only Paris beats it. Each year, some 5,000 Arab migrants enter the US through Detroit, with the majority settling only a few miles away, in Dearborn.

There is an intensity to the cultural taste and texture to be sampled in these small communities. In the United States, the inhabitants of a county, a state or even a region display characteristics ascribed to earlier, older folkways. The strong social welfare programme in Minnesota is influenced by the Nordic populations who settled there. At the other end of the spectrum, the North Britons who settled in the Appalachian and Ozark Mountains have maintained a deep and enduring xenophobia: they use the word 'foreigner' in its Elizabethan sense to refer to someone of the same nationality but not from the immediate area.

It is tempting to think that the xenophobic curmudgeon has been reduced to a cipher – a cliché, a bogeyman figure creeping on to the stage in such films as *Deliverance* (1972). However, this is not the view of many white, middle-class, middle-aged men who – to all intents and purposes – personify the assimilation of ethnic minorities in to mainstream America. According to

Jim, a senior FBI agent, there are still clubs in New Orleans that he cannot join as an Italian. Bob worked for Coca-Cola before joining the Department of Homeland Security (DHS) as an assistant secretary; he is an archetypal American: a lean, grey-haired guy who gets up at 5.30 a.m., goes to the gym at 6.30 a.m., trains for the US Marines Marathon, and then goes in to work. He is also a Catholic of Polish origin who described a posting to Montgomery, Alabama, on a project that took him to other Southern cities as quite an experience:

> I was white but Catholic, Polish and from the northeast, with somewhat liberal views. Could there have been anything else wrong about me? I did not fit in to what was the accepted norm. Those people down there are still smarting from losing the war!

In the case of those seeking refuge from persecution, there were even more reasons to celebrate and promote difference, since this was why they had come to America in the first place. The Amish and Mennonite communities of Lancaster County, Pennsylvania, represent one example, but the most enduring and successful community of asylum-seekers are the Jews. Their relationship with America was defined by a letter that George Washington wrote to Moses Seixas, head of Rhode Island's Hebrew congregation, in 1790. Here he asserted that the government of the US was one which 'gave bigotry no sanction' and he acknowledged America as a sanctuary for Jews. In return, he asked only that the Jews should be good citizens. However, the relationship has not been without difficulty. In 1818, Maryland's Jew Bill sought to overthrow a state constitution that required public-office holders to declare their belief in the Christian religion. During the Civil War, General Ulysses S. Grant expelled 'Jews as a class' from territories of Kentucky, Mississippi and Tennessee (an order that Lincoln was swift to rescind in 1863). And visitors to the John Brown Museum in Harper's Ferry will be surprised by a photograph on display showing uniformed ranks in what looks at first glance to be Adolf Hitler's Nuremberg Rally: in fact, this shows a 1930s gathering of 20,000 members of the anti-Semitic American Nazi Party in Madison Square Gardens. The huge icon displayed on the banners is not Hitler, but George Washington.

It is instructive to look at the treatment of German-Americans during the First World War. Don Heinrich Tolzmann has shown that the German immigrants of the nineteenth century had – despite Frederick Jackson Turner's theory – failed to melt. In 1837, the Pittsburgh Convention called together the first national gathering of Germans in the United States, with the aim of preserving their language and culture. This resistance to Anglo-centric ways continued until the 'Americanization Crusade' of the First World War, when German-Americans became targets of anti-German hysteria. Almost every state, and many communities had a 'Security League', 'Patriotic Citizen's League' or some similar form of vigilante group that attacked anything German in their area. Street names were altered, books were burned, theatres were closed and the German language was banned by state councils from schools, churches, telephone conversations and semi-public spaces. Over-zealous patriots smeared the homes of German speakers with yellow paint or forced German-Americans to kiss the flag on their knees to prove their loyalty to the United States. Many German-American businesses, societies and individuals anglicized their names. The first case of a lynching of a German-American took place on 5 April 1918 in Collinsville, Illinois, when Robert Prager was strung up by a mob. Overall, more than 6,000 German-Americans who had not yet received their citizenship papers were interned for the duration of the First World War. A similar fate lay in store for over 100,000 Japanese-Americans in the Second World War.

However, the United States does not need to be at war to trigger heightened levels of ethnic intolerance and animosity. Take the experience of Hispanics living in the country (the number is difficult to pin down, but in 2009 it was over 40 million and rising). 'Latinos' have replaced blacks as the country's largest minority: in 1970, they represented less than

5 per cent of the population; in 2010 this is expected to be closer to 15 per cent. US Government projections see this trajectory continuing to the point when almost 25 per cent of the population – over 100 million – are Hispanic in 2050.

The Latino issue was the dominant migration question in the opening decade of the twenty-first century, with the 2006 American Community Survey showing that 40 per cent of foreign-born residents in the country were Hispanic (i.e. some 14 million people out of a population of 35 million immigrants). Spanish surnames featured for the first time among the top ten family names in the country, in the 2000 census (see Chapter 8 for further details).

The history of Mexican-Americans represents an instructive case study (although Puerto Ricans, Cubans, Dominicans and El Salvadorians have their own stories to tell). After the 1846–48 war with the United States, Mexico gave up territory that would become California, Utah, Nevada, New Mexico, Texas and even parts of Colorado and Wyoming. The resident population of Mexicans effectively became US citizens overnight. They did not fit the classic pattern of immigrants: they did not pass through the border – the border passed through them. As with the Native Indians, they soon found that their property rights and other promised privileges were worthless in the face of an Anglo-American onrush.

Millions of Mexicans have subsequently migrated to 'El Norte'. With Mexico in such close proximity, and with the existence of 'little Mexicos' throughout the southwest, these migrants have retained the language and cultural practices of their homeland. They continue to eat their favourite food (tripe, tongue, pinto beans) flavoured with Mexican herbs and spices. Distinctive Mexican networks of co-parents (*compadrazgo*) are sustained in baptism and wedding ceremonies. They listen to Mexican folk songs and ballads, and belong to devotional societies, such as the Virgin of Guadelupe, which organize the same religious parades and the Christmas shepherds' play – *Los Pastores* – as they do at home. Irish-Americans have St Patrick's Day, German-Americans have the Oktoberfest, but Mexican-

Americans commemorate *Cinco de Mayo* – the victory over French occupational forces in the Battle of Puebla on 5 May 1862.

Today, these migrants provide the cheap labour that drives companies like Wal-Mart; they disembowel cattle in slaughter-houses and pick fruit in orchards; they provide middle-class families with janitors, hedge-trimmers, leaf-blowers and valet-parkers. They do the jobs that other Americans don't want to do. As with their forerunners on the Bracero ('hired hand') Program, which was operated by the US Government from 1942 to 1964, they experience poor housing, inadequate food, periods of unemployment and anti-immigration violence. For many in the United States, the word 'Mexican' is synonymous with 'illegal immigrant'. This sentiment was reflected by angry comments made by David – himself a migrant from Israel – a young cook who had abandoned the hunt for work in New York and was planning his own restaurant in Cape Cod:

It is hell working in Manhattan. You work 16 hours a day and they want more. It is sucking the life from me. And for what? They pay us a pittance. It's because of the Mexicans – illegal immigrants. They will work for $4 an hour. I'm worth $45 an hour ... how can I look them in the face when they are dragging the market price down. They just don't care.

By 2006, the Mexican-American Association was arguing back: it organized protests and marches in a number of US cities, demanding the 12 million illegal immigrants working in the United States should now be documented ... because they want to become Americans too. Meanwhile, there were increasing reports of white supremacists and vigilantes patrolling the border, spurred – no doubt – by headlines like this in Associated Press on 4 May 2007: 'More Mexicans migrating to U.S. than die in Mexico.' Mexico's demographics agency had found that an average of 577,000 people migrated to the US each year from 2000 to 2005, compared to 495,000 deaths a year in the same period.

A new Immigration Bill became the subject of intense debate within the country: the proposal was to establish a guest-worker programme and provide the means for millions of illegal immigrants to stay in the country (and possibly become citizens), but it would also strengthen border security, with 370 miles of triple-layer fencing along the Mexican border. A complicated three-tiered system would determine who could stay and more jail cells would be built for those awaiting deportation. In a gesture that offended many Hispanics, the Bill also declared English to be the country's national language. The Bill was finally killed off in the Senate in June 2007: hours before the vote, the Capitol's switchboard was reported to be jammed by thousands of calls from groups and individuals arguing for and against the measures, signalling its deeply divisive nature.

In April 2009, gasoline was added to the fire by the northward spread of 'Mexican Swine Flu'. The Americans for Legal Immigration Political Action Committee (ALIPAC) called on Congress to close the southern border to all non-essential traffic and to deploy the military. William Gheen of ALIPAC said, 'We have thousands of illegal immigrants entering America each night and we can't contain or slow the progression of the latest Mexican outbreaks with that happening.' For the author of the 'Stop the invasion of Oregon' blog, disease is one more evil to be inflicted on the citizens of his state by Mexican illegals, in a list that includes rubbish-tipping, rape, car crashes and drug dealing. Like the scapegoat of ancient Judaism, the illegal immigrant comes to carry – for some – all the iniquities of the world.

Given the depth of feeling over the issue, it is telling that President Obama chose Mexico as a venue to reaffirm (in August 2009) his promise to institute comprehensive immigration reform. 'We have a broken immigration system,' he told a news conference in Guadalajara after attending with his Mexican and Canadian counterparts. 'It's not fair, and it's not right, and we're going to change it.' Obama wants an amnesty for illegal immigrants, providing a pathway to citizenship, 'so that they don't have to live in the shadows.'

*   *   *

As we struggle to make sense of that troubling formula, *e pluribus unum*, it brings little comfort to know that when the Founding Fathers composed that phrase they harboured no vision of today's pluralist, multi-ethnic nation. Thomas Jefferson opposed large-scale immigration – even of whites – into Virginia, regarding this as a threat to the social bonds and homogeneity of the place and to the genius of the people. As Garry Wills has shown in *Inventing America: Jefferson's Declaration of Independence*, he also wanted to exclude black freedmen in the state (drafting laws for the state that were so harsh that his countrymen refused to pass them). If a white woman like Barack Obama's mother had given birth to a black man's child in Jefferson's dystopia, she and her baby would have twelve months to leave the commonwealth or become outlawed – to be killed with impunity.

The question of American identity is even more of a riddle today. Americans themselves struggle to make sense of it all. In conversation, many argue – with a puzzled and reflective look – that there probably is a distinctive national identity. Others say that there is not, and talk about their nation as a collection of melting pots, or a rainbow, or a stew. Greenwood, the educational publisher, has created a website called 'American Mosaic' to document the multi-ethnic experience. By July 2007, the site had expanded from an original focus on African-Americans and Hispanics to include sections on American Indians, Arab Americans, Asian Indian Americans, Chinese Americans, Dominican Americans, Filipino Americans, German Americans, Haitian Americans, Irish Americans, Italian Americans, Jewish Americans, Korean Americans, Mexican Americans, Polish Americans, Scandinavian Americans and Vietnamese Americans. Germans feature as one rare example of a group that has completed the process of transformation and integration, their distinctiveness almost entirely expunged save for their Teutonic surnames; except in Oldenburg, Indiana – referred to above – whose population of 647 shows a remarkable commitment to Germanic ways.

An example of the popular culinary view of national identity is found on the Amazon website where – in November 2006 – a

user called 'The Old Lady "Just Me"' from California reviewed
Arthur M. Schlesinger's *Disuniting of America*:

> The country was at one time like a rich stew, and now has
> become a bunch of individual plates of foods or ingredients
> that don't want to even touch each other. Each ingredient
> yells out how important it is, and not realizing that carrots
> alone, wonderful as they may be, have not reached the
> potential they can when mixed with potatoes, meat,
> tomatoes, spices and lovingly blended into that rich stew.

This isn't the world of Symilus, kneading his ingredients into a
paste, but the world of *dissimilis* – where difference dominates.

This paradox of identity is only one of several inner
contradictions that bedevil the US today. However, it is a
fundamental issue because it lies, like a watermark, inside the
fibre of the national existence. In reality, American identity is
both First Person Singular and Plural. It acts like one of those
optical puzzles where an image can switch – before your eyes –
from a candlestick to the profile of two faces, and back again.
From one angle, we see the national style that is applied like a
veneer by those who aspire to power, influence and wealth as
corporate members of a new republic of liberated citizens.
Look again and you see a nation composed of idiosyncratic
villages, each with its own distinctive ethnic and cultural
identity. This phenomenon has never been better expressed
than by the great African-American writer and activist, W.E.B.
Du Bois, when he wrote of a 'double-consciousness' in *The
Souls of Black Folk*:

> One ever feels his two-ness – an American, a Negro; two
> souls, two thoughts, two unreconciled strivings; two war-
> ring ideals in one dark body, whose dogged strength alone
> keeps it from being torn asunder. The history of the
> American Negro is the history of this strife – this longing
> to attain self-conscious manhood, to merge his double self
> into a better and truer self. He would not Africanize

America, for America has too much to teach the world and Africa. He would not bleach his Negro blood in a flood of white Americanism, for he knows that Negro blood has a message for the world. He simply wishes to make it possible for a man to be both a Negro and an American . . .

Social anthropology can help to explain the conundrum. It deflates the commonly held view that ethnicity is all about objective cultural differences. The work of Fredrik Barth, in particular, has led us to concentrate on the boundaries between groups, rather than on the 'cultural stuff' contained inside them, showing that there is a continuous flow of people and information across ethnic frontiers. Out of this insight, anthropologists have developed the idea that an individual's identity is fluid and relative, depending on the situation he finds himself in.

If ethnic identity is about relationships, it is possible to see the United States' fixation with the question of race as a struggle to draw comprehensible boundaries around the challenging notion of being American. A political experiment may have begun with the Declaration of Independence; but along the way the game-plan changed (with a massive influx of migrants from every nation in the Old World) and the moral vision of the Enlightenment became eroded and distorted, as increasing emphasis was placed on the person not the people. Today, the Declaration is seen to delineate a nation composed of individuals making their own unhampered choices within an arena where the citizen can pursue personal goals free from the constraints of race, religion or class. However, the magnitude of this challenge is daunting and it comes as no surprise that people flit between two identities – Old and New, kin and country.

Over time – as demonstrated by the descendants of German migrants – the safe-harbour can be abandoned and the familiar channels of the Old World ways silt up. But for some the passage is hard – especially those Indians and blacks who never chose to walk the American Way in the first place. Tellingly, the above quotation from Du Bois concludes: 'He simply wishes to make it possible for a man to be both a Negro and an American without being cursed and spit upon by his fellows, without having the doors of Opportunity closed roughly in his face.'

Obama may promise to fulfil the dream of a post-racial America, but the quest for self-realization and self-definition remains a daunting prospect. The American citizen is required to venture from the security of 'tribal' ethnicity into the realm of personal liberation, equipped for the venture with rich and complex systems of belief, including the articles of faith associated with the Temple of Trade.

CHAPTER TWO

The Temple of Trade – On Consumerism

It is December 2008, Christmas is approaching and a church congregation might reasonably be reflecting on the Holy Trinity or assembling a Nativity scene with the Three Wise Men kneeling before Baby Jesus in the manger.

However, a very different triad stands before the altar of the Greater Grace Temple in Detroit. Three burnished sports utility vehicles – a Chevrolet Tahoe, a Ford Escape and a Chrysler Aspen – represent three unwise leviathans of the US auto industry that are in dire financial straits as the credit crunch bites. Pentecostal Bishop Charles H. Ellis III stands beside the gas–electric hybrids and calls on God and Congress to salvage these businesses. Then the choir launches into a vigorous rendition of the gospel song 'We're Gonna Make It' as the Bishop anoints workshop fitters, company executives and car salesmen with consecrated oil.

Welcome to the Temple of Trade.

Commerce is as old as human society. The exchange of goods is a defining feature of social intercourse. In the deltas of South America, the jungles of Africa, the valleys of the Himalayas, the archipelagos of the Pacific and the souks of the Maghreb, don't men and women seem to trade as they do in the canyons of New York City?

The answer is no. Barack Obama himself has acknowledged that it would be hard to find a country on earth that's been more consistently hospitable to the logic of the marketplace than the United States: 'Our Constitution places the ownership of private property at the very heart of our system of liberty. Our religious traditions celebrate the value of hard work and express the conviction that a virtuous life will result in material reward. Rather than vilify the rich, we hold them up as role models.'

Commerce is indeed different in the United States. It is different in scale. The United States has the largest economy in the world: its Gross Domestic Product, despite the concussive effects of the credit crunch in 2008–09, is predicted to reach $15 trillion by 2010, when the second largest national economy will be Japan (with GDP worth a mere $5 trillion). The nature of commerce is also different. In most societies in the world, trade is about the exchange of goods within a social network, with the emphasis on human relations; in the States, the emphasis is on price and value in a free market with the focus ultimately on the individual consumer.

Commerce has also taken on an almost spiritual value of its own: somewhere along the American Way, the free market spirit of the Virginia Company (the pursuit of Gold) merged with the puritan spirit of the Pilgrims (the pursuit of God) to elevate trade to a higher plane where it is associated with the greatest achievements of mankind. You will find this sentiment beautifully expressed in that most auspicious of chambers – the Reading Room in the Library of Congress. Looking up, the visitor will see an allegory of 'Human Understanding' painted on the ceiling of the great dome which, in turn, appears to be supported by eight pale, powdery, Pre-Raphaelite women personifying the 'Endeavours of Civilization'. There are the usual suspects here: 'History', 'Art', 'Philosophy', 'Poetry', 'Law', 'Science' and 'Religion'. But the eighth seems entirely out of place to a visitor from the Old World: 'Commerce' stands there, no less pallid or powdered than the rest, but her presence is puzzling: what has trade to do with Human Understanding? It is as if a street-walker had stepped in to join blue-stockings at their tea-time tutorial. The European's cultural and moral compass is liable to spin further on reading the accompanying inscription – indeed, it is likely to draw a stifled cry of disbelief from anyone whose sensibilities have been sharpened by the horrors of 9/11. Beneath the figure of 'Commerce' the caption says, 'We taste the spices of Arabia, yet never feel the scorching sun which brings them forth.'

However, the exchange of goods and services is not merely equated with cultured endeavour in the States. It is also likened by some to a religion, as if trading-houses were temples, salespeople were priests and consumption was a form of communion. This twinning of God and Mammon was emblemized in a mural, crudely daubed on a warehouse wall in New Orleans in the months after 9/11. The art depicted an image that has achieved iconic status – three firemen raising the Stars and Stripes over the ruins of the World Trade Center – and a text was written in capital letters beneath:

THE DESTRUCTION AND RUIN OF THE TEMPLE
DOES NOT MEAN THAT OUR FAITH HAS GONE.

This equation of a trade centre with a temple, and commerce with faith, seems anomalous, even blasphemous. Prophets and profiteering do not go together. There is no holy liturgy, creed, ritual or sacred space associated with the business of exchange. Christ drove traders from the temple in an unprecedented exhibition of force, while in the Sermon on the Mount he told his followers: 'You can't serve both God and Mammon.' On this basis, Mammon – the false god of avarice, and the personification of the worship, pursuit and acquisition of riches – should be the antithesis of all that is held dear by America's church-going millions.

However, the muralist of New Orleans was not alone in expressing this sentiment. Take the following extract from the blog of Bill Petro – an IT specialist from Colorado Springs – written the week after 9/11:

Terrorists struck the emblem of US military might and the symbol of American economic power. As in 70 AD when the Jewish Temple in Jerusalem was destroyed, the destruction of America's temple of trade does not spell the end of a people, but it does change them.

It may be tempting to dismiss these effusions as the over-emotional reaction to the shock and carnage of terrorist atrocities. Yet the motif has appeared both before and some years after 9/11. For instance, on 29 July 2001, Peter House, the Summer Minister at the Unitarian Church of Rochester, gave a sermon on 'The Religion of Consumerism':

> I often tell people that I was raised Catholic when they ask me what religious tradition I was raised in. But I really should tell them that I was raised Consumerist. I can rattle off advertising copy quicker than I can the passages from the Baltimore Catechism that I memorized . . . Consumerism permeates our society and in many ways it is the religion of America.

In 2003, Andrew Stephen, US editor of the *New Statesman*, expressed the view that 'malls have become sacred temples, inseparable from the American way of life'; he quotes Jim Farrell in *One Nation Under Goods*, who describes the mall as a place where Americans make statements 'about the good, the true and the beautiful'.

Some commercial enterprises sound theological as they expound their value-laden 'mission statements' – Google's motto, for instance, is 'Don't be evil'. The intention can be tongue-in-cheek, as in this statement from Burger King on its website in September 2006:

> Have It Your Way. You have the right to have what you want, exactly when you want it. Because on the menu of life, you are 'Today's Special.' And tomorrow's. And the day after that. And . . . well, you get the drift. Yes, that's right. We may be the King, but you my friend, are the almighty ruler.

Amway, the leading practitioner of 'Multilevel Marketing' (using a network of 'independent business owners' to sell its products), is far more pious as it enunciates a vision statement that is all about helping people live better lives. Its founding principles are carved in stone outside its world headquarters – a building that it boasts is over a mile long – in Ada, Michigan:

> Amway will always offer HOPE to the individual, will support the fundamental FREEDOM of people to determine their own future, allowing them the time and resources to protect and nurture their FAMILY, and receive REWARD in proportion to their efforts.

The company's founder, Richard DeVos, is a committed Christian, establishing Third Century Publishers to print educational literature for Christian fundamentalists and evangelicals. There are also Amway networks that mix business with Christian prayer meetings. Steve Butterfield, a former distributor, has described the operating style of Dexter Yager – one of Amway's leading salesmen who sold goods worth $2 billion in 1994: Yager would inject a strong Christian element to his quasi-religious business rallies, where the Lord would be praised for bringing commercial success to his followers. All of this has led to the rumour that the company is not named after 'The American Way' (as the founders assert), but is a reference to Jesus' 'I Am the Way'.

The established view in the nation today is that commerce and Christianity go together. Apologists will point to the Bible's endorsement of the ownership of private property: the eighth commandment warns against stealing it, the ninth prohibits coveting it. Matthew 25 and Luke 19 show that Jesus approved of honest workers who invest wisely and accepted that the poor would always be present. Kerby Anderson, the National Director of Probe Ministries of Richardson, Texas, wrote an essay entitled 'A Biblical View of Economics' in 2001 in which he argues that our ability to choose between competing products and services is an aspect of the rationality endowed upon us as beings created in the image of God; and that private property shows Man following God's commandment to subdue the earth and have dominion over creation.

'Christian Capitalism' has been invoked in Concord, North Carolina, where the First Assembly of Concord Baptist Church bought a mall on the assumption that shoppers can fulfil their spiritual as well as retail needs in one place. The *Christian Science Monitor* reported on 9 July 2002 that this congregation belonged to 'a growing number of Christian groups trying to transfer the Bible's message from the pulpit to the retail rack'.

Investing commerce and consumption with sacred virtue is not confined to the Christian faith in the United States. For centuries, Jews have used items of luxury on their holy days to deepen the distinction between the sacred and mundane spheres of life, blessing – it is said – the humblest men and women with a foretaste of God's splendour. However, Andrew R. Heinze has shown that such distinctions collapsed in the United States, where luxuries were routinely converted into necessities: newcomers found that American abundance added a dimension to the holidays that anchored Jewish identity in the new world. On Sukkot, they adapted celebration of God's bounty to include the feat of American manufactured affluence; Chanukah became infused with the spirit of shopping that characterized the American Christmas; and Passover was reoriented, so that this festival of festivals came to reflect the anticipation of higher living standards as well as the remembrance of spiritual captivity and liberation.

Of course, there are those who, like Peter House, look upon the merging of God and Mammon with distaste or disfavour. The Watchman Fellowship is a 'counter-cult ministry' that has condemned the style of religious practice exhibited by Dexter Yager of Amway as 'prosperity theology'; and Bill Leonard, dean of the Wake Forest Divinity School in Winston, Salem, NC, has criticized the emergence of the 'shopping-mall monastery'. But these voices are too still and too small to be heard above the commotion generated by the crowds in the Temple of Trade.

*   *   *

J.K. Galbraith (the leading liberal economist who died in 2006, aged 97) was in no doubt that selling had become a formidable force in the United States by the mid-twentieth century. He wrote in *The Affluent Society* that 'many of the desires of the individual become so only as they are synthesized, elaborated and nurtured by advertising and salesmanship'. Advertising and sales were now some of the nation's most important and talented professions, boosted – in keeping with the pseudo-religious language associated with commerce – by President Woodrow Wilson when he addressed a salesmen's convention in Detroit in 1918:

> Lift your eyes to the horizon of business with the inspiration of the thought that you are Americans and are meant to carry liberty and justice and the principles of humanity wherever you go, go out and sell goods that will make the world more comfortable and more happy and convert them to the principles of America.

There is a view that inherent value sells itself. This is encapsulated in the dictum, attributed to Ralph Waldo Emerson, that if you build a better mousetrap the world will beat a path to your door. In the doctrine of the free market, the salesman performs an ethical job ensuring that the consumer is equipped with information to make rational, efficient decisions.

However, boosting had been a prominent feature of life in the US for many years. A young English pioneer, Evelyn Hertslet, encountered the phenomenon shortly after she arrived in the Napa Valley in the 1850s. The record of her adventures in America can be scrutinized in the Reading Room of the Library of Congress (beneath the approving gaze of pale, powdered Commerce) where one discovers her surprise at the town's undertaker putting an advertisement in the local news-sheet: 'cholera is coming, so buy your coffins now, while stocks are plentiful and prices low!'

This anonymous undertaker unwittingly demonstrated the 'AIDA Rule' decades before it was expounded by E. St Elmo

Lewis – one of the founding fathers of the advertising industry. Lewis, who is memorialized in the 'Advertising Hall of Fame', cut his teeth as head of marketing for National Cash Register Company and Burroughs Adding Machine Company in the early years of the twentieth century. In 1900 he devised his rule: 'attract Attention, maintain Interest, create Desire, get Action'.

Another revered ancestor for the 'ad-men' is Helen Lansdowne Resor – renowned for her work as a copywriter with J. Walter Thompson, the agency that came to dominate the advertising industry in the twentieth century. Her style, which aped the look and layout of popular magazines, has been described as 'aesthetic and intuitive'. A typical Resor page would combine a picture with persuasive copy that contains arguments for buying the product and an offer of a free or cheap sample by mail. Her most famous advertisement – for Woodbury's Facial Soap in October 1921 – shows a handsome couple in evening dress, with the man pressing his chin to her cheek, and the headline 'A skin you love to touch'. It is credited as the first commercial to use sex appeal, with seven paragraphs of copy that told the reader:

> Your skin is changing every day! As the old skin dies, new skin forms in its place. *This is your opportunity*. By using the proper treatment you can keep this new skin so active that it cannot help taking on the greater loveliness you have longed for.

Fewer than 300,000 people are employed in the American advertising industry, but their work imposes itself on every individual in the land and they generate substantial revenue – $220 billion in 2005 (close to the revenue of America's powerful defence sector). Posters and billboards create a grand canyon of hype through which any journey takes us: our attention is drawn to the merits of this product and that service by messages plastered across once redundant surfaces or inserted into once open spaces. Billboards separate the traveller on the freeway from the natural world, as if the insurance policies, white goods or beauty products that they sell deserve our attention more than the prospect of forests and hills that lie behind them. The messages are repeated on the flanks of trailers, trucks and buses, and projected via posters, banners and multimedia fibre-optic screens at subway stops, airports, escalators, street corners and crossroads. The traveller will find no sanctuary in newspapers or magazines and, when they open their front door, they are bound to find a catalogue or similar mail-shot waiting for them. (Direct mail accounts for the biggest earner of all for the advertising industry, at some $55 billion per annum.)

The very commodities that people crave to own in their homes – radios, televisions and computers – act as channels for more advertisements. Upbeat voices urge us to eat cheesy snacks, rebundle our debts and sleep soundly on new mattresses. Cures are offered for flatulence, impotence, coronary disease and low energy levels (before the voice descends into monotonous overdrive to deliver the obligatory small print about unpalatable side-effects that all too often seem to induce low energy levels, coronary complications, impotence or flatulence).

Wealthier households pay to exclude the worst of the ads by procuring TV channels like Home Box Office. (They are like the elite in Orwell's *Nineteen Eighty-four* who number among their privileges the ability to turn off the machines that spout forth propaganda.) The majority must sit through banal, repetitive promos that play half-hour after half-hour, month in, month out, as if the mind was a stone on which the drip-drip-drip of marketing will ultimately make an impression. Ads for cars, trucks and fast food predominate. Offers of 'cash-back', together with promises of extended '0 per cent finance', must leave the buyer believing this truly is the American Dream – come home from the shops with a Honda Civic *and* more money in your pocket! Healthy hikers are seen driving their SUVs across deserts and up mountains suggesting that ownership of these 4x4 gas-guzzlers will unleash the elusive freedom that every American craves – to roam a wilderness that is, in fact, fenced in and picketed with 'No trespassers' signs. Fast-food ads emphasize the quantity and economy of the meals on offer, with nuclear families excited and fulfilled at the chance to consume super-size chicken nuggets at less than $1. A commercial on the cartoon channel has a child's voice declaring what might be a clause from the Manifesto of American Consumerism: 'It's every girl's right to change her shoes and her skirt again and again and again!' The ad – echoing the high-minded tone of Burger King, quoted above – promotes Happy Meals at McDonald's (whose 'golden arches' are branded on the built environment of every town in the country), where girls are tempted by a give-away plastic doll called Betty Spaghetti with different costumes to clip on.

The advertising industry is now turning to the internet, as the proportion of Americans with regular access to the world wide web has climbed to 72.5 per cent by the end of 2008. 'History shows that advertising ultimately follows the audience,' says Tom Hyland of Price Waterhouse's New Media Group. 'We believe advertising budgets will continue to shift more online.' Revenue from commercials on this new medium confirms this: it grew from $6 billion in 2002 to $23.4 billion in 2008.

Sport has become another pack-horse for advertisers. A commercial net enfolds the major events in American football, baseball, NASCAR races, tennis and golf. By 2009, advertising companies were paying $3 million to broadcast a thirty-second commercial during the Super Bowl Final on *Super Sunday* – the summit of the American Football season with almost 100 million domestic viewers. An hour's play is stretched to over three and a half hours, partly to accommodate all the commercial breaks. There are plenty of college kids who admit they are drawn to watch the tournament not for the sport, but for the spectacular new ads made especially for the occasion.

Companies also raise awareness through sponsorship of both sporting events and teams. They do so, for instance, in the stock car racing that is immensely popular with both TV audiences (coming second to American Football) and spectators. NASCAR races – named after the National Association for Stock Car Auto Racing that manages the sport – draw some of the biggest crowds, typically on a Sunday: more than 13 million people went to over a hundred races in 2004. Nextel Communications, the mobile phone company, is spending $75 million a year over ten years to get 'naming rights' for the flagship championship. The main sponsor for each of the forty-three teams will pay $10–15 million a year and altogether 1,100 companies – including 102 from the Fortune 500 – are backing the NASCAR phenomenon, inspired by the adage: 'Win on Sunday: Sell on Monday.'

One reason for building the link between product and sport is to develop a brand image – a novel concept developed by the advertising industry at the turn of the twentieth century. Early in America's history, a brand was the mark of ownership burned on to the hide of an animal with a hot iron (with darker connotations, beyond the realm of cowboys and ranches, of the branding of slaves and criminals). However, in the Temple of Trade a brand has become the symbolic embodiment of all information connected to a company, product or service, evoking in the consumer's mind the notion that a product has unique and appealing qualities. This phenomenon emerged in the burgeoning age of industrialization, when the producer was far removed from the consumer: the brand provided some compensation for the loss of trust that followed the disappearance of local production networks. Campbell's Soup, Coca-Cola, Juicy Fruit Gum, Aunt Jemima and Quaker Oats were some of the first products to be 'branded', carrying the reassurance of quality and helping to build 'brand loyalty'.

In the 1940s, manufacturers realized that consumers were developing psychological relationships with their brands (rather than the product), associating them with values such as youthfulness, fun or luxury. Furthermore, the association of an individual or lifestyle with a particular product could affect its brand image, although the first recorded instance of a film star having this effect had a negative impact on the marketplace: in 1934 the sight of a vest-less Clark Gable in *It Happened One Night* sent sales of vests plummeting – manufacturers of this undergarment had to await Marlon Brando's appearance in *On the Waterfront* (1954) to restore the balance. Today, there are marketing companies dedicated to product placement in films, television dramas and even computer games. The urban slang phrase 'Brand Slave' has been developed – seemingly oblivious to the sinister association between those two words – to describe someone who will only buy or wear clothes because of their brand (the Tommy Hilfiger flag, the Lacoste crocodile) regardless of value, taste or style.

Today, it is estimated that almost a fifth of Coca-Cola's market value is based on the 'familiarity and favourability' deriving from its brand. As with other major companies (such as General Electric, Microsoft and Wal-Mart), this value – a symbol of trust and faith that in pre-industrial societies might be invested in a deity or saint – is measured in tens of billions of dollars.

'Our life is brands,' Michael Shvo has asserted. This Israeli immigrant owned taxis before becoming reputedly one of New York City's biggest estate agents by incorporating brand into the mix. In 2006 he was promoting his transformation of the Chase Manhattan building in Pine St into the Armani/Casa whose apartments were equipped with products designed by the Italian fashion icon, Giorgio Armani. The launch of the sales campaign was timed to coincide with the payment of Wall Street's January bonuses and it was reported that one-third of the flats were snapped up within days for prices between $800,000 and $10 million. For some, Shvo came to personify Manhattan's real-estate bubble in the mid-2000s. However, he was still riding high in May 2009, combining bubbles and brands as he was reported to have sprayed $90,000 of Dom Perignon champagne over brunchers at Bagatelle's in the Meatpacking District of New York City.

Recently, the US's largest house-builder, KB Homes, has joined forces with Martha Stewart, the 'Queen of Homemaking' who has achieved celebrity through TV programmes and journals such as *Martha Stewart Living*. (Her star status barely wobbled when, in 2003, she was indicted on charges of securities fraud and obstruction of justice. She eventually served five months in Alderson Federal Prison Camp in West Virginia.) The houses are based on three of Stewart's New England homes, complete with Stewart's choice of interior decor and furniture and with concrete driveways stamped to resemble cobblestones. In early 2006, KB Homes completed the first of 650 houses, each costing $250,000–$500,000, on a site called Twin Lakes in the suburban community of Cary, North Carolina. Hundreds of buildings based on design-patterns associated with the 'domestic goddess' – 'Lily Pond', 'Dunemere', 'Skylands' and 'Katonah' – are now being sold by KB in Greater Los Angeles, Houston, Denver and Orlando Florida.

Bigger names – bigger even than Giorgio Armani and Martha Stewart – have lent their images to the branding industry. One might be forgiven for thinking that Saint Valentine and Saint Patrick have been enrolled into the American Advertising Federation. On St Patrick's Day we are expected to sprinkle powdered blarney stone on our corn flakes, if the salespeople are to be believed. One internet service provider tells its clients, 'You don't have to be Irish to get into the spirit of St Patrick's Day. Your eyes will be smiling after trying some touch o' green recipes or learning about shamrocks, leprechauns and Irish customs.' We are urged to enjoy the 'Luck o' the Irish' by clicking on links that lead to the 'all new St-Patricks-Day.com website dedicated to the Irish diaspora around the world', with the pages fringed with more commercials.

The festivals of Christmas, Thanksgiving and Halloween also provide emotional buoyancy to advertising campaigns: the themed commercials begin weeks before these special days, in a bid to inspire sales. Rites that were once heavily imbued with spiritual, patriotic or religious significance are now vehicles for promoting commodities. It was Marx who wrote of the revolutionary nature of capitalism: 'all fixed, fast-frozen relations, with their train of ancient and venerable prejudices and opinions, are swept away, all new-found ones become antiquated before they can ossify. All that is solid melts into air, all that is holy profaned.'

Any reflection on the state of marketing in the United States encounters a 'chicken and egg' conundrum. What came first: the purchase or the sale? There is more than enough evidence to suggest that Americans go out of their way to look for goods, rather as their forebears went out to hunt and gather. Those who doubt this should listen to the deafening footfall in the mall.

Consumer spending accounts for two-thirds of America's economic activity. The 2000 census revealed that 20 million people were employed in supporting this consumption through their work in the wholesale and retail trade (making it the largest industry in the country) and there are 20 feet of shelf-space per head in the United States (ten times the amount in Britain). The United States has led the world in the innovation of the shopping experience. The nation has invented new kinds of credit and currency (postal money orders, travellers' cheques, credit cards and instalment plans) and new forms of marketing (the department store, mail-order catalogues, the supermarket, the mall, outlet parks and internet trading).

Malls come in different shapes and sizes. Downtown, they range from an enclosed arcade to a multistorey complex with cinema, food outlets and underground car-park. In the suburbs, there are discreet crescents of terraced shops with dedicated car-parking. Out of town, they form an encircling eczema of 'outlet stores' and 'retail parks' – cavernous, insulated warehouses with extravagant signs surrounded by acres of parking connected to four- or six-lane highways. When Mall of America of Minneapolis (the country's biggest mall with 4.2 million square feet of space) opened it was predicted to attract more people in the first year of business than the Grand Canyon.

It comes as no surprise, then, that contemporary artists have been inspired by this phenomenon: David Opdyke's sculpture USS Mall appears to be an aircraft carrier, until closer inspection reveals the hull of the ship to be rock and stone (as if sliced out of the earth); the deck is a car-park with tiny automobiles; and the superstructure is made up of outlet stores. Meanwhile, Barbara Kruger has explored in her work the slogan 'I shop therefore I am', and it is true that Americans spend an average of twelve hours a month in these emporia – more time than they devote to any activity other than sleeping, eating, working and watching television (where, of course, they ingest hours of commercials).

The day after Thanksgiving carries a particular weight: 'Black Friday' is so named because retailers believe this is when their accounts move out of 'the red'. Its dimensions are frequently measured out as if to demonstrate the nation's economic potency. Rumours will circulate of crowd-sizes in the malls which – in the Orient – would be associated with religious festivals in Mecca or on the Ganges: in 2002, for instance, it was said that over 600,000 people visited Potomac Mills, Virginia, in the first hour of trading. News channels report official sales figures collected by specialist companies like ShopperTrak (monitoring thousands of outlets) and special attention is paid to one emblematic company – Wal-Mart. The media reported Black Friday turnover for this chain amounting to $1.46 billion in 2002, rising to $1.52 billion in 2003. Sadly, in 2008 news channels reported a grimmer story, when a worker – Jdimytai Damour – was trampled to death by shoppers chanting 'push the doors down' as they stampeded across the threshold of a Wal-Mart store on Long Island. One witness described the crowd acting like savages: 'When they were saying they had to leave, that an employee got killed, people were yelling "I've been on line since yesterday morning!" They kept shopping.'

Wal-Mart is the biggest name in retail and in 2007–08 was competing with Microsoft and Exxon for the title of Biggest Company in the World (each with a market capitalization of between $250–300 billion). Sam Walton established his first shop in Rogers, Arkansas, in 1962; by 2008, his company had 4,100 stores across the US and the estate was growing at a rate of 10 per cent a year. Facts are frequently presented by the media to illustrate Wal-Mart's status:

- It is like a country in a country, with turnover comparable to the GDP of many sovereign nations (ranking ahead of Pakistan, for instance); group sales for 2007–08 were $374.5 billion, when profits rose to $12.73 billion.
- About 112 million shoppers pass through a Wal-Mart every week, spending, on average, $35 each; 80 per cent of all households visit Wal-Mart at least once a year.

- 8 per cent of all expenditure in US retail outlets (excluding spending on cars and car parts) goes through its cash registers, and it sells more than one in four of all shampoo bottles and nappies bought in the US.
- Wal-Mart's trade with China exceeds that of Russia or Australia, and its imports account for 10 per cent of the US trade deficit with China.
- It employs 1.4 million staff (out of a national workforce of 138 million): there as many Wal-Mart employees as there are US military personnel, or Estonians, or residents of Washington, DC, and Boston combined.

If Wal-Mart stores are truly temples of trade, their icon is the lemon-yellow smiley face that signifies salvation through price 'rollbacks' and 'every day low prices'. Sam Walton's philosophy was to compete aggressively on price in the sale of basic goods: 'Always Low Prices – Always' is its motto. Price and turnover dominate this mass retail industry and business schools make much of the techniques developed by Wal-Mart to optimize these. The company's obsessive drive to cut prices is said to save American consumers $80–100 billion a year.

However, the nation's shopper is not entirely in thrall to the cut-price store. Travelling through the country one encounters victories for the little retailer. In Taos, New Mexico, in 2003, for instance, citizens voted to turn down the chance for a Wal-Mart and cities like Annapolis, Maryland, and Santa Barbara, California, feature small shops opening on to the street in the European tradition. In a society as rich and variegated as the United States, there are outlets to suit all tastes and persuasions. For lovers of literature, there are havens like Square Books in Oxford, Mississippi, where visitors can take a volume, a coffee and a homemade cookie out on to the veranda to while away the hours, watched over by photographs of local authors William Faulkner and Eudora Welty. For collectors of ethnographic curiosities, there are the Indian crafts of Eagle Plume in the Colorado Rockies. Eastern Market, close to the Capitol in Washington, DC, provides shoppers with a traditional covered market where game (pheasant, duck, partridge, turtle-dove) is sold as well as farm-reared birds such as turkey and chicken. At a stall specializing in salamis and sausage, the mustachioed vendor speaks German to his clients and – around Christmas time – an old lady who might have stepped from the pages of a Charles Dickens novel sits by a brazier selling vegetables.

Boutiques range from traditional clothes shops to specialists in niche markets to purveyors of the twee and bizarre. In the gay enclave of Provincetown, the laws of gravity have been overturned by the dizzying levity of the *double entendre*: confectionary shops sell 'sexy sweets to pucker up to'; soap and perfume is for sale at Good Scents; Binky's Ice-Cream offers 'the Best Licks in Town'; and Board Stiff has clothes for men promoted by images of handsome models with well-filled boxers asleep on the shore. (In case we don't get the allusion, the pants are trimmed with the words 'B Stiff'.)

Pet-owners are lavish shoppers and there are emporia throughout the country dedicated to their needs and whims. They can buy costumes (clip-on devil's horns and mortar boards are particularly popular) and beauty products for their beloved creatures. Chains like Petco charge $50 to wash, trim and comb a dog, squeeze its glands and clip its nails; and a shop in Santa Barbara has sweetmeats arranged on the counter which dogs select by pointing their nose through the glass. Laney exemplifies the fusion of dog-love and commerce. She is the proprietor of a dog-walking service in Eastham, Cape Cod, and drives a car with 'The Pampered Paw' on its door. Her goal, she says, is to 'saturate Cape Cod'. Her pamphlet – blue card with black paw-prints dotted over it – contains a number of references from satisfied customers such as that of R. Ryan from Brewster: 'I went away for 10 days and Laney took care of both my toy poodles. It was a good feeling to know my little boys were well taken care of.'

Testimonials like this touch on what Americans themselves regard as an essential feature of their consumer society – customer service. Complaint is an essential element in an ethos which emphasizes the primacy of the customer (and appears to be another outcome – like the brand – of the loss of personal enduring relationships that are such a feature of the traditional marketplace). People regularly return goods they are dissatisfied with, expecting to be compensated. Liz, who managed the shop in National Geographic's headquarters, described the man who walked in with an atlas he had bought there, asking for a replacement because the spine was damaged. The problem, she pointed out, was that this was 2001 (two days after 9/11) and he had bought the book in 1957. She could not countenance a replacement since it was reasonable to expect some wear and tear after forty-four years! Her customer disagreed and threatened to write to the president of National Geographic unless he got satisfaction. Liz was delighted that she could give some service at last: 'Let me spell his name for you,' she said.

This disgruntled shopper might have been more at home in the network of second-hand shops that exist – like a shadowy underworld – to serve the penny-wise wealthy as well as the deserving poor. Washington, DC, has been described as a 'city of closet thrift-seekers', where socialites, judges, ambassadors and politicians hunt for bargains in consignment shops such as Secondi in Connecticut Avenue, Secondhand Rose in Wisconsin Avenue, and Once Is Not Enough in Macarthur Boulevard. Somewhere out there, you can probably buy pieces from the wardrobe of Nan Kempner, the New York socialite and dedicated *haute couture* shopper, who said memorably (in a line that deserves to be the motto of God & Mammon Partners Inc.): 'I want to be buried naked! I know there'll be a store where I'm going!'

With all this shopping, all that engorgement, something has to give. There are certain events that play an almost ritualistic part in the purging process, when consumers relieve themselves of acquisitions. In suburbs across the country, the weekend after Labor Day is a popular time for garage or yard sales (suitably aligned with Black Friday, so that the gorging can begin again a few weeks later). These sales are typically advertised in the immediate vicinity of the home, with a few handwritten fliers distributed by the children. But the news spreads far and wide – as if transmitted by the telegraph poles that carry the posters.

All manner of goods are available at knock-down prices, attracting bargain-hunters who crowd streets that are normally serene and orderly. There are 45 rpm records, a bread-maker without the instruction manual, diaper-bins, a long-shaft engine for a motor-boat, the glass lining to a vacuum flask, a cooker, books, toys and so on.

Then, at the end of a life well spent, there is the estate sale. This is, in essence, a super-sized yard sale. The same handwritten posters appear on street corners, though now the event may be organized by professionals (such as Diener Jewelers in Washington, DC). Buyers will walk through the door to hear how an old widow has passed on: 'She accumulated a huge amount of stuff,' the sales staff will say. 'She must have been a shopaholic. The house is crammed with stuff she never used. Her husband was a doctor. He earned a packet!'

Everything is for sale. Everything has a price. The estate sale, like the yard sale, is indeed one of those rare occasions when Washington, DC's social boundaries become porous: professionals from the immediate neighbourhood – white and middle-class – mix with African-Americans from the ghetto and car-loads of Chinese diplomats. An elderly gentleman addressed as a 'General' manhandles his acquisitions out of the house and loads them into a car. Other buyers wander through rooms full of furniture, clothes, knick-knacks, old golf clubs, rugs, crockery. 'If something hasn't got a label with a price on, you ask!' an assistant says. But most items are marked up, usually in the simplest terms: 'Tallboy', one label states bluntly. A frosted glass vase has a tag of $2,500: 'That's an art-glass work. Very popular. Look on the internet.' There is even a dressing-table with vanity mirror, carrying a message scrawled in capital letters with a felt-tip pen that seems to snub the pedantic prose of a Sotheby's catalogue: 'ME LOVE YOU LONG TIME IF YOU BUY ME.'

The consignment shop, the yard and estate sales, and now – in these days of the world wide web – eBay, represent links in a chain of exchange that runs through society and punctuates human existence – the American answer to the gnostic's 'Circle of Life'.

We have touched on the breadth of commerce in America in our review of the dominant position held by buying and selling in society. Now it is time to feel the quality.

In the middle of the twentieth century, J.K. Galbraith – in *The Affluent Society* – felt compelled to call on America to free itself from an idea that he regarded as the 'central problem of our lives': production. From the beginning, America has been a source, not a sink, for raw materials and commodities. The intention of the adventurer companies who set sail across the Atlantic was to produce. They were to harvest the New World for all the natural and mineral riches that it had to offer. As early as 1602, Bartholomew Gosnold, the Suffolk sea-captain credited with naming Cape Cod, had undertaken a voyage to 'Northern Virginia' and returned with a profitable cargo of fur, cedar and sassafras (a popular cure for syphilis at the time). In Jamestown, John Rolfe began to cultivate a ceremonial plant procured from the Indians. The first substantial cargo of tobacco amounted to 105 lbs, and exports rocketed, with 2,300 lbs in 1616 rising to 3,000,000 lbs by 1638. Tobacco became the only commodity not regulated or controlled by the English government, and the weed dominated the economy of tidewater Virginia and Maryland for centuries.

Further south, exports of indigo, rice, wheat, tobacco and cotton brought immense wealth to the plantation owners, although this was only made possible by that most egregious of imported goods – the slave. Further north, New England traded with markets as far afield as Arabia, China and Japan, creating the nation's first millionaires in the early nineteenth century in Salem; many of them resided in Chestnut Street – one of the finest manmade vistas in America, with handsome houses built with the fortunes accrued by sea-captains and their widows.

By the twentieth century, the United States was a manufacturing powerhouse and production was, indeed, the key indicator of national prowess. This was the era when branded 'consumer durables', 'convenience items' and 'comfort goods' spearheaded an American invasion of overseas markets. Galbraith blamed producers for generating synthetic demand. He likened American society to a squirrel in a cage racing to keep up with a wheel propelled by its own efforts. He argued that, 'If production creates the wants it seeks to satisfy, then the urgency of the wants can no longer be used to defend the urgency of this production.' There were more pressing needs that society was failing to address because of the way in which priorities were set: social housing, for instance, or the health and education of the poor.

In one sense, the United States of the twenty-first century has heeded Galbraith's advice. It has relinquished its dominant role as a producer, with the mantle passing to the tiger economies of Asia. However, the consumption continues and Americans seem to be proud of their capacity for acquisition. This is nothing new. When Tocqueville visited the country in 1831, he found that 'the desire of acquiring the good things of this world is the prevailing passion of the American people'. In 2003, President George W. Bush praised those attending a dinner to raise funds for his re-election by suggesting he was among 'the haves and the have mores'! A telling statistic was published in the *Financial Times* that same year: 19 per cent of the US population believe they are in the richest 1 per cent bracket of the country; a further 20 per cent believe they will eventually get there. This reveals the optimism and aspiration of the American people and how well off so many people feel.

It is no accident that American economists have developed a model called 'hedonic pricing' for better assessing the value of goods and services by accounting for all the benefit and value that accrues from a possession. We shall examine later the extent to which the pleasure principle at work here is establishing a culture of immediate gratification. It seems that the acquisition of goods and services does seem to serve a deeper, symbolic function: it helps to construct 'self' and provide 'security' in a society where there is confusion about identity and where the liberated citizen has to navigate through unpredictable waters. Brands have become 'personal philosophies', allowing the consumer to express and affirm their values, viewpoint and standing in the world. A comment by Michael Shvo is instructive here: he has said of the Wall Street traders who pay premium prices for an Armani/Casa apartment: 'It's the new money that really feels they want to be a part of something. It's the assurance of feeling like they belong.'

This insecurity about identity extends to self-conservation. Americans show excessive interest in restoring the body when it ails, but also in preserving and improving it. This may seem at odds with what Americans do with all other goods – use, dispose, replace. However, the body is the one thing they cannot easily dispense with, so they treat it the way that Europeans care for their chattels. Teeth, breasts, blood, heart and faces are all conserved. The importance of the smile is a case in point. Americans take no little pleasure in baring their whitened fangs at the state of European – and especially British – mouths (a running gag, for instance, in the Austin Powers films). It is no accident that the world's first dental school began in Baltimore in 1839, but dentistry really took off in the States after the Second World War. Dentists rank as some of the country's highest-paid professionals, with orthodontists ensuring that teeth are straight and that white enamel is used so that no unsightly fillings show.

A distinctive aspect of the American way of health is the practice of going directly to specialists. The doctor who is a 'general practitioner' continues to play a prominent part in the life of the Old World, providing continuity and cohesion in the most broken of communities – a source of ritual healing in societies bereft of magicians and ministers. In the US, it is far more common for the customer to self-diagnose and then call upon the services of a cardiac, skin or liver specialist. This reveals something about how Americans regard the body – as a collection of disparate parts or goods rather than a holistic whole. The mind represents one such product that might merit a workout or more remedial treatment: hence the prominent role that the 'shrink' has to play in the lives of many.

The luxury of cosmetic surgery is gaining popularity in the United States. A familiar sight at the smarter cosmopolitan parties is the line-free sheen on the faces of older women who direct their taut grins towards the bee-sting lips and silicone breasts of their ex-husbands' new 'trophy wives'. The men, more likely, will be members of the 'zipper club', having had open heart surgery to replace a valve or bypass some veins; they may have had a stent inserted to open a blocked artery, or they may simply be on statins to reduce the 'bad' cholesterol and increase the 'good'.

A procedure involving botox, implants and a chin-tuck is one thing, but a procedure that relies on the lucrative but illegal trade in body parts is something else. In his 1979 film, *Clonus*, Robert S. Fiveson painted a macabre picture of the future where clones (thinking, feeling human beings) are created and matured for the sole purpose of being harvested to replenish and revitalize their 'sponsors': they live in a colony and a select few win a lottery to go to a promised land called 'America'. (Incidentally, the director was reported to be considering a lawsuit against the makers of *The Island*, a 2005 blockbuster with a similar theme. One film about the horrors of cloning would appear to have been, itself, cloned!)

As yet, the dystopian vision of *Clonus* may be a fantasy, but the United States is already becoming the world's trade centre for human 'egg donation'. The Government's Center for Disease Control and Prevention has tracked a 60 per cent surge in the use of donor eggs, from 10,389 in 2000 to 16,976 in 2006. (Stem-cell research, still in its infancy, is expected to add to demand for donor eggs.) Donors undergo three weeks of hormone injections followed by a surgical procedure to remove some fifteen eggs from their ovaries. The standard fee – described as compensation for the donor's time, effort and discomfort – ranges from $3,000 in the countryside to $8,000 in New York. However, prices skyrocket for special requests: it has been reported that an advert posted in campus newspapers at Ivy League universities in 1999 offered $50,000 for the egg of a woman with top test scores who was at least 5ft 10in. tall; more recently, a full-page spread in Stanford University's student newspaper promised $100,000 to a Caucasian woman under thirty 'with proven college-level athletic ability'. There are now 'egg brokers' who will add to the base fee by $500 if a previous donation has resulted in a pregnancy or $250 if the donor gets good grades at university.

There is also a macabre and illegal trade in organs of the dead. Commerce has made a commodity out of our mortal remains. In December 2005, British sensibilities were bruised when news broke of the theft of the journalist and broadcaster Alistair Cooke's cancerous bones, hours before his cremation. There is a grim irony to this treatment of Cooke, whose weekly *Letter from America* on the BBC gained iconic status for British listeners over many decades. He suffered a surprisingly common American crime – one of hundreds of corpses illegally plundered for profit in the United States' organ transplant and body tissue industry. The ensuing investigation by the Brooklyn District Attorney centred on a New York undertaker and the manager of a body-tissue processing company, amid allegations that they harvested bones, veins, skin, heart valves and other body parts from corpses before selling them on to unwitting and reputable surgical transplant companies. The body of one woman, exhumed in the investigation, had plastic plumbing tubes put under her shroud instead of legs.

There is even a market for virtual bodies. The internet hosts a number of American-created make-believe worlds within which users can operate through the medium of a computer-generated avatar. These avatars gain in value as their skills develop over time, and they can be traded in online markets. An avatar's rank (based on overall competence) is by far the most marketable attribute, but other characteristics that affect price include gender and class (e.g. being a wizard rather than warrior).

This is a society that celebrates immediate, rather than deferred, gratification. However, there are unintended consequences as technology and market forces enable desires to be satisfied ever more quickly and cheaply. The drive to bring down the price of Levi-Strauss jeans has led to the closure of factories in the United States, but clothes that cost half what they used to deteriorate faster, lasting no more than five years compared with the fifteen-year life of the originals. Commerce has adapted to the changing needs of a society that no longer values long-lasting goods – the fashion will pass on well before those flared trousers do. In the same way, there is little point in building houses, or creating their interior décor, to endure since Americans value what is new: it would be rare to find a kitchen in middle-class America whose units outlived a pair of old-fashioned Levis!

There are claims that intellectual activity is affected by the pursuit of easy gratification. In the corridors of power, serious decisions are as likely to be taken on the basis of a PowerPoint presentation (the 'fast-food' medium of the hard-pressed bureaucrat) than an extensive policy paper; and Camille Paglia, professor of humanities and media studies at Pennsylvania's University of the Arts, has noted that interest in and patience with long, complex books and poems has diminished among college students in the US. The use of narcotics and other illegal stimulants fits with this model of the rise of easy gratification. Statistics published by the Drug Enforcement Agency show that adults aged 18–25 are particularly prone to using proscribed narcotics: in 2005, 28 per cent admitted using marijuana in the previous year, and 6.9 per cent admitted taking cocaine.

Meanwhile, appetite for some legal substances – salt, animal fats and, above all, sugar – is taking its toll on the nation's health. In 2006, for instance, the Institute of Medicine estimated that 33 per cent of US children are at risk of obesity and in 2007 the Federal Trade Commission released a report that was not unrelated: half of the ads for junk food, sugary cereals and soft drinks are on children's programmes.

American consumerism is also anathema to conservation. Sixty years ago, Geoffrey Gorer wrote of the disastrous con- sequences of the American attitude to land and its products: 'the vegetable world is spoken of and treated as though it were a mineral world'. Crops were extracted, land was mined and wood was extricated until the vein was exhausted. Gorer's concern was with a particular phenomenon of his era – the dust-bowl. At the dawn of the twenty-first century, ours must be with the globe, with the carbon emissions generated through the production and transportation of goods.

This danger was powerfully and awfully illustrated in the events that unfolded around New Orleans on 1 September 2005. It is of passing interest that 62 per cent – by value – of all consumer goods sold in the United States flow through the port of New Orleans; the thirteen 'South Louisiana Ports' on the Mississippi River alone handle 290 million tons of cargo a year. The links between this activity and global warming are attenuated and complex: those who sow the wind will not necessarily reap the whirlwind. Nevertheless, as Labor Day 2005 approached, the sea-temperature off the Gulf Coast reached 30°C (86°F), and this was the engine that drove Hurricane Katrina into Mississippi and Louisiana, leaving more than 2.3 million homes without electricity, and towns like Biloxi and Gulfport, to the east of New Orleans, wiped from the map.

Those who could do so had evacuated the area before the storm struck, leaving behind an impoverished, mainly black, underclass numbering tens of thousands. People sought shelter, paradoxically, in the city's two centres of entertainment and commerce – the Superdome and Convention Center. Here, it was said, they were dying of hunger and dehydration, but armed gangs were spotted when helicopters tried to bring aid and pilots refused to touch down. These gangs, it seemed, were intent on living the American Dream, only this retail therapy was enacted in a Theatre of the Absurd against a backdrop designed by Hieronymus Bosch. Rioters with automatic weapons chased fire-fighters away from a burning shopping mall in Gretna. Gangs waded through flooded streets emptying shops of televisions, jewellery and guns. They emerged pushing the shop furniture itself – massive metal display cases that run on roller-ball wheels, packed with goods spoilt by the oily, polluted waters of the Mississippi (itself contaminated with the spill-off of much of America). Few of the looters had homes in which to install these commodities and there was no electricity to power them. This was postmodern shopping, deconstructed to the point where it became a form of performance art – an end in itself.

A vengeful anarchic mob had taken over the Big Easy within hours of the thin veneer of law and order being removed. Penny, an officer with NOPD who remained on duty throughout, says she knows to the minute when the moral fabric of the city fell apart. She spent the next week with a team of colleagues protecting hundreds of refugees who were holed up in a multistorey car-park, with police communications out and armed vandals trying to break in: 'By Day 7, we were almost out of food, drink and ammunition.'

The anger and appetite of the hurricane's wrath may have been engendered by the radiation of a consumer society, but in turn it exposed the anger and appetite of an underclass that knew no other values than those preached in the Temple of Trade. But Americans did not have to wait for Katrina to find this underclass. In 2000, 11.3 per cent of the population of the United States was living in poverty; by 2007, this had risen to 12.5 per cent, or 37 million people. In a society that lacks a free health service comparable to Britain's NHS, 47 million Americans are without health insurance coverage; and in May 2008, over 28 million people were registered with the Food Stamp Program (an indicator of hunger in the nation). There is no Wal-Mart or five-and-dime store to serve the needs of the underclass. They must rely on charity.

In a society where government is largely removed from the provision of social services, the philanthropist has a major contribution to make. Universities flourish as a result of donations from alumni, and billionaires like Bill Gates and Larry Ellison have created medical foundations that challenge the more conservative approach represented by the National Institutes of Health, and promote high-risk research.

Charitable giving is found at almost every level of society. According to *Giving USA*, the yearbook of philanthropy, contributions in 2005 amounted to over $260 billion (2.1 per cent of GDP – more, it should be acknowledged, than revenues from advertising). This included contributions of over $7 billion to three major natural disasters at home and abroad. Most households claim to have contributed to a charity, with the donors giving to churches and religious organizations (50 per cent), disaster relief organizations (47 per cent), community groups (35 per cent) and human service organizations (34 per cent). Despite the absence of major natural disasters in 2006, a record $295 billion was given in that year and 65 per cent of households with income less than $100,000 gave to charity.

There are tens of thousands of benevolent women and (to a lesser degree) men who have created their own charities. Given the dominance of commerce in this society, it is interesting to see how many of the great public art collections around the country were assembled not by aristocrats or manufacturers, but by shopkeepers or tradesmen or – tellingly – by their daughters. This is the case, for instance, in Salem (the Peabody Essex Museum), Boston (where Isabella Stewart Gardner's father made his fortune in the Irish linen trade), Baltimore (with its collection by the Cone sisters, whose fortune came from grocery and textiles) and Richmond, Virginia (the Lewis family). The Bartlett family acquired their wealth through a hardware store that flourished in Chicago in the nineteenth century: Frederic Clay Bartlett endowed the city's Institute of Art with glorious Impressionist works. His sister, Maie Bartlett Heard, founded the Heard Museum in Phoenix, Arizona, in 1926, and Florence Dibell Bartlett founded the Museum of International Folk Art in Santa Fe, New Mexico, in 1953. The trend continues today with Alice Walton (whose personal Wal-Mart fortune is valued at $18 billion) supporting the new Crystal Bridges Museum in Bentonville, Arkansas; the museum, designed by Moshe Safdie, will focus on American painting and Native American art when it opens in 2010–11.

Philanthropy has given the United States so much more. The

Yellowstone and Acadia National Parks, the world-class exhibits of the Smithsonian Institution and the high-quality broadcasts of National Public Radio have all been 'made possible' through private donations. Yet, to the jaundiced eye of the anthropologist tutored in rites of conspicuous consumption (like the *potlatch* of the Haida Indians in the Pacific Northwest), charity can all too easily appear as another form of image-building, especially when public display is a prominent feature. Philanthropy will, for instance, procure for the more extravagant donor – who allows his or her name to be associated with acts of tax-efficient generosity – a place on the 'Washington Social List', gaining privileged access to the rich and powerful in countless events through the year (private parties, fundraisers, balls, galas, art openings, book launches and movie premieres).

In a society that claims to be classless, it is also instructive to observe how often a public 'pecking order' is used to rank benefactors. Take, for instance, the annual rodeo organized by the Snowmass Western Heritage Association in Colorado which badges its benefactors according to size of donation: Rancher – $15,000; Marshal – $10,000; Buckaroo – $5,000; Cowboy – $2,500; Wrangler – $1,000; and Posse – $500. The Aspen Festival, nearby, operates with rather more gravitas but applies a similar scheme: Premier Associates – $25,000; Associates – $10,000; Benefactors – $6,000; Patrons – $3,000; Sustainers – $1,500; Affiliates – $500; Friends – $250; Contributors – $100; and Subscribers – $50.

A powerful driver behind the compulsion to consume is the need for identity and status in a society that offers little of either. However, there may be other factors to be taken into account. Poet Cole Swensen attributes consumerism to a need that is, she believes, peculiar to Americans – the need to act: 'It is the act of buying that matters, not the acquisition.' Bill Bryson, in *Made in America*, analyses the demographics of the mid-twentieth century (1946–60) when the US population rose by 40 per cent and the number of teenagers grew by 100 per cent. In the mid-1950s, 16.5 million teenagers had $10 billion to spend, buying 9 per cent of all new cars, 40 per cent of all radios, records and cameras, and over 50 per cent of movie tickets. Many features of contemporary American culture and mores, then, seem to have formed in this hormonal crucible of adolescent extravagance and exuberance.

There is also the collective memory of periods of privation. Each year, at Thanksgiving, schoolchildren re-enact the story of hungry Pilgrims rescued by Indians. The 'Starving Time' of 1609–10 is especially emblematic, with a population of 500 Virginia colonists reduced to sixty survivors, many of whom were described as 'crazed for want of food', digging up graves to consume corpses and eating human excrement. Things were not much better in 1623, when Richard Frethorne wrote, in a pitiful letter home to his parents from Jamestown, Virginia: 'And when we are sick there is nothing to comfort us; for since I came out of the ship I never ate anything but peas, and loblollie (that is, water gruel).'

As late as 1739, George Whitefield was collecting supplies in London to take to a thousand needy souls who represented the population of a fledgling colony called Georgia. His cargo contained necessities to survive in the sandy scrubland of Savannah. This catalogue of aid to America is worth setting out, to understand the level of privation in the land at that time:

Stockings, shoes, caps & hats; canvas breeches, striped flannel waistcoats, handkerchiefs, tapes, laces, buttons; paper, quills, sealing wax, copybooks, pencils, tin pots, tinder boxes, ink-pots & ink-horns, corks & corkscrews, knives, gunflints & gunpowder, shot, scissors, buckles, combs, spoons, porringers, claw hammers, nails, gouges, gimblets, axes, files, chisels, planes, hatchets, saws, shovels, spades, locks, hinges, fishing tackle; butter, cheese, lemons, barrels of raisins, hogsheads of white wine, cinnamon, sugar, brimstone, cloves, mustard, pepper, oatmeal, oranges, potatoes, sage & onions.

To the present day, of course, some migrants come to the United States seeking refuge from famine, pogroms and poverty in the Old World. Meanwhile, Americans have not forgotten the profound impact that the Great Depression – lasting for at least a decade from 1929 – made on the lives of their parents and grandparents, when 25 per cent of the workforce (15 million) became unemployed and pandemonium broke out on the trading floor of the New York Stock Exchange on 'Black Tuesday', 29 October 1929.

The United States has travelled a bumpy, uneven road from famine to feast – from the ordeal of the 'Starving Time' to an era when starvation diets are pushed as a way of managing weight and reducing obesity. In the process, commerce – the selling and buying of goods and services – has come to dominate American culture. It is deeply engrained, today, into the habits, practice and fabric of American life. Commerce is the defining American cultural construct, providing imagery that saturates everyday dialogue. Commerce is commonplace, a feature of the quotidian world, where money – as the media mogul Ted Turner has said – 'is how we keep score'.

Yet there is something about the scale, the all-encompassing presence, the dominance of that invisible market force, that adds another dimension to the way people think and feel about it. It is a spiritual force: it is a calling and evokes devotion. Consumerism in America is not just business – it is belief, and it is hard-wired into the nation's value system. For most Americans, this is one of the ways in which they define themselves. If pressed to explain, they will typically refer to the line that Thomas Jefferson inserted in the Constitution. Everyone knows about 'the pursuit of happiness' since who could be happier than those who can gratify their wishes, desires and appetites? There are, of course, citizens who eschew materialism, advocating a self-denying lifestyle where enlightenment is achieved through literature, music, or the call of the wild. However, American fulfilment rarely flows from the sort of purification that comes with an ascetic religious tradition; fulfilment comes literally through filling up.

The anthropologists Mary Douglas and Baron Isherwood remind us that 'Overconsumption is more serious and more complicated than personal obesity, and moral indignation is not enough for understanding it.' People buy goods for material and psychic welfare, and for display; but goods also act as a form of metaphorical reasoning: 'Goods are neutral, their uses are social; they can be used as fences or bridges.' Consumption makes categories of culture both visible and stable.

However, the beliefs and practices pursued within America's Temple of Trade are not without consequences. Those looking to benefit from what Émile Zola termed the 'democratization of luxury' submit to a demanding work ethic that puts pressure on family values: those in work are employed 395 more hours a year than the British (a fact cited by apologists for each nation to demonstrate superiority over the other). The consumerist creed of an ownership society engenders a candy-floss culture, dominated by the drive for instant, but insubstantial, gratification. The fall-out from this includes obesity, debt, poverty and pollution.

The spirit of consumerism – aerated by the Jeffersonian mandate to pursue 'happiness' – falls like kerosene on the torch of liberty. While the ensuing conflagration will warm and enlighten many, it must scorch and blind countless others.

CHAPTER THREE

Trick or Treat – On Belief

America is self-consciously modernistic in its outlook, with its face set firmly towards an infinite future. However, on the last night of October each year, one ceremony in the nation's festal calendar recalls the timeless rites of pre-modern societies.

There is an early premonition weeks before, with homes across the country undergoing a ritual make-over. This may be quite simple, with the threshold decked out with little more than a bale of straw, a sheaf of corn and the ubiquitous pumpkin carved into a grinning jack-o'-lantern – its tangerine hue reflecting the changing colours of fall. Mock gravestones appear on lawns, carrying gloomy inscriptions ('Here Lies Jack', 'Dying to Meet You', 'I Told You I Was Sick'). Skeletons hang from windows, witches appear to fly through trees and richer households may install elaborate displays of deep blue or purple lights that flicker mysteriously.

Halloween is one of those egg-white occasions that unite the country: it covers the cracks between ethnic and class divisions, and binds together the generations. Mardi Gras may hold a special place in New Orleans, but this is the closest the whole nation comes to carnival, or the Saturnalia of Ancient Rome. On the night, as darkness falls, the roads of the nation fill with small children dressed as witches and demons (led in crocodile-file by attentive parents) or packs of teenagers, boisterous in their disguises. Colleges put on costume parties; hotels and clubs arrange balls; downtown bars and restaurants run themed events; and Manhattan is one of many cities and boroughs to organize a Halloween Parade.

The festival has come to be associated – first and foremost – with the secular age of American consumerism. 'Halloween is all about scaring grown-ups so they give you sweets,' kids hear on a festive episode of *Rugrats*, and this is a version of the lesson their parents learnt from Disney's *Trick or Treat* (1952) when Huey, Dewey and Louie tried to shame Donald Duck into giving them candy with the help of Witch Hazel.

Not only does Halloween facilitate the ingestion of vast quantities of candy, but it also involves extensive expenditure on costumes and decorations. Halloween ranks as the second festival of the nation's calendar in terms of consumer spending. Polling data show that in this first decade of the twenty-first century, 80 per cent of adults hand out sweets and 93 per cent of children go out to deliver the doorstep challenge 'Trick or treat!' In 2008, the National Retail Federation found that the average American planned to spend $66.54 on the holiday and total Halloween spending was estimated to reach $5.77 billion.

However, this event is more than a children's sugar-fest and another chance to party. It is linked to two old Christian festivals: All Saints is still a Holy Day of Obligation in the Roman Catholic calendar and All Souls (or 'All Hallows' – hence All Hallows Eve or *Halloween*) was traditionally the occasion when the faithful prayed for the dead. In Washington, DC, a United Methodist Minister tells his congregation that sweets should be collected to commemorate the lives of the departed and especially the souls of dead relatives. The Hispanic communities of the southwestern states can be found celebrating the 'Day of the Dead' and in southern California, for instance, Roman Catholic priests ceremonially bless the Halloween costumes to be worn in that pageant.

There is another layer to Halloween, connected to a darker heritage. Many churchmen reject or condemn the festival for saluting – even celebrating – the presence of evil in the world. They point to its roots in the pre-Christian fire festival of *Samhain*. The Celts believed that on this night the dead revisited the mortal world, so they lit bonfires to ward off evil spirits. This image of Halloween feeds the fear that evil lurks around the corner: the manicured lawns and white picket-fences of suburbia could mask a minatory, Gothic underworld. One evangelical pastor told his flock in Washington, DC, in 2003, 'The festival of Halloween is beyond redemption.' He described the Druid feast, where householders waited in trepidation for a knock on the door from priests requesting food: one of those who answered the door would be selected for ritual sacrifice by disembowelling on the capstone of the Neolithic tombs.

This remains a special night for the Church of Satan and the Wicca (or witchcraft) cult. They call it 'Devil's Night' in Detroit – a city that has suffered decades of economic deprivation and racial tensions – where a favoured activity is the torching of abandoned buildings. Up to 800 buildings would burn each Halloween in the 1980s; by 2007, the figure stood at around 150 (thanks to a 'youth curfew' imposed by the city authorities, who also deploy tens of thousands of volunteers to patrol the neighbourhoods). At the other end of the social spectrum, the Stanley Hotel in the Rockies became notorious for its Halloween Ball, inspiring Stephen King's novel, *The Shining* (1977); the season closes with this ball, and when a psychic was recently employed to report for the local radio station on the big night, she left before the end, saying, 'I've never known so many spirits in one place! I am never going back there again.'

Many ministers rail against the demons, devils, witches, zombies and tormented ghosts who parade – in the company of Frankenstein's monster, Fester, Morticia, and Cruella de Vil – through the city blocks, suburbs, main streets and prairie trails of the nation. The American Tract Society, publisher of religious pamphlets since 1825, sells almost 3 million 'Halloween outreach' items a year, for handing out to unsuspecting trick-or-treaters when they knock at a Christian's door – a righteous equivalent to those chocolate-coated sprouts that tricksters hand out to fool their callers! Wayne Braudrick, senior pastor of Frisco Bible Church near Dallas, Texas, urges his congregation to 'stay home on Halloween and wait by the door! I believe we are recapturing the holiday for the Lord.'

This militant language suggests that Halloween has become a theatre of operations in the 'culture war' – that metaphorical crack that has appeared on the surface of America's Liberty Bell in recent years. Although the term is used to describe the polarized views of entrenched Republicans and Democrats, it is more commonly perceived as a division between the religious faithful and liberal sceptics. This theme gained traction in the closing years of George W. Bush's presidency, when Dan Gilgoff published *The Jesus Machine* (2007), arguing that evangelical America was 'winning the Culture War'. In 2008, Paul Auster published a novel – *Man in the Dark* – that depicted a parallel universe where the Twin Towers still stood, but where cultural divisions had led the nation into a second civil war.

Despite the election of an emollient Barack Obama, attention is still paid to these divisions and they were emblemized at the end of the first decade of the twenty-first century by emotive arguments about abortion laws and the legalization of same-sex marriage. However, we have to avoid the temptation to descend into caricature here, contrasting the born-again evangelical from the rural Midwest with the East Coast urbanite watching *Sex in the City*. America's metaphysical life is more complicated, more nuanced and more profound than this. The numinous and the sacred are given expression in the mundane fabric of everyday life. We can observe, for instance, the spiritual depth and life-enhancing energy of African-American gospel music or the enlightened relationship between the faith of American Jews and their patronage of fine art and music. We can stand in awe at the humbling display of loving-kindness shown by the Amish of Nickel Mines, Pennsylvania, publicly forgiving the homicidal maniac who slaughtered their daughters before ending his own life in the classroom that he had transformed into an abattoir. We can witness, across the nation, thousands of voluntary associations pursuing benevolent, charitable and spiritual goals: groups like the Greater Pittsburgh Community Food Bank whose 11,000 volunteers distribute 1,000 tons of food through food pantries and soup kitchens to 120,000 people in south-western Pennsylvania.

Halloween provides a fitting point of departure for a survey of the rich and complex cultural amalgam surrounding questions of belief in twenty-first-century America. On this day, the Sacred and Profane, Ancient and Modern, Good and Evil mix, repel and co-exist like so much oil, vinegar and mustard poured over the American salad. In this chapter we shall examine each of these paired dyads, as we survey the nation's metaphysical life.

Sacred and Profane

In 1967, Herman Kahn and Anthony Wiener, the authors of *The Year 2000 – A Framework for Speculation on the Next Thirty-Three Years*, looked forward to the dawn of a new millennium when the United States would be empirical, this-worldly, secular, humanistic, pragmatic, utilitarian, contractual and hedonistic. Five years later, Sydney Ahlstrom seemed to sound the death-knell for traditional, God-centred faith in America in his magisterial *A Religious History of the American People*. He was writing, he said, at a time of doubt about the supernatural and the sacral. There was a 'galloping' awareness of the contradictions in American life between the ideal and the actual, leading scepticism to stand in place of faith. Ahlstrom was, of course, penning his *magnum opus* at a troubled time in the nation's history. Religious institutions seemed powerless and ineffectual in a country mired in the blood and napalm of Vietnam, shaken by a counter-cultural revolution, choking on the smoke from race riots that left cities burning, high on marijuana tokes and amphetamine hits, with the president's authority shortly to be rocked by the Watergate crisis.

This view seemed to be affirmed by small instances of non-deference that amounted to a hail of buckshot peppering the flanks of the righteous. G. Thomas Sharp – a science teacher and pastor of a Baptist church in Alabama at the time – recalls that in the 1960s:

Bible believing families throughout the US were suffering the loss of 60 per cent to 70 per cent of their sons and

daughters to secular thinking by the time they reached 15
years of age [and] church going families were experiencing
a 40 per cent + divorce rate!

In his view, the teaching of Darwinian evolution had overthrown, in the name of science, the dominance of the Bible as
the foundation of America's world view.

Meanwhile, the witch – that scourge of seventeenth-century
New England – was transformed into a comely young housewife
called Samantha, newly married to advertising executive Darrin
and acting 'mortal' in the suburbs. *Bewitched* – one of America's
most popular TV sitcoms – used this conceit to examine the
social and moral foundations of Middle America in the 1960s.
This witch was a force for good, using her powers to overcome
human frailties and promote the American Way: a neighbour's
son gains the confidence to pitch awesome baseballs; the
alcoholic Mr Zeno – failed magician and entertainer – recovers
his self-esteem and learns that age-old virtue of self-belief; and
in a Halloween theme, we are taught not to stereotype
minorities (be they witches or Jews) in a story about the picture
on the wrapper of a Halloween candy called Witch. This was the
decade when *The Munsters*, a family of lovable freaks living in
suburbia, and *The Addams Family*, a grotesque inversion of the
ideal nuclear family, had their screen debut (although their
origins go back to the 1930s and 1940s).

A number of syndicated spin-offs followed. *Tabitha* was the
witch-daughter of Samantha and Darrin, working in television
in Los Angeles. *Buffy the Vampire Slayer* has proved to be a
popular 'postmodern Gothic' pastiche where – according to
creator Joss Whedon – vampires, werewolves and zombies
represent the personal anxieties associated with adolescence and
early adulthood. The demons of the past are here used quite
explicitly to provide guidance to teenagers about dealing with
their emotional and psychological problems while growing up
in the world.

The annual rash of Hollywood 'horror' releases at Halloween
seems to confirm that the supernatural has been reduced to a

sub-class of mass entertainment. Following in the footsteps of Nathaniel Hawthorne and Edgar Allan Poe, we have a cleverly contrived exercise to manipulate our fears in a pleasing way, drawing in box-office receipts in the process. This is fundamentally a secular business process as described by Graham Baker, the British director of *The Final Conflict* (the third film in Hollywood's 'Omen' trilogy about the Devil's incarnation on earth as Damien):

I had few theological discussions in making OMEN THREE, and those mainly with the writer and a couple of the actors. Elsewhere it all seemed pretty hokey and superficial in the way one expects such a commercial project to be treated. The word fundamental springs to mind here, if not Manichean. There was a certain amount of discussion in several religious journals, quotes from which Twentieth Century Fox used in the publicity for the picture.

Today, the Council for Secular Humanism claims that some 31 million Americans belong to what it calls a 'Community of Reason', representing the second largest belief group in the United States. The country rests on pillars of civic law and humanist values, and its pursuit of happiness has created a consumerist paradise. America has progressed from the bite in the apple to the byte in the Apple; from the Book of Job to the I-book of Jobs.

The progress that the US has made in accommodating these secular, rationalist beliefs would not have surprised the Founding Fathers, because it reflects their direction of travel. They may not have shared Voltaire's revolutionary wish to see the Last King strangled with the guts of the Last Priest, but they did subscribe to the notion of a civic nationalism, based on what has been called the 'American Creed' and its principles of liberty, democracy, individualism and the rule of law. There is room for a deity in their vision, but God comes across as a just, reasoning technocrat who manages the machinery of the universe from a distance. George Washington rarely cited the Bible and never spoke of Christ, preferring terms – in keeping with his Masonic credentials – like the 'Grand Architect', 'Superintending Power' and 'Great Ruler of Events'. Thomas Jefferson spent hours of his retirement compiling *The Life and Morals of Jesus* in an effort to extract the ethical content of the Messiah's teaching. He judged his grandchildren and their peers would die Unitarians – rejecting talk of the Trinity as nonsense and promoting the principles of liberty, reason and free inquiry.

It was not to be. By the dawn of the twentieth century, George Willis Cooke, author of *Unitarianism in America* (1903), was struggling to explain why this progressive religion had failed to replace the backward-looking sects that dominated the American scene. Unitarianism, he concluded, was too modern in its spirit and insufficiently populist to find ready acceptance among those who were influenced by backward-looking beliefs:

> The religion of the great majority of persons is determined by tradition or social heredity, by what they are taught in childhood or hear commonly repeated around them. Only persons who are naturally independent and self-reliant can overcome the difficulties in the way of embracing a form of religion which carries them outside of the established tradition.

A century later and nothing has really changed. Sydney Ahlstrom was wrong. People today speak of the US being caught up in a fourth Great Awakening. In doing so, they refer to those waves of spiritual and religious frenzy that sweep across the nation. Tocqueville experienced this when he toured the country in the early nineteenth century, leading to a chapter in *Democracy in America* entitled 'Why Some Americans Manifest a Sort of Fanatical Spiritualism'. The breadth and depth of religious belief in twenty-first-century America is remarkable – especially when compared with the secular ways of twenty-first-century Europe. Some 270 million Americans subscribe to a personal God who answers prayers. Recent polls reveal that

'Belief in God' trumps all other personal values – even freedom and family. Religious practice proliferates in the US. Leander – a property developer in Maryland – is no Bible-thumping fundamentalist, but his experience is typical:

> I think it's said that 95 per cent of Americans believe in God – either Christian, Jewish or Muslim. Just about everybody I know is a churchgoer, from all walks of life. Toby, our black handyman, is deeply religious, attending a black Baptist church: he is convinced non-Christians will go to hell; his two sons have become preachers at their own churches; his sister comes to work carrying a Bible. All my business associates go to church: my accountant is a Presbyterian; even the builders who work for us – young men. It's not a big issue because it's normal: in conversation it'll slip out, 'When I was in church the other day . . .'

Degrees of scepticism and religious fanaticism vary in the country, and the ethnic and cultural differences of this hyphenated society affect the style and content of worship. In Manhattan, Judaism and Roman Catholicism dominate. Lutheranism flourishes in the prairie-lands of Iowa and Minnesota. Quakers persist in much of Pennsylvania but the denizens of Lancaster County are Amish. Methodists and Baptists have built up a strong following in the South, with African-Americans developing their own churches (such as the Colored – later the Christian – Methodist Church, the African Methodist Episcopal [AME] and AME Zion churches). Mormons hold Utah; Roman Catholics are inevitably in the ascendant in the Hispanic southwest; and Unitarians and Episcopalians retain a foothold in the old eastern cities of Boston and Washington, DC.

Throughout the country, preachers, ministers, priests, rabbis and mullahs play a prominent role in sanctifying those life-ceremonies that mark the course of an American's life. The nation's holy men – 352,000 people were registered as 'clergy' in the 1999 census, 86 per cent of them male – officiate at major rites-of-passage such as baptism, bar mitzvah, marriage and funeral; and they contribute to other punctuation marks in the book of life such as retirement. Take the blessing, for instance, offered at a lunch celebrating the retirement of Ray – a law enforcement special agent – in 2002 at a Virginia military base. Ray's brother, a minister who had flown over from California, opened the proceedings with prayers: he praised God for the good that Ray had done, making America a safer place to live; he thanked God for the gift of parents who taught their children right from wrong; and he asked God to bless Ray's colleagues in their work.

Of course, the standing and influence of churchmen is enhanced by the constitutional separation of Church and State: religious education must be provided away from the established educational system, so children attend Bible studies and Sunday school arranged by their ministers. Churches play a considerable role in collecting charitable donations from US households, and these institutions also supply care and social services within a society that does not see this as a function of government. Churches provide clubs to keep teenagers amused and occupied, and they organize summer camps for the kids: Noah's Ark, for instance, specializes in outward bound courses on the Arkansas River for church youth groups; they organize prayer sessions on rafts as they float down river and they are readily identified by their lifejackets that carry the commandment 'Thou shalt not steal'.

If the topography of the United States' religious landscape followed that of the capital's skyline, the Episcopalians would be in the ascendancy. Their National Cathedral in Washington, DC, dominates the horizon, its massive Gothic form rising above a bluff to the north of the Capitol. In fact, this American branch of Anglicanism had been eclipsed by Congregationalists and Presbyterians by the end of the colonial period and it has continued to decline, proportionately, ever since. The Episcopalian Church is still associated with the WASP ('White Anglo-Saxon Protestant') hegemony and those attending its services tend to belong to a privileged class ('St Columba's in

Washington, DC, is full of wired Episcopalians who run the country,' one congregant said). However, the church has a dwindling membership of 2.5 million and its liberal views (including the appointment of a gay bishop) are out of kilter with the dominant strain of conservatism among Christians in the country.

The Roman Catholic Church, by contrast, cares for one in four souls in the US, making it the nation's largest belief-group. Yet its influence on American society fails to match its size. A large, hierarchical organization is out of line with the 'voluntary' traditions of the country – especially one that owes allegiance to an outside authority. Furthermore, the Catholic Church has a long association with the underclass – the German, Irish, Polish and Italian communities of the nineteenth century, and the Hispanic migrants from Central and South America today.

The dominant religious culture of the US is evangelicalism, expressing values that are quintessentially American: patriotic destiny, self-help, freedom, innovation and renewal. It is epitomized by the National Association of Evangelicals – an umbrella organization covering 45,000 churches with a combined congregation of over 30 million souls. It embraces Pentecostals, Methodists, Baptists, Presbyterians, Congregationalists, Pietist groups, Reformed and Lutheran Confessionalists, Churches of Christ and Anabaptists such as Mennonites.

A modern feature of evangelical practice is a studied avoidance of entanglement in too many doctrinal disputes. This is at odds with the hackneyed image of the fiery fundamentalist. The focus is on pluralism, not separatism. Groups like World Vision and Campus Crusade for Christ emphasize their interdenominational nature. This can, however, lead to the ecclesiastical equivalent of supermarket shelves packed with competing brands of baked beans or corn flakes, where the most distinctive difference is in the design of the label. Chicago's thriving Willow Creek Church exemplifies the non-confrontational approach, telling its membership that 'there are many areas of faith and practice on which intelligent and Godly believers hold different views (various end-times scenarios, charismatic issues, predestination and free will debates to name just a few)'. Congregants can hold their own opinions on these matters provided they remain respectful in any dialogue.

Above all, American evangelicalism is about the individual: his or her relationship with the church, but more importantly his or her relationship with God. In a tradition that dates back to colonial times, church life depends on voluntary support of a committed laity, with a democratic, local church-group the norm. The individual is the primary religious unit and this creates a more dynamic – some might say turbulent or chaotic – scene where sects will splinter under pressure of ideological disputes or clashes of personality. (It is paradoxical – at a time of a perceived culture-clash with Muslim fanatics – that this formula closely approximates to that followed by Sunni Islam.) There are, for instance, forty Methodist denominations in addition to the United Methodist Church, with its 9 million members, and countless variants of Lutheranism over and above the Evangelical Lutheran Church in America (5 million members).

As a consequence, a distinctive feature of American religious practice is the phenomenon of worshippers 'shopping' between churches to find one that fits their particular needs. There are many examples in the 'Temple of Trade' of people trading in temples. Jennifer was brought up Episcopalian, though her mother was Catholic; she turned to Congregationalism in New England because she and her husband Peter liked the preacher – he gave the best sermons; but now she is back with the Episcopalians in Bethesda. Valerie, a government archivist, is drawn to the Unitarian Church: she likes the fact it doesn't require members to believe in God; she has worshipped in three Unitarian churches, each reflecting the local heritage – lapsed Mormons from Utah, lapsed Jews from New York and lapsed Catholics from Maryland.

Marilyn, by contrast, started worshipping at a Unitarian Church (decorated with images from the five world religions), but changed her mind when her daughter was born: 'I felt the need for Jesus in my life. I tried various churches and liked what the Presbyterians had to offer.' She applauds the independence of her parish and the fact that the community is not very strict: 'The congregation gets restless if the minister's sermon goes on too long.'

Mark started with the Presbyterians but now worships with the African Methodist Episcopalians (AME), a church that began on the African continent but is flourishing in the US, especially among African-American communities. Meanwhile, Meng Hao was brought up as a Buddhist in Shanghai. Now she lives in Rockville and has started to attend the Chinese Christian Church there: she doesn't see any conflict between the two religions, and opting for the Christian institution helps her connect with her new American roots.

Kathleen, the daughter of a Church of God pastor from Indiana, says:

We went to a Church of God to begin with, but when my husband's job took us to Minneapolis, it was a long way to go to get to the nearest Church of God and we were the only young ones there: everyone else was old. My husband John wanted to be in a congregation of people closer to our age, so we moved to the United Methodists.

She pauses for a moment before adding, with a gentle smile: 'We do a lot of church-shopping in the States.'

Ancient and Modern

Given the ecclesiastical marketplace that exists in the US, and an abiding preference for novelty in the American Way, it is inevitable that religious practice in the country is modern and forward-looking. Religious leaders have rarely shied from the pursuit of new ways of promoting themselves and they have exploited contemporary channels of communication in their eagerness to bring salvation to the common man.

Developments in the first decade of the twenty-first century include the Saddleback Church Internet Campus (complete with blog, Facebook and Twitter) and Groundwire, which claims to connect a generation to Christ by delivering 'a line of 60-second Christ-centered radio spots that aggressively promotes the love of Christ' through secular radio to a weekly audience of over 10 million people on five continents, backed up on the world wide web. These innovations belong to a long tradition: in the 1940s, the *Old Fashioned Revival Hour* had the largest radio audience in the country; in the 1980s and 1990s, 'televangelist' preachers raised tens, if not hundreds, of millions of dollars a year for their ministries through eponymous programmes like *Oral Roberts*, *Dr James Kennedy*, *Ken Copeland* and *Jimmy Swaggart*. Today, Kenneth Copeland's Trinity Broadcasting Network boasts 5 million viewer-households per week in the US and was generating $200 million in revenue in 2004; and in 2009 *The Lutheran Hour* claimed to be heard by 1.2 million people a week on over 800 stations nationally. The latter is the longest-running Christian radio programme in the world, starting in 1930.

The trend is away from pulpit-thumping dogma and towards a more inclusive, populist salvation theology. Pastors in this tradition can leave the impression that style is more important than substance. There is a surprising amount of theatre associated with evangelical practice. In many of the 'exurbs' of Southern and Middle America, thousands gather to worship in 'seeker-friendly mega-churches' that seem to have more in common with retail outlets than traditional ecclesiastical architecture. The high-definition digital screen has replaced the stained-glass window; instead of pews there are cushioned stacking chairs. The 'worship leader' does not officiate at an altar but performs on a stage, and the church organ and choir are likely to have been replaced by a rock group leading the congregations in praise songs.

Christmas services can be particularly spectacular. In 2002, one Baptist church in Houston entertained its congregation of 3,500 people to *tableaux vivants* of the birth of Christ that included an angel competition: the winner, suspended by wires on a frame that was wheeled on to the stage, was wearing great white feathery wings. In a nearby mega-church, the Tooth Fairy,

Spider-Man and Superman appeared before the congregation to complain about a lack of attention from the kids; then the minister and his wife intervened to tell the story of Christmas, illustrating their narrative with a performance that re-enacted the Nativity (including a live camel), Jesus' miracles, and the Passion with Jesus on the cross.

The New Life Church at Colorado Springs has taken spectaculars of this sort to a new level with its production of *The Thorn* – a theatrical extravaganza performed in its worship centre during Lent. It re-enacts Passion Week, but its creator, John Bolin, also looks 'behind the scenes at the supernatural battle that was most certainly raging at the same time'. The web-based trailer shows dark clouds boiling in the sky, announcing between bolts of lightning:

> Since the dawn of time
> a battle has been waged
> between the darkness
> and the light.

In recent years, this church has also staged a version of the play for children called *The Crown*, which is described as an adventurous story of the life of Christ seen through the eyes of a child: the website announces, 'So this Easter season bring the entire family to enjoy the life and sacrifices of our Lord.'

Events like the Easter performances in Colorado Springs and the Christmas shows in Houston remind us that religion can also be business. The specialized Christian music industry has an annual turnover of $300–$500 million (more than 5 per cent of total retail revenue from music), with sales of over 55 million albums and singles in 2008. That year, it was claimed that 'Contemporary Christian' radio – with 945 stations – was the second most popular radio music format in the US after 'Country' music, with a further 322 'Southern Gospel' stations; a Country/Christian variant forms the staple diet for listeners to National Public Radio in many parts of the nation on a Sunday morning through the *Stained Glass Bluegrass* show.

There is a flourishing market in Christian symbols and phrases that feature on clothes, calendars, greetings cards, lapel pins, coffee mugs and bumper stickers. The simple 'Jesus Saves' badge of the 1970s has turned into the window transfer with a Superman emblem containing the letters JC and the words 'Jesus Saves' beneath ($2.99 from the Christian Zone of Sticker-Giant.com). You can buy a label stating 'Real men love Jesus' or a button showing a sportsman, with 'Jesus Team' on his vest, lifting his arms in triumph under the words 'I got picked!!' Vehicle licence plates carry cryptic variants such as 'GOD RCKS', 'GODCANN', GET2HVN', 'BOW2HIM', 'PRZ2GOD' and 'B4GIVEN'. T-shirts provide the canvas for expressing more complex images and ideas. The cross features on many: it may be accompanied by the words 'Jesus beat the Devil with a BIG UGLY STICK!' or depicted over the Stars and Stripes above the words 'Cross Country'. This use of the double-meaning, so popular with advertising executives, is used to telling (if tasteless) effect in the image of Christ nailed to the Cross: 'Body piercing saved my life'.

At the heart of the extravagant worship and merchandising there lies the concept of salvation, with many mega-churches around the country emphasizing personal spiritual growth (although this may be a reaction to the heady mix of pious ecstasy and materialism exhibited by the televangelicals in the closing decades of the twentieth century). Examples include Bill Hybels' 'seeker-friendly' Willow Creek Community Church in suburban Chicago and Rick Warren's Saddleback Church in Lake Forest, California (with congregations of 17,500 and 20,000 respectively). Saddleback notes on its website that Warren's manifesto for Christian living in the twenty-first century – *Purpose Driven Life* (2002) – has been recognized as 'the bestselling non-fiction hardback book' in history, selling 16 million copies in the first seventeen months with the help of warehouse stores like Wal-Mart.

There is also, of course, a history of charismatic personalities starting new religious enterprises – the sacerdotal counterpart to the entrepreneurs and city-fathers who built the nation with such zeal. Just as the landscape is littered with ghost towns, and just as the archives of the Inland Revenue Service are packed with bankrupt companies, so America's metaphorical altar is covered in the empty husks of defunct or near-defunct cults (like the 'strange sects . . . which endeavour to strike out extraordinary paths to eternal happiness' that Tocqueville described). Visitors to Jerusalem in New York State can drive past a tall federal-style building that bears the name of Jemima Wilkinson – the first American-born woman to found a religious group. The Society of Universal Friends housed her body here after her death in 1819, waiting patiently for her to be restored to life until the congregation was overtaken by disappointment, disillusionment and old age. Many sects like this have either died out or struggle to survive – the Shakers, for instance, or the Church of Christ, Scientist.

However, the homegrown Mormon faith – the Church of Jesus Christ of Latter-day Saints (LDS) – continues to flourish with some 6 million American followers: in 2007, LDS was said to be the nation's fastest-growing religion, even making in-roads into African-American communities like Harlem. Its founder, Joseph Smith, claimed God sent an angel to lead him to a book of golden plates buried in a hillside in western New York, written by the prophet Mormon who had lived in America in the fourth century AD. The thirteen articles of faith presented in this book contain many elements that conform – superficially – to the Christian tradition, but there are also differences: Mormons believe, for instance, that God and Jesus Christ have physical bodies; and their doctrine includes the baptism of the dead as a way of reclaiming the souls of ancestors. There is a distinctive American nexus to the religion, seen in the Mormons' tenth Article of Faith:

We believe in the literal gathering of Israel and in the restoration of the Ten Tribes. That Zion (the new Jerusalem) will be built upon this (the American) continent. That Christ will reign personally upon the earth, and that the earth will be renewed and receive its paradisiacal glory.

This mythology of angels and sacred texts in New York State remind us of the paradoxical way in which threads of archaic and arcane doctrine are woven into the modern fabric of American religious practice. Among the articles of dogmatic faith that continue to find favour, there are the concepts of Predestination, Millenarianism and Biblical Inerrancy.

Predestination presumes that unconditional salvation is promised to a chosen few – the Elect, whose souls will be welcomed into God's sanctuary whether they know it or not, leaving the rest of us to rot in hell. It dominated as an idea in New England in the early colonial days and it was turbo-charged by an influx of Scottish and Irish Presbyterians in the eighteenth century. George Whitefield (whom we met in 'The Temple of Trade' chapter supplying aid to Georgia) is credited with igniting the first Great Awakening in the 1730s: he drew massive crowds on his tours of the Eastern Seaboard, delivering open-air sermons in which he maintained a strict line over Predestination.

However, others leant towards the modified Calvinism of Jacobus Arminius, who emphasized the role of free will in the process of salvation. John Wesley, founder of Methodism, rejected Predestination in his sermon 'On Free Grace' and started publishing the *Arminian Magazine* in 1778. He and his followers believed that God loved every human soul and wished for the salvation of everyone, not just an elect few. Salvation was to be gained through faith, displayed at the moment of conversion when the 'born-again' soul responds to the Word of God. This philosophy has proved to be better attuned to a society where free will and the idea of success based on personal endeavour are articles of faith. Predestination is too bitter a medicine for these saccharine times. The New World has warmed to the notion of ecstatic salvation for all.

Millenarianism enjoys greater popularity. The scale of its canvas is more panorama than portraiture: it addresses the fate of the universe. In the theological debate about the 'End-Time' there are competing pre- and post-millennial interpretations of the Bible that can result in serious doctrinal dispute between different sects. However, the 'churched' of Peoria, Illinois – that city which, because of its geographical position and demographics, has acquired legendary status as the yardstick of the nation – are less concerned with the small print and focus instead on the major elements of the contract: they are likely to live in dread of the Tribulation (when they believe the Antichrist will be in dominion), in anticipation of the millennial Second Coming (when Christ will return to Earth), and in hope of the Rapture (when the redeemed ascend to heaven). Indeed, the 'Calendar of Events and Sermons' at the El Vista Baptist Church in Peoria in 2007 showed – under the banner 'Are you ready if the Lord Jesus would return in 2007?' – that a 'Second Coming Prophecy Conference' was scheduled for 16–18 September. (It must be coincidence that the word 'tentative' followed this entry in parentheses.)

Proof of the interest in the Second Coming is found in the bestseller charts. The book of the 1970s was Hal Lindsey's *The Late Great Planet Earth* with its prediction of the rule of Anti-Christ, followed by the Second Coming: 28 million copies had been sold by 1990. In the *Left Behind* series, Tim LaHaye and Jerry Jenkins tell of the struggle of non-believers who remain on Earth – after true believers disappear in the Rapture – under the seven-year rule of the evil Nicolae Carpathia. The authors betray their political views by making this Prince of Darkness hold the post of Secretary General of the UN. A group of Christian converts form the Tribulation Force under Tsion Ben-Judah – a rabbi, former Israeli statesman and guerrilla evangelist. Over 62 million copies of the *Left Behind* books had been sold by 2004, with the final volume published in April 2007.

The Millenarian debate is not confined to literature. In his commentary on Hurricane Katrina, Billy Graham said:

> We are living in a period that Jesus predicted would be a very serious and difficult time, and as we approach the end of the age, it is going to get worse and worse . . . But at the end, it's going to be the coming of Christ, and that's the hope we really have.

Likewise, a ride with an African-American taxi-driver can be accompanied by a radio programme in which a 'brother' deals with a caller asking about the length of a tribulation: the presenter agrees this is important, since we are about to enter such a period; but he admits to some confusion because two different tribulations appear in the Old Testament – one lasting twenty-four years, the other 120. The important thing, he concludes, is not the length of time, but that it is going to happen.

Rapture Ready is a web-based service offering a 'prophetic speedometer' to measure the state of tribulation in the world. It takes account of forty-five factors indicating end-of-time activity including earthquakes, inflation, moral standards, floods, plagues, false Christs and liberalism. The results are registered against an index of prophetic activity pointing to the imminence of Rapture: below 85 – slow; 85–110 – moderate; 110–145 – heavy; over 145 – 'fasten your seat belts!'

Dominionists occupy the extreme end of Millenarian opinion and enjoy far greater prominence in text-books than the size of their support-base can justify. They argue for the seizure of temporal power by the Church as the only means through which the world can be rescued, enabling Christ to return to rule and reign. Organizations like Coalition on Revival produce 'world view documents' that describe how to apply dominion theology to such spheres of social life as education, economics, law and entertainment.

Reconstructionism represents an even rarer species within the Dominionist genus. It is associated with two think-tanks – the Chalcedon Foundation, established by Rousas John Rushdoony, and the Institute for Christian Economics, established by Rushdoony's son-in-law, Gary North. They advocate the imposition of an Old Testament style theocracy – a theonomy – complete with capital punishment for such offences as adultery, homosexuality and blasphemy.

The concept of Biblical Inerrancy, in which the Bible is considered to be without error, is expressed by many religious institutions, including the American Association of Christian

Schools (AACS). AACS may have no more than 170,000 students and teachers in its thousand schools, but many mainstream evangelical churches pay lip-service to the doctrine. For instance, Willow Creek in Chicago says in its statement of faith that 'we hold that the Scriptures are infallible and inerrant in the original manuscripts'; and one of the nation's largest communities – Saddleback Church in California (whose pastor, Rick Warren, was chosen to deliver the invocation at Barack Obama's presidential inauguration) – declares its belief that the Bible is 'God's perfect guidebook for living'.

Of course, the number of Americans who accept the validity of every word in the Bible and apply it with rigour to their life is small. When taken to extremes, this can affect everyday life in the strangest ways: for instance, born-again students will debate whether it is right to dress a man in girl's clothing for a college skit-show, given the prohibition in Deuteronomy XXII.5: 'The woman shall not wear that which pertaineth unto man, neither shall a man put on a woman's garment: for all that do so are abomination unto the Lord.' The 'Old Order Amish' of Lancaster County, Pennsylvania, are renowned for their archaic ways, observing an Anabaptist theology dating back to six-teenth-century Switzerland. They travel by horse and cart, reject all forms of modern technology and wear eighteenth-century clothing: the women have long, plain-coloured dresses with aprons and shawls, with their hair scraped back under bonnets; the men have long beards (but no moustaches – these are associated with the military) and are dressed in broad-brimmed hats and dark suits with wide trousers held up by braces. Clothes are fastened by buttons or pins – zips are prohibited.

The influence of Biblical Inerrancy is most obviously seen in the wide support for 'creationism' in the nation. A 2005 poll by the Pew Forum on Religion and Public Life found that only 26 per cent of the population sees Darwin's theory of evolution providing the best explanation; a further 18 per cent believe that evolution occurred with divine guidance; 42 per cent subscribe to the origin of the world according to Genesis. Christian bumper stickers express it well. Some show a big fish ('Jesus') swallowing a small fish ('Darwin') under the tag-line 'Survival of the Fittest'. Others declare 'Science: The Study of God's Creation' and 'Big Bang Theory: God said it, and BANG! It happened'.

This issue was emblemized in the 1925 'Scopes' monkey trial' when schoolmaster John Scopes of Dayton, Tennessee, was found guilty of violating a new state law that prohibited the teaching of Darwin's theory of evolution in public schools. The judgment was overturned on a technicality and the law was repealed in 1967, but in many parts of the US the debate continues and Dayton remains a community where fundamentalist Christian beliefs predominate. In the nation at large, organizations like the Institute for Creation Research, the Creation Truth Foundation and the Discovery Institute of Seattle are dedicated to promoting the biblical explanation for the origins of the universe. In April 2006 a Museum of Earth History opened in Arkansas, describing dinosaurs and humans in co-existence; sister museums are being built in Texas and Kentucky; and the Creation and Earth History Museum in Santee, California promotes a similar line. The latest term for this hypothesis is 'Intelligent Design'. There have been legislative attempts in thirteen states to have intelligent design added to the school curriculum.

One indicator of separatist sentiment is to be found in the number of families that are home-schooling their children in preference to what many regard as ungodly, un-Christian teaching in public schools. David – a 'born-again' software engineer – said that 7 per cent of children received home education in the US. He explained his reason for schooling his four children at home in Boca Raton, Florida: 'I am a Christian and I don't want them being taught that homosexuality is OK. I would accept them becoming gay, but I want them to understand that they can choose an alternative to the secular lifestyle.'

Research by the Institute of Education Sciences in 2007 suggests that David's estimate is inflated. Nevertheless, its analysis shows that 2.9 per cent of students in the country are home-schooled (amounting to 1.5 million children), up from 2.2 per cent in 2003. This may reflect – perhaps – the influence of movements such as the Southern Baptist Convention, which in 2004 urged members to remove their children from public schools and either home-school or place them in private Christian establishments. The Evangelical Association of Christian Schools International (ACSI) – 'striving to effectively educate children and young people with the mind of Christ' – boasts 4,000 schools in its directory for the US, from the '91st Psalm Christian School' in Phoenix, Arizona (with 141 pupils), to the 'Zuni Christian Mission School' in New Mexico (enrolment: 65). Ken Smitherman, president of ACSI, remarked in his 2005 report that 750,000 children were involved in his association's programmes, representing more than 1 per cent of the nation's pupils.

It is difficult to assess the proportion of Americans who subscribe to these fundamentalist views. Humans are capable of holding incompatible values more or less simultaneously and fanatics are prone to exaggerate the facts. In twenty-first-century America, it is the more tolerant, all-inclusive 'neo-evangelicalism' that holds sway. This dates back to April 1944, when a movement called Youth for Christ was established by businessman George M. Wilson; he aimed to hold a new kind of Christian rally at the First Baptist Church at Minneapolis, Minnesota, believing the Gospel 'could reach servicemen and un-churched civilians, if clean excitement was linked with an uncompromising Christian message'. (It must be a coincidence that this same month saw the premiere of *Fancy Free*, a ballet choreographed by Jerome Robbins to music by Leonard Bernstein, about three sailors fighting over two girls in a New York bar.) Youth for Christ flourished, with rallies held across the US: these were Saturday events (different from the traditional Sunday service), operating under the banner 'Geared to the Times, Anchored to the Rock'. The aim was to engage with the modern world while remaining above worldliness: the leaders wore loud hand-painted ties and bright suits, proclaiming to the world that theirs was no dreary faith. There was light, laughter, high drama and music, such as a sonata for 100 pianos performed in Minneapolis.

An early rally in Chicago featured a young theology student called Billy Graham. Today he enjoys a status in the land akin to a religious prophet and leader: he has spoken of being engaged in a 'crusade to bring America to her knees in repentance of sin and faith towards God'. He remains active, fifty years after an authorized biography spoke of him preaching to over 50 million people and converting a million. His views are clearly aligned to those American values of freedom and individualism: God's will works in conjunction with human will; salvation is the product of the grace of God and the faith of individual believers who freely choose to surrender to Jesus. The essential precursor to this vision of salvation is the rejection of sin.

Good and Evil

Good and Evil have been battling it out in America from the earliest days, although opinion has varied as to whether Evil was resident or imported. In 1642, a Plymouth man called Thomas Granger was executed having been 'detected in buggery with a mare, a cow, two goats, five sheep, two calves and a turkey'. Granger, it was asserted, had acquired the 'knowledge and practice of such wickedness in old England'. Governor William Bradford, leader of the separatist settlers, blamed traders for failing in their responsibility to transport godly persons to the plantation: business instincts led them to make up their freight and advance their profit, 'car[ing] not who the persons were, so they had money to pay them. And by this means the country became pestered with many unworthy persons who . . . crept into one place or other.' However, for Cotton Mather, the puritan minister who came to particular prominence in the Salem Witch Trials, the 'squalid, horrid, American desert' had been a diabolical realm until the arrival of Christians. In *Wonders of the Invisible World* (1693) he addresses the need to counter a plot against New England being hatched by the Devil.

Satan was aggrieved, he wrote, because 'the *New-Englanders*, are a People of God settled in those, which were once the Devil's Territories'.

Notions of Good and Evil, Saints and Sinners, have continued to flourish in twentieth- and twenty-first-century America. They are, for instance, encapsulated in *Hellbound Train* – an African-American film from 1930 that likens man's spiritual journey to a train ride where each carriage represents a particular sin; viewers are warned to avoid jazz music, dancing, intemperance, sex, disobedience in children, theft, murder, gambling, Sabbath-breaking, dishonesty in business and back-sliding. In a final dramatic sequence, the train speeds towards hell as the title implores, 'Get off this train by repenting, believing and being baptized, before it's too late.'

Seventy years later, we find a similar message relayed by *Unshackled!* – the longest-running radio drama in history; it started in 1950 and is produced by the Pacific Garden Mission in Chicago, broadcasting its religious message around the world over 6,500 times a week on over 1,550 radio outlets. Its website offers the following steps on how to get to Heaven: 1. Admit you are a sinner. 2. Realize the penalty of sin. 3. Accept God's provision for your sin. 4. Personally receive Jesus Christ as Saviour and Lord.

The novels of Frank Peretti describe angels and demons still battling it out in the US: a spirit of perversion holds San Francisco, for instance, and a spirit of greed disrupts missionaries in San Jose. These demons, who are led by Rafar of Babylon, an intimate of Lucifer, have slimy, black hides and breathe in sulphurous gasps. The angels, by contrast, are giant warriors with beards and swords held in scabbards strapped to their legs; their wings burn like lightning and they dress in tan military fatigues. These works reached a wide audience of Christian evangelicals in the 1990s, with *This Present Darkness* alone achieving sales of 2.8 million.

The public comments of twenty-first-century leaders continue to assert that Good and Evil are operating in and around the United States. In 2002, President George W. Bush spoke of the need to counter 'an axis of evil' overseas. In an interview with Larry King on Christmas Day 2005, Billy Graham said:

> I can't explain 9/11, except the evil of man. I think there is a force in the world, a force of evil. There are two great forces, God's force of good and the devil's force of evil, and I believe Satan is alive and he is working, and he is working harder than ever, and we have many mysteries that we don't understand.

Two months later, *Newsweek* published an interview with Graham on 'God, Satan and Katrina'. He noted that Job's suffering was caused by the Devil and that suffering was relieved by God. The Devil may have had nothing to do with Hurricane Katrina, but Graham does believe that there is a personification of evil at work in the world, contending against God: 'The Scripture teaches that there is a devil, and his name is Satan, which means "destroyer".'

In August 2008, Barack Obama attended a forum hosted by Rick Warren at his Saddleback Church in Orange County, California, at which the pastor asked the presidential candidate: 'Does evil exist? And if it does, do we ignore it, do we negotiate with it, do we contain it, or do we defeat it?' Obama replied that evil is everywhere – in Darfur, in our streets, in our own hearts, in parents who abuse their children. We cannot, he said, 'erase evil from the world. That is God's task. But we can be soldiers in that process, and we can confront [evil] when we see it.' But he also called for humility, since so much Evil has been perpetrated in the name of Good.

The vocabulary of Good and Evil features in exchanges between a conservative coalition (whose 'Moral Majority' includes evangelicals, Catholics and Mormons) and liberal humanists. In 1981, for instance, the evangelical philosopher Francis Schaeffer published *A Christian Manifesto* that called for Christians to use civil disobedience to restore biblical morality and overthrow the secularists who had pushed America in an ungodly direction with legalized abortion and the removal of religious education in public schools. Freemasonry – that movement favoured by so many of the Founding Fathers – is also periodically condemned by Christian fundamentalists as a cult of the Devil. Some have found proof for this within the very street layout of the nation's capital which they claim contains the Masonic symbols of square, compass, rule and pentagram (incorporating the Satanic goat's head).

The 'Saga of Roy's Rock' gripped the nation in the summer of 2003. Alabama's Chief Justice, Roy Moore, installed a granite monument of the Ten Commandments in the rotunda of his Supreme Court one night. A TV crew from Coral Ridges Ministries filmed the judge dressed in his robes unveiling the two tablets of stone and reciting one of his trademark poems that called on the faithful to stem an 'evil tide' that includes children poisoned by cocaine, abortion on demand, and godless judges who throw reason out the door:

> Too soft to put a killer in a well-deserved tomb,
> but brave enough to kill that child before it leaves the womb.

Moore may not hold a torch to fellow versifiers T.S. Eliot, e.e. cummings and Ezra Pound, but he was lionized by Christian conservatives and bus-loads of church groups from towns around the state arrived daily to view the monument. However, it was condemned as a violation of the First Amendment by groups like the American Civil Liberties Union, Southern Poverty Law Center and Americans United for the Separation of Church and State. After a Federal Appeals Court hearing in August 2003, the monument was removed to a private room in the courthouse and Moore was removed from his office.

Further ambiguity is added to an already complicated picture by the counter-intuitive view that Evil lurks within the religious establishments who aspire to set the nation's moral tone. The Roman Catholic Church has been blighted by revelations of child abuse by priests, and in December 2002 Cardinal Bernard F. Law of Boston resigned in the face of growing anger among both Catholic laity and priests about the crisis: his archdiocese was threatened with bankruptcy in the face of a multiplicity of civil suits by the abused. In July 2007, the diocese of Los Angeles was reported to be paying out over $600 million to over 550 alleged victims of sexual abuse.

For many right-wing evangelicals, the appointment of a practising homosexual to an Episcopalian bishopric is evidence of the decadence of that church. However, homosexual intrigue is also one of several categories of scandal that periodically engulf the evangelical movement. With its emphasis on charismatic leadership, self-promotion and mass communication, it is unsurprising that the fallible creatures who stand in the electronic limelight should fall prey to temptation: celebrity, money, ego and testosterone form a volatile, intoxicating compound. There have been a number of high-profile televangelicals who have proved to be less than perfect, but the problem is larger than that according to Pastors.com: in 2002, it found that 64 per cent of pastors or church staff struggled with sexual addiction or compulsion, and 25 per cent admitted to having sexual intercourse with someone besides their wife while married.

The downfall of Ted Haggard, pastor at the New Life Church in Colorado Springs who became head of the National Association of Evangelicals in 2003, received extensive airplay. He was listed by *Time* magazine as one of the most influential evangelicals in the US in 2005, but a year later this outspoken critic of homosexuality was accused of engaging in sex and drug abuse with a former male prostitute. He resigned from both his ministry and the association, and in February 2007 the 'Restorers and Overseers' of his church wrote to the congregation about Haggard's moral default: 'we have done extensive fact-finding into his lifelong battle with a "dark side" which he said in his confession letter has been a struggle for years'.

The investigation uncovered other staff within the Church 'struggling with unrelated sin issues'. The Overseers concluded:

As we prepare ourselves for the Easter season, we all have a choice today: Will we live as captives of the past, the grave and sin, or will we shake ourselves, cleanse ourselves, and rise up to be a powerful new Body? . . . *'Where sin does abound, grace does much more abound'*, and that means much grace is being poured out upon us right now! . . . Like an army that suffers a setback, they re-focus, re-tool, and rebound.

In the popular mind, sin is made manifest by the frenzied pursuit of instant gratification and the satiation of appetite through consumption, and the image of cannibalism has become a powerful trope for this in American narratives in recent years. For instance, in Cormac McCarthy's post-apocalyptic novel *The Road* (2006), a devastated America is plagued by bands of cannibals who scour the land in search of prey. The nation is locked in the grip of a nuclear winter: ash covers the earth and obscures the sky, and almost all plants and animals are dead. As father and son travel through this dystopia, the older man clings to the thought that there must be an ethical core surviving in humanity, despite all indications to the contrary.

Other examples of cannibals in popular culture include 'Hannibal' Lecter; Cardinal Roarke and Kevin in *Sin City* (who eat prostitutes for their inner light); Sylar, in the TV series *Heroes* (who acquires the super-powers of his victims by eating their brains); and the vampire Bill Compton in the TV drama series *True Blood* (based on the *Southern Vampire Mysteries*, first published in 2001); and Edward Cullen, the 'vegetarian vampire' in *Twilight* (2008).

Notions of good and evil may guide individuals on the path to individual salvation, but these concepts are not confined to the churched in the US. Secular America has replaced God and his Saints with a pantheon of supernatural beings who are dedicated to fighting wrongdoers – the super-heroes that have featured in the pages of DC and Marvel Comics since the appearance of Superman in 1938. In January 2009, Marvel celebrated the inauguration of Barack Obama (a self-professed fan of Spider-Man) with a story that teamed the president-elect with the super-hero: the story takes place in Washington, DC, with one of Spider-Man's foes – the Chameleon – attempting to thwart the Inauguration of the Forty-Fourth President of the United States.

The popular 'grindhouse' movies of the 1970s are far removed from the super-hero comics read by the prepubescent. But this genre – typified by quantities of sex and violence, with plots that bizarrely mix the Gothic, the Baroque and the surreal – address those questions of Good and Evil that abound in America; and when this genre is transformed by the genius of Quentin Tarantino we are offered a masterclass in moral philosophy and practice. His films – ranging from *Reservoir Dogs* (1992) to *Inglourious Basterds* (2009), and including such classics as *Pulp Fiction* (1994) – follow a grindhouse tradition in depicting a world stripped of meaning and value. Tarantino's debt to the genre is exemplified by naming his 2007 double bill with Robert Rodriguez *Grindhouse*.

The presentation of violence as an aesthetic – one might almost say a cosmetic – performance shocks the viewer into seeing Tarantino's universe as one occupied by cold, insensate automatons. In *Kill Bill* (2003), for instance, the business of killing an enemy is slotted into the suburban routine of child-rearing, like another domestic chore. However, his characters are not like the soulless androids in *Blade Runner* (1982) or *Terminator* (1984). They exhibit cool humour and hot honour, laughing in the face of death and driven by just vengeance. The ethical boundary in a Tarantino film may shift as protagonists pursue their pipedreams, but a solid core is eventually reached and a moral order is re-established in the face of callous nihilism. For instance, Jules, the hired assassin in *Pulp Fiction*, finds redemption when he finally listens to the quotation that he spouts ritualistically before despatching his victims: 'Blessed is he, who in the name of charity and good will, shepherds the weak through the valley of darkness, for he is truly his brother's keeper and the finder of lost children.' He recognizes that he has been representing the tyranny of evil men; now he wants try to become 'the shepherd'.

It may be tempting to portray the humanist and Christian

evangelical traditions in the US as adversarial, but – as Tarantino's films illustrate – personal fulfilment lies at the heart of both. Each struggles with that same enduring challenge that has preoccupied 'classical' American philosophy: how to construct and sustain a set of beliefs – a moral framework – that accommodates the individual and the community. Above all, there is a shared understanding about the meaning of Good and Evil that revolves around values that counter the threat of nihilism stripping the world of meaning.

These shared concepts of Good and Evil also provide some explanation for those shocks to American society that seem to lie outside human control. In acknowledging the 'dark side' at Halloween, Americans recognize the existence of harmful external forces that cannot be controlled: terrorists, rapists and psychopathic killers; hurricanes, typhoons, tornadoes and earthquakes. This is an important pressure valve in a society that takes control so seriously.

It does not, then, come as a surprise that a twenty-first-century bogeyman has been given a part to play in the festival. As early as October 2001, a toy fair in Hong Kong was selling Osama bin Laden masks, anticipating a market for Halloween parties. Sales were brisk in many parts of the world outside the US (especially Brazil) and one American retailer expressed a willingness to sell the masks provided they were being bought 'for the right reason'. Within three years, a subsidiary of the New York Times Company (the About.com website) could run a poll asking: 'Is it wrong to wear an Osama bin Laden mask for trick or treating or for Halloween masquerade parties?' The site offered one of two answers (with over 70 per cent of responses favouring the second):

Yes. To wear a bin Laden mask is to display insensitivity towards the victims of September 11 and to trivialize the menace posed by terrorism.

No. If anything, wearing a bin Laden mask signifies revulsion towards bin Laden, essentially equating him with the Devil.

Superficially, Halloween appears to demonstrate that ancient rites and primeval fears of the Old World have been sublimated to the appetites of the free market and a generalized pursuit of happiness. The genial, tongue-in-cheek festivities, the conspicuous consumption, the 'spook-tacular' ghost stories and crafted horror films all seem to make this another manifestation of the nation's sceptical, secular credentials. Halloween expresses both the solidarity of neighbourhood communities and the pursuit of individual self-interest. The game of 'trick or treat' equates to those rites of misrule that anthropologists have recorded around the world, providing a social pressure valve as children break the bounds of propriety by demanding gifts from their elders and betters, and exhibiting behaviour that elicited witchcraft accusations in seventeenth-century New England.

However, we have seen things are more complicated than this. Despite a superficial veneer of secularism, the US is remarkable for its strength of attachment to religious values. Tocqueville could only explain American bouts of religious exuberance by resorting to spiritual language. He wrote simply, 'The soul has wants that must be satisfied.' More recently, Barack Obama has described the deep need for spiritual comfort that he has identified in so many of his fellow citizens:

> They want a sense of purpose, a narrative arc to their lives, something that will relieve a chronic loneliness or lift them above the exhausting, relentless toll of daily life. They need an assurance that somebody out there cares about them, is listening to them – that they are not just destined to travel down a long highway towards nothingness.

Want undoubtedly lies at the heart of the matter, but the cultural anthropologist will prefer to speak of the need for symbolic structures that serve to bring a sense of order in a disordered universe, intelligibility in the face of incomprehension and levers of power in the face of impotence. The phrase 'In God we trust' may have appeared on coins since 1864, but the free market in which that specie is spent has little room for other relationships of trust; the individual is all too readily isolated in the face of an unforgiving marketplace and an anonymous bureaucracy. Only the evangelical contract offers certainty: give yourself up to Jesus and you shall be saved. Americans may not have a Lord of the Manor, as in feudal societies, nor an all-providing government as in the socialist polity, but they can rely on a relationship with a nurturing Jesus Christ.

The much-vaunted values of the American Way are accommodated, even promoted, in the process. Church membership provides a sense of community for men and women who appear like agitated molecules in America's dynamic, mobile society. Meanwhile, the myth is sustained that members of free congregations enjoy free will under God and bear responsibility for their own destiny. While the 'Dream' suggests that anyone can make it to the top through hard work and application, the realities are different for many. Submission to Jesus is an appealing alternative to the challenge of pulling yourself up by the bootstraps.

In this narrative, the practice that liberates the soul of the individual also controls their worst egoistical traits. Concern with salvation cultivates a hedge around the anti-social sins of self-gratification; self-centred behaviour is curbed, and vices (pride, gluttony, lust, etc.) are suppressed. However, in reality, the churched have reached an extraordinary accommodation with the material world, imbuing commerce and consumerism with a semi-sacred lustre. We have seen this circle squared in the 'Temple of Trade'. We see it again in the congeries of paradoxical beliefs expressed at Halloween in the rites of 'trick or treat'.

CHAPTER FOUR

The Lattice Constant – On Innovation and Enervation

'Yes We Can!'

This slogan, deployed by Barack Obama in his successful bid for the US presidency, became a chant repeated again and again by the crowds who flocked to hear him. It formed part of an innovative campaign that led Steve Strauss, writing on the 'Huffington Post' website, to describe Obama as 'the best entrepreneur in the world'.

It was, however, Obama's predecessor, George W. Bush, who captured the quasi-religious gloss that is applied to the nation's 'can-do' creed, when in February 2007 he described the US as 'entrepreneurial heaven ... a great place to take risk and to realize your dreams'. In the process, he combined praise for the nation's spirit of innovation with condemnation of its nemesis, 'pork-barrel politics', where legislators appropriate federal funds to benefit vested interests. All too easily, it seems, the innovating energy of the entrepreneur can be obstructed by the enervating antics of the power-brokers.

There was something emblematic about the president's choice of venue for his speech. George Bush was opening a semiconductor factory in Manassas, Virginia, after it had undergone a multibillion dollar makeover to improve the purity of its production-line. Semiconductors are the engines driving America's Electronic Age: the pitch-perfect scale of their crystalline structure – known as the 'Lattice Constant' – ensures the free flow of energy through the system. However, these crystals are vulnerable to impurities that block or divert the electrons. This was the trope operating beneath the president's narrative: the Lattice Constant of America's entrepreneurial heaven can be contaminated by privileged power-blocs whose interests are antithetical to a truly free society.

Here, then, is another crash-spot along the American Way. Freedom clashes with control, energy with power. The entrepreneur may be a source of continuous revolution but this is not enough to defeat resourceful interest-groups that flourish in society. 'Yes We Can', the one may aver. 'No You Can't', the other will retort.

There is nothing novel about novelty in the United States. In a nation that began with revolution, the word 'new' carries as much symbolic freight as 'freedom' and the two notions are inextricably linked. New art and new music make liberty manifest in the Land of the Free; spiritual salvation is defined as being 'born again'; and innovation is used indiscriminately to raise footfall in the Temple of Trade.

It may be an oxymoron to refer to a tradition of innovation, but the US has it. Images of invention, creativity, 'groundbreaking design', 'continuous improvement', 'the latest fashion' and 'this year's model' are woven into the cultural fabric. This tradition is symbolized in the Great Seal – dating back to 1782 – that appears on every dollar bill: its Latin inscription speaks of 'A New Order of the Ages' and its image of an unfinished pyramid is said by the US Department of Treasury to signify that the US will always grow, improve and build.

Innovation is taken to be a distinguishing characteristic of the nation. In every state and in every generation, there have been men who have gained – or lost – a fortune trying to make things work better, solve problems and liberate their fellow men and women by easing their lot. The US Patent Office – one of the few buildings in Washington, DC, spared the British torch when they burned the city down in 1814 – is itself an example of innovation becoming hard-wired into the establishment. This institution started with three 'utility' patents registered in 1790 and applications for patented inventions have grown to a record 456,321 inventions in 2008. The first patent – issued on 31 July 1790 – was signed by George Washington and Thomas Jefferson and went to Samuel Hopkins for a production process for potash and pearl ash – compounds used to make fertilizer and soap. This is one of 2,845 'X Patents' which survived a fire in 1836 (over 7,000 others were lost). The first patent issued under a new numbering system (established by the Patent Act in 1836) went to Senator John Ruggles of Maine, whose cog mechanism for train wheels was designed to give 'tractive power to the locomotive and to prevent the evil of the sliding of the wheels'.

Sir Harold Evans has argued that the adaptive genius of Americans is not simply invention, but inventiveness put to use. He writes in *They Made America* (2004), 'Practical innovation more than anything else is the reason America achieved pre-eminence, while other well-endowed landmasses lagged or failed.' Evans is not alone in identifying this characteristic. Geoffrey Gorer cites 'know-how' as a peculiarly American phenomenon: this society, he argues, is endlessly ingenious in transforming things to man's use, enjoyment and profit. He was, in turn, echoing the observations of Tocqueville, a century earlier, that Americans think about nothing but ways of changing their lot and bettering it.

Evans' 500-page book can be likened to those hagiographies of medieval Europe that extolled the lives of saints. He starts with John Fitch (steamboat) and ends with Larry Page and Sergey Brin (Google); along the way, readers encounter such luminaries as Eli Whitney (cotton gin), Samuel Colt (pistol), Cyrus McCormick (mechanical reaper), the Wright brothers (airplane), Henry Ford (car) and Philo T. Farnsworth (TV).

However, it is Thomas Edison (1847–1931), above all others, who has attained mythical standing in the nation. He was a man lionized in his own lifetime. When the following headline appeared on the front page of the *New York Graphic* on 1 April 1928 – 'Edison invents a machine that will feed the human race' – many readers were said to have accepted the story until they took a closer look at the date (April Fool's Day): this played on a common view that Edison was a man who could work miracles. A recent biography, written by George Sullivan and produced for American schoolchildren (*Thomas Edison*, 'In Their Own Words' series, 2001), describes him as the greatest inventor in American history:

> Edison amazed people with the first practical electric light-bulb. The phonograph was another of his successes. He invented a movie camera and projector, and was one of the first people to produce movies. Edison also did much more. He invented the business of inventing. He brought together teams of scientists and engineers. He used them to solve problems [and] in doing so, Edison introduced the idea of the modern research laboratory, which many companies use today.

Edison's papers have been methodically catalogued and preserved by Rutgers University. In a society that reveres the written word, this is the equivalent to preserving the relics of medieval saints – it honours the man and offers his followers direct access to and contact with his genius. There are also shrines to his memory at the Edison National Historic Site in West Orange, New Jersey; the Edison Winter Home in Fort Myers, Florida; the Edison Birthplace Museum in Milan, Ohio; the Thomas Edison House in Louisville, Kentucky; and the Edison Memorial Tower and Museum in Edison, New Jersey. Visitors to these places will learn that in addition to being granted 1,093 patents in his lifetime, he patented a number of memorable quotations, including the oft-cited line that 'genius is one percent inspiration and ninety-nine percent perspiration'. His can-do ethos was exemplified in his words to employees working on developing the electric light-bulb: 'The trouble with other inventors is that they try a few things and they quit. I never quit until I get what I want.' The story is still told of the last day of the year 1879, when he laid on a display of electric lights strung from one tree to another leading to his laboratory at

Menlo Park; every room, indeed, was lit with his lamps and the many visitors were fascinated by being able to switch the electric flow on and off. This, the *New York Tribune* declared, was 'progress on the march'.

Progress was something that inspired Edison. He was excited by the arrival of the horseless carriage, saying that the automobile woke America up, energizing the nation: 'It has caused them to move, to stir themselves, to get out and away.' But then improvement to all forms of communication – the canal, the railroad, the airplane, the telegraph, the radio – has always excited the American imagination (undoubtedly because the country for so long has felt the need to embrace and bestride its limitless tracts). Nathaniel Hawthorne expressed the sense of freedom that came with the locomotive when he wrote in *The House of the Seven Gables* (1851): 'These railroads . . . give us wings; they annihilate the toil and dust of pilgrimage; they spiritualize travel!' He was equally effusive in his paean to electricity and the telegraph, painting a picture that seems to presage the world wide web.

If Sir Harold Evans is the hagiographer of American innovation, the early-twentieth-century economist Joseph Schumpeter is the theologian – he is described as the *Prophet of Innovation* in the title of a 2007 biography by Thomas K. McCraw. Schumpeter regarded the entrepreneur as the most conspicuous figure in the capitalist process, distinct from the manager who is focused on administrative direction and the capitalist who risks his wealth. The defining characteristic of entrepreneurial enterprise was the doing of new things or the doing of things that are already being done in a new way. Schumpeter argued that the entrepreneur was inherently revolutionary, destroying old, traditional, atavistic social structures: 'Not until the process we term the Industrial Revolution did the working masses, led by the entrepreneur, overcome the bonds of older life-forms – the environment of peasantry, guild and aristocracy.'

Today, internet users can browse millions of records lodged in the US Patent Office by these revolutionaries. Search engines allow us to scrutinize the records by inventor, category or date, using portals such as Patent Storm, whose home page bears Edison's elegant drawing of an electric light-bulb (Patent No. 223,898, dated 27 January 1880). While the new grants featured in May 2009 were expressed in words that a layman can comprehend – an improved livestock feeder, a new method for making a wind-turbine blade root and a new imaging system for locating subcutaneous blood vessels – the language of invention can possess an incantatory power and magic that holds our attention, even though the meaning is difficult to fathom: 'piezoelectric resonator filter'; 'method to predict and identify defocus wafers'; 'skew cancellation for source synchronous clock and data signals'; 'Nonhuman model animal of Th2-mediated hyperimmune response'; 'adding microscopic porosity to a microcoil's surface for medical implantation'; 'methods and systems employing intracranial electrodes for neuro-stimulation and/or electroencephalography'.

One of the main reasons for registering a patent is, of course, to secure monopoly rights in the invention for twenty years, with the hope of reaping financial rewards as well as scientific kudos. However, in reality, fewer than 10 per cent of patents achieve commercial success and fewer than 1 per cent can be considered to be of seminal importance.

Mark Zuckerberg, twenty-three, has certainly achieved the former. He is upheld as the latest example of an entrepreneur-inventor, having started to develop Facebook, the social network website, in his Harvard dorm room in 2002. He and two business partners moved their operation to an apartment in Palo Alto, California, after Bill Gates (the founder of Microsoft and America's wealthiest citizen) had urged his Harvard class to take time off school to work on a project. In October 2007, Microsoft paid $240 million for a 1.6 per cent stake in the company – which had 40 million users and registrations doubling every six months – putting a value of $15 billion on the company.

Zuckerberg stands close to the pinnacle of the Great Seal's unfinished pyramid. Max – a nervous twenty-three-year-old from Chicago – is more typical of those populating the base. He has completed his studies in French and German at a California university, and is now rooming with three friends as they launch their unique business proposal:

> We are taking the Christian fish symbol somewhere else. You know, that *ichthus* logo that Christians put on their cars ... We want to develop that motif. How about the Darwinian fish – with legs and the words 'I'm evolving'? What about fish that wear the colors of your favourite sports team? Then you can have a big Orioles fish swallowing a Chicago White Sox; or vice versa. The possibilities are endless.

Max has prepared a 150-page business plan and is looking to raise $1.75 million of start-up funds from venture capitalists.

Max will probably discover that the free-market waters in which he is swimming contain more piranha than *ichthus*: whatever the merits of his piscine vision, the scales are tilted against him. However, for Americans there is something admirable about entrepreneurial failure: if he falls, Max will be expected to pick himself up and start over again. 'In Silicon Valley we don't ask how close to the cliff? but where do the skid-marks begin?' says Allen Morgan, the managing director of Silicon Valley's oldest venture capitalist firm, Mayfield. He estimates that 50 per cent of the enterprises that his company invests in will fail: 'There is no shame in failure – it is evidence of experience.' Max belongs to a group of aspiring businessmen and -women who are – it has been said – sustaining revolution in the US. That was certainly the view of Schumpeter, who insisted that an entrepreneurial initiative did not have to be of spectacular, historical importance: 'It need not be Bessemer steel or the explosion motor. It can be the Deerfoot sausage'. Or even an *ichthus* in the White Sox strip.

J.R. Simplot embodies this tradition. When he died, in May 2008 at the age of ninety-nine, he was billed as the US's oldest billionaire, worth $3.6 billion. He was an all-American 'rags to riches' story: a farm-boy who grew up in a log cabin before striking out on his own to create an empire of businesses employing 10,000 people (making his largest fortune from frozen french fries). Simplot had walked away from his family's Idaho farm at fourteen after an argument with his father: he went into the potato-growing business, using money acquired from selling hogs raised on his own slop formula of horsemeat and potatoes. He adopted new growing and processing techniques and was a millionaire by thirty. During the Second World War, the young entrepreneur reportedly supplied one-third of the dried potatoes and onions consumed by American troops – weighing in at some 38 million pounds. Simplot's company came to dominate the postwar boom in frozen and packaged foods, as he converted his equipment to handle frozen chips, instant potatoes, dried hash browns and frozen shoestring potatoes. In the mid-1960s, he signed a contract with Ray Kroc to supply fries to the burgeoning McDonald's restaurant chain.

The 'Potato King' echoed Edison whenever he was asked the secret of his success: 'Work hard – that's all. Don't listen to others. If I'd have listened to my attorneys and bankers, hell, they'd have had me broke before I got started.' In 1980, aged seventy-one, he moved into the high-tech field of semiconductors, buying 40 per cent of what would become Micron Technology. He might almost have written the script that President Bush used when opening that Micron factory: he told a reporter some time ago, 'America is the greatest country in the world. I've proved that you can be a success. I made it – and I started from scratch.'

Government statistics show that about 10 per cent of the US workforce owns a business. This in itself is not significant: agricultural societies in the Old and New Worlds (Greece, Italy, Portugal, Spain, New Zealand, Ireland) have higher rates of self-employment, reaching up to almost 20 per cent. However, a striking feature of the American Way is the generation of new business. In 1996–2005, for instance, new companies were launched by an average of 437,000 people a month.

David Giles represents one such adventurer walking that perilous path between success and failure. He is the English inventor of FastShip – a revolutionary vessel which promises to carry a 10,000-ton payload across the Atlantic between Philadelphia and Cherbourg in less than four days in almost all weather conditions. This could almost halve the journey-time for the movement of freight and offer a credible alternative to air-transport (with its costs and threats to the environment). He says:

> I left England because of the bureaucracy and the attitude of the Admiralty towards my design. In contrast, there was interest from the US Navy and from one wealthy individual who saw the opportunity for improving his own world-wide logistics. In America you find open minds and a drive to make things better.

Fred Smith of FedEx was prepared to stake $10 million as seed capital in the enterprise.

Simon Fittall is another British-born businessman drawn to the US. His company, PharThinking, has developed Bayesian inference models to evaluate opportunities in the pharmaceutical and biotech sectors. He argues that he is prospering as a start-up in the US because of the tax regime and can-do culture; but he also believes that America's innovative edge is sustained by immigrants: 'American growth would be zero if it wasn't for zero-generation Americans like me.'

One migrant who has achieved the zenith of this entrepreneurial heaven is Max Levchin. He is the founder of PayPal – an e-commerce business that allows payments and money transfers to be made through the internet. He was born in Ukraine and came to the US when his parents migrated. He has described how he turned himself into an American at high school: his fellow students coached him on the right haircut and clothes, but above all he made a deliberate effort to become enterprising because that, he was convinced, was the American Way.

The Current Population Survey does, indeed, confirm an

entrepreneurial bias within the migrant community. In 2005, 350 out of 100,000 immigrants started a business each month compared to 280 out of 100,000 native-born Americans. More detailed research has shown that at least one key founder was foreign-born in a quarter of all technology and engineering companies started between 1995 and 2005 – mostly from India, the United Kingdom, China, Taiwan, Japan and Germany. Nationwide, companies like this produced $52 billion in sales and employed 450,000 workers in 2005.

The Nobel Prize provides another index of American enterprise and innovation. No other country has had as many Nobel Prize recipients. In October 2003 a monument was dedicated in Theodore Roosevelt Park, Manhattan, honouring almost 300 Americans who have won the prize. The migrant also features strongly in the list of laureates: for instance, almost one in three of all American Nobel Prize-winners in medicine and physiology were born overseas (twenty-seven out of the eighty-seven prize-winners).

It would appear that the American Dream is self-sustaining: enterprising foreigners are inspired by the myth and come to make it a reality. However, only a tiny proportion of foreign-born founders of American businesses actually entered the country with this purpose in mind: educational and job opportunities drew them in, and research shows that they only founded companies after living in the United States for some thirteen years. Education – especially in the STEM fields of science, technology, engineering and mathematics – is often an essential component in the mix, with 53 per cent of the immigrant founders of technology and engineering companies completing their highest degrees in US universities. This has led the Kauffman Foundation to argue that the nation would benefit from more enlightened immigration policies, attracting and retaining highly skilled foreign workers to sustain the dynamic spirit of American entrepreneurship.

The pattern of settlement of these university-bound migrants may be one explanation for the extraordinary variation in the genius of individual states (when measured by business start-ups and the registration of patents). Vermont, Colorado, Montana, Wyoming and Idaho are found to be the states with the highest rate of entrepreneurial activity, with three times the average rate of business start-ups compared with those states at the bottom of the league table – Delaware, West Virginia, Alabama, Kentucky and Pennsylvania. As a general rule, levels of entre-preneurialism are concentrated in the Mountain states and Pacific and northeastern regions of the US, while rates are lower in the Southern and Midwestern states.

A similar trend emerges in the chart at the end of the chapter, which ranks each state by relating the share of registered patents (2001–05) with share of the national population. Utah emerges as the benchmark, with 0.8 per cent of both population and patents. California appears to be almost twice as inventive with a 12 per cent share of the population but 22.4 per cent of all patents. But Idaho's population of 1.5 million (0.5 per cent of the nation) punches way beyond its weight with over 2 per cent of all patents.

In this list of winners and losers in the innovation stakes, there is a striking contrast between the West and Northeast, and the Southern states who appear disinclined to dabble with innovation (despite a reputation for literary creativity). There will be cultural and historical differences at work here – evidence, perhaps, of the gulf between North and South that brought about the Civil War, or evidence of the consequences of victory and defeat. However, it would be a mistake to assume that the 'genius of states' is about the priorities and innate skill of individual citizens. The reality is that most of the innovations registered as patents are institutional, generated by companies, universities and government departments rather than by individuals. The records of the US Patent Office for 2006 show that only 15,247 patents – out of 102,343 issued to applicants based in the US – went to independent American inventors. So it is almost certainly the case that Micron Technology – the company that had supplied the venue for George W. Bush's speech about Entrepreneurial Heaven – provides the reason why Idaho tops our league table.

Corporations like Micron, IBM, Hewlett-Packard, Intel, Microsoft and Texas Instruments embody a tradition of corporate research and development dating back to the creation of DuPont and Kodak Research Laboratories in 1911. The term 'R & D' was recorded in the dictionaries as an Americanism by the 1960s, but statistics have been assiduously retained measuring the amount of money spent on research and development since the 1930s, and the pioneer American industrial research laboratory was founded by General Electric in 1900.

Innovation is judged to be important for corporate entities because – it is said – they need to rejuvenate to survive. This notion dates back at least to the early twentieth century, when Willis R. Whitney – a pioneer in the development of General Electric's laboratory – argued that major enterprises had to remain innovative: 'Our research laboratory was a development of the idea that large industrial organizations have both an opportunity and a responsibility for their own life insurance.'

John W. Gardner (who died in 2002) was another powerful advocate for dynamic change. He worked as secretary of health, education and welfare under President Lyndon Johnson and wrote numerous books on improving leadership in American society. In *Self-Renewal* (1963) he urged readers to sustain a spirit of adventure as they grew older, testing out new business models: 'We pay a heavy price for our fear of failure. It assures the progressive narrowing of the personality and prevents exploration and experimentation.'

Gardner belonged to a cadre of experts – academics, politicians, commentators and management consultants – who have contributed to the construction of a symbolic universe in which enterprise, innovation and entrepreneurialism are promoted as distinctive features of the American Way. The management consultant – often referred to as a 'guru' or 'company doctor' – is one of those 'ritual specialists' within the American culture who operate in a liminal space – in this case between the creative, individual innovator and the corporation. The Bureau of Census shows that almost 400,000 people were employed as management analysts in 1999. The Census reports:

As business becomes more complex, the Nation's firms are continually faced with new challenges. Firms increasingly rely on management analysts to help them remain competitive amidst these changes. [They] analyze and propose ways to improve an organization's structure, efficiency and costs.

The industrialization of innovation sits uncomfortably with the mythical narratives that champion the independent entrepreneur, but this is the reality. An equally important role has been played by the federal government over the years. Barack Obama has pointed to the Morrill Act – signed by Lincoln in 1862 – as a key milestone here. This spawned the land grant colleges, establishing a model for universities to serve as research and development laboratories for the nation. Today, the US government regularly features in the top ten of American organizations registering new patents. For instance, in 2005 it received 696 utility patents, ranking it eighth in the table, after many of the usual suspects listed above; and the success of the US's electronics industry dates back to a huge expansion in governmental science and engineering investments during the Second World War.

The lives of tens of millions of Americans living in the plains and prairies of the Midwest have been affected by a modest government initiative since 1914, when the Department of Agriculture created the Cooperative Extension Service (CES). The CES established a network of clubs for boys and girls that became known as 'Four-H Clubs' (the letters stand for Heart, Head, Hands and Health). The aim was to teach rural youth the practical skills of farming, and experimentation was an early feature with competitions to see how many bushels of corn could be raised on a plot of land through introducing the latest techniques. Today, there are almost 100,000 Four-H Clubs in the country with over 9 million members aged 5–21: their motto resonates with the spirit of innovation – 'To Make the Best Better!'

The engine of war has been especially powerful in driving forward innovation in the country. The Defense Advanced

Research Projects Agency (DARPA) exemplifies this. Its mission is 'to maintain the technological superiority of the US military' and it claims bragging rights to such developments as the Stealth fighter, the Drone (or unmanned aerial vehicles) and even the internet. The agency's overriding imperative is said to be 'radical innovation for national security', so its 2007 strategy talks about importing entrepreneurial programme managers:

> To maintain an entrepreneurial atmosphere and the flow of new ideas, DARPA hires program managers for only 4 to 6 years because the best way to foster new ideas is to bring in new people with fresh outlooks. New people also ensure that DARPA has very few institutional interests beside innovation, because new program managers are willing to redirect the work of their predecessors – and even undo it, if necessary ... Another element of DARPA's strategy is to cultivate entrepreneurial performers in university and industries by funding ideas that represent revolutionary, vice evolutionary, technical achievements.

However, successful innovation is hard to achieve or sustain within a corporate or institutional environment. Before it was declared bankrupt in late 2001, Enron – the Houston-based company whose interests extended to electricity, natural gas, communications, pulp and paper companies – was named 'America's Most Innovative Company' by *Fortune* for six consecutive years. It employed 22,000 people and its accounts registered revenues of $111 billion in 2000. Twelve months later it was revealed that Enron's accounts were based on institutionalized, systematic and creatively planned fraud; in the ensuing fire-sale, even the iconic 'crooked E' logo – made of stainless steel and neon – had lost its value, selling for $8,500 (when it was estimated to have cost $50,000).

Enron's collapse was one of three substantial bankruptcies that occurred in the US between December 2001 and July 2002 (the others being WorldCom and Global Crossing), and it has been said that all these failures were partly due to the innovative use of complex financial instruments known as derivatives. The economists behind these new mathematical models had gained international recognition in 1997, when Myron Scholes and Robert Merton received the Nobel Prize in Economic Sciences for 'a new method to determine the value of options'. (Fischer Black would have joined them, had he not died in 1995.) The work of these extraordinary men – who oscillated between academia and trading houses such as Goldman Sachs, Saloman Brothers and the ill-fated Long-Term Capital Management – fuelled a massive increase in such instruments as equity options and currency or interest-rate swaps in the 1990s. However, the financial sector found itself riding a high-speed train without sufficient understanding of the controls and without the track to support it. As early as 2002, Warren Buffett, the American investor acclaimed as 'The Sage of Omaha', wrote that derivatives posed a grave threat to the global financial system: 'We view them as time bombs, both for the parties that deal in them and the economic system. Derivatives are financial weapons of mass destruction, carrying dangers that, while now latent, are potentially lethal.'

Other commentators were far more sanguine. In February 2004, Gene Callahan and Greg Kaza argued (in ReasonOn-Line.com – motto 'Free Minds and Free Markets') that derivatives were playing 'a central role in the flowering of innovation that financial markets have enjoyed during the last two decades'. However, by 2009, the nation, like the rest of the world, was suffering from the mother of all hangovers created by the production of ever more elaborate and innovative credit derivatives such as collateralized debt obligations and credit default swaps (CDS) that minced and repackaged loans in an attempt to manage risk and make more money. At the height of the madness, the value of the CDS market allegedly reached over $60 trillion – almost four times larger than the total capitaliza-tion of all the stocks traded on the New York Stock Exchange. When Lehman Brothers fell on 15 September 2008, the avalanche began.

There is a paradox here – a mismatch in the Lattice Constant. The US may have industrialized the process of innovation, but the independent inventor/entrepreneur and the corporate business enterprise are by their very nature poles apart, like (to sustain our metaphor) silicon and germanium. The instincts of the innovator are revolutionary. The instincts of the corporation are conservative. The US may have sought to institutionalize the habits of innovation, but any institution or organization must inevitably be drawn into the preservation and promotion of the interest-group. Here we encounter one manifestation of a phenomenon that is as pervasive in the US as in any other society – politics and power-games.

In *The Power Elite* (1956), C. Wright Mills described a class of men within American society:

> whose positions enable them to transcend the ordinary environments of ordinary men and women . . . they are in command of the major hierarchies and organizations of modern society. They rule the big corporations. They run the machinery of state and claim its prerogatives.

It is this institutional feature of power that makes it so different from the creative energy of the innovator. Political power is rarely, if ever, the property of an individual: it corresponds to the human ability to act in concert. Power-brokers develop and exploit social capital – a resource deriving from a durable network of more or less institutionalized relationships – to channel power to benefit a minority.

Social capital takes many different forms in twenty-first-century America. The gang culture of the nation's impoverished wards represents one example, with estimates putting the number of gangs nationwide at 30,533, with 815,896 members. (Los Angeles tops the list with nearly 8,000 gangs and at least 200,000 gang members.) A less brutal, but not necessarily less cruel, variant is found in the discriminating high school cliques that form around 'jocks' and 'cheerleaders', 'emos' and 'goths'.

However, for those who wish to develop political stature in society, the process frequently begins with college honour (or 'Greek') societies. These groups, with their arcane rites of allegiance, are similar in purpose and function to the sects of traditional cultures and the guilds and Masonic lodges of medieval Europe.

Statistics illustrating the special status of honour societies are openly published. In the autumn of 2008, for instance, the homepage of 'Greek Life' on the website of the University of California drew on data produced by the 2006 North American Interfraternity Conference to claim that 'Greeks' represent: 3 per cent of the US population (i.e. 9 million people); 30 per cent of *Fortune* 500 executives; 30 per cent of congressmen/women; 40 per cent of all US Supreme Court justices; 42 per cent of all senators; 48 per cent of all US presidents.

Membership is typically an affiliation for life, so students are not normally allowed to be initiated into more than one sorority or fraternity. The Phi Beta Kappa Society is the most prestigious of these, claiming that enrolment is one of the highest honours that can be conferred on an undergraduate. Its Greek-letter name stands for *philosophia biou kubernetes*, meaning 'love of learning is the guide of life'. It is an exclusive society that aims to foster and recognize excellence in the arts and sciences. It is also the oldest honour society in the US, being founded at the College of William and Mary on 5 December 1776 – five months after the Declaration of Independence. Phi Beta Kappa introduced a code of high ideals, secret rituals and handclasps, membership badges and oaths that have come to characterize all 'Greek letter' societies. Today it has over 500,000 living members, 276 chapters and 58 alumni associations.

There is no indication that Barack Obama is affiliated to an honour society (despite speculation on the web that he was pledged to the Kappa Alpha Psi Fraternity, with its strong African-American credentials). However, Alan D. DeSantis (professor of communications, University of Kentucky) has

found that 'Greek' social organizations produce a dispropor-
tionately large percentage of power-brokers in business and
government. Phi Beta Kappa boasts that its membership has
included seventeen presidents (including George Bush Snr and
Bill Clinton) and seven out of nine current Supreme Court
justices. Through the alumni associations, members can continue their 'active affiliation' with the society after graduation,
with an emphasis on supporting scholarship and learning.
However, it is inevitable that those outside the privileged circle
will suspect this is a group that works to promote the interests
of members.

The traditional appeal of the fraternity society is nicely
expressed in an article in 'Punchline' (an online newsletter
serving readers in Richmond, Virginia) where a writer using the
pseudonym 'Senior Cranky' recalls:

> I was active in the now defunct Mu Mu Pi chapter at Xavier
> University back when fraternities had something to do with
> dignity and honor . . . I learned quickly that the only way
> to get anywhere in life is to make friends early and take
> advantage of them later. The University's Greek society was
> the best place for a young man in my day to begin climbing
> the social ladder. If you wanted an ounce of respect, you
> rushed your fraternity of choice right after unpacking your
> clean underwear and wool socks. The last thing you wanted
> to be was a goddamn independent. Sure we were lured by
> the mystery of a secret society and we wanted to see what
> all the strange rituals were really about, but the real appeal
> was the way that a fraternity could clinch you an instant
> circle of friends. What a difference it made to walk across
> that wide lawn snuggled into a fraternity sweater vest. Oh,
> that magic cashmere did make the ladies swoon.

A different image of a fraternity is presented in the film
Animal House (1978): the emphasis, here, is on kegs of beer,
bouts of boozing, toga parties, the punishing rites of initiation
('hazing' – popularly depicted as beating on the bottom with a

paddle) and sexual escapades with sororities. Hank Nuwer, who recently retired from the Indiana University School of Journalism, has criticized this culture in *Wrongs of Passage* (1999), where he examines 'the dark side of college fraternal life', while DeSantis has argued that 'Greek culture' instils conventional gender stereotypes: the 'real men' of the fraternity are unemotional, promiscuous, violent and aggressively masculine; the 'nice girls' of the sorority are nurturing, passive, domestic and purely feminine.

It is claimed that a distinguishing feature of the 'Greek' system is the process of selection, where many are called – in an event called 'The Rush' – but few are chosen. Statistics show that only one in ten college students belongs to a fraternity or sorority, but with the national figure peaking at 400,000 in 1990 there are indications that many students are rejecting the process (rather than being rejected by it). It is not surprising that many Americans hold 'frats' in contempt or suspicion – a view reinforced by media stories of hate crimes against African-Americans or homosexuals. Nevertheless, the system continues to flourish. Some of the societies are associated with ethnic or other interest-groups, but the majority are linked to a chosen vocation, such as aerospace engineering (Sigma Gamma Tau), osteopathic medicine (Sigma Sigma Phi), anthropology (Lambda Alpha), forensics (Pi Kappa Delta), computer science (Epsilon Delta Pi) and religious studies (Theta Chi Beta).

There are a number of other college societies that have gained a particular reputation for secrecy. The most renowned of these is Skull and Bones at Yale, described as an organization aiming to create bonds among future leaders of the US. Another group surrounded by mystique and some suspicion is the Seven Society at the University of Virginia. Members are only revealed after their death, when a wreath of black magnolias in the shape of a '7' is placed at the gravesite, the bell tower of the University Chapel chimes seven times at seven-second intervals on the seventh dissonant chord when it is seven past the hour, and a notice is published in the university's alumni news and the *Cavalier Daily*. The group contributes financially to the university, announcing donations with letters signed only with seven astronomical symbols in the order: Earth, Jupiter, Mercury, Mars, Neptune, Uranus and Venus. Saturn is not included. The society also gives scholarships to the university each year in quantities that include the number 7, e.g. $777 or $1,777. In addition to granting spontaneous gifts, it sponsors an annual $7,000 graduate fellowship award for excellence in teaching. Students supposedly are 'tapped' for admission during their third year and become members during their fourth year. The only known method to successfully contact the Seven Society is to place a letter at the base of the Thomas Jefferson statue inside the university's historic Rotunda.

All this arcane mystery inevitably feeds the public imagination and these organizations have acquired a sinister reputation, sustained by films like *The Skulls* (2000), which shows a college senior from a poor background join an elite college fraternity, hoping to gain acceptance into Harvard Law School; a series of strange incidents, including his best friend's suicide, leads him to uncover the true nature of the group. Robert De Niro's 2006 film *The Good Shepherd* – about the early years of the CIA – includes a key flashback in the narrative when the hero (Edward Wilson) is initiated into the Skull and Bones, revealing a deep secret as a way of demonstrating a bond of trust; later, at a Skull and Bones retreat on Deer Island, Edward is invited to join the Office of Strategic Services.

Periodically, one is told, even by rational public servants, lawyers or financiers, that X or Y has gained preference or advancement thanks to his or her affiliation to a secret society (the Tabard Society, founded in 1987 in the University of Pennsylvania, is a 'pseudo-Greek' society for women, which has developed the reputation for having a strong network of sisters working in positions of authority). These casual comments and reflections occupy one end of a spectrum of opinion that holds these societies to be part of a conspiracy to contain and channel political power and influence. At the other extreme, there are books like *America's Secret Establishment: An Introduction to the Order of Skull and Bones* (1983) by Antony C. Sutton, with volumes entitled 'How the Order Controls Education' and 'How the Order Creates War and Revolution'. The author tells us that his work explains 'why we go to war, to lose; why Wall Street loves Marxists and Nazis; why the kids can't read; why the Churches have become propaganda founts; why historical facts are suppressed, why politicians lie and a hundred other whys'.

A more recent article by Artevia Wilborn, published in December 2006 under the headline 'Secret Societies: They Are Not Just at Yale – They Are Running a University Near You', explores the phenomenon of powerful secret societies within the nation's public universities. She examines organizations like Spades (Auburn University, Alabama), Order of the Bull's Blood (Rutgers, New Jersey), Mystical Seven Society (Wesleyan University, Connecticut), The Order of Gimghoul (University of North Carolina at Chapel Hill), and Burning Spear (Florida State University):

> what societies like Spades aim to do is build an ever growing web of influence; and like a bunch of spiders they position themselves in key places on their web so that their slightest touch affects the entire college web . . . Machine, University of Alabama's secret society, has used all manner of illegal tricks and threats to both win university elections and discourage opponents from running against them.

For Wilborn, these societies fight to control the political makeup of their universities in pursuit of power. They control student organizations' budgets and place people on the student judicial board. They write legislation that affects the student body and hold representatives in every college or school on their university's campus. They allocate funds for student festivities and events and safeguard the interests of groups like fraternities and sororities, of which many secret-society members also hold membership. Furthermore, the networks they establish continue into the arena of adult politics: 'like the members of Skull and Bones these secret societies members on public university campuses go on to powerful positions in local, state, and federal government, they become successful business men, and continue the ever connecting web of power'.

In this vision, secret societies become a nursery for power-brokers preparing for a life of political machinations in the country at large, being described by one commentator as 'hotbeds of future success'. This reinforces a deep antipathy towards 'big' government that is already well embedded in the country. The Pew Research Center has found that in 2007 only a third of Americans agreed with the statement 'Most elected officials care what people like me think' (matching a twenty-year low in 1994 and down from 44 per cent in 2002). There is a mythical depiction of the Executive as a sinister machine spying on its own citizens in order to advance the interests of a powerful and shadowy cabal. Hollywood regularly taps into this vein, with films like *All the President's Men* (1976), and *The Bourne Ultimatum* (2007). *Enemy of the State* (1998) – with its tagline 'It's not paranoia if they really are after you!' – depicts a national security agency that is capable of directing satellites to gather imagery on an individual at a moment's notice, at the whim of a corrupt executive.

In the beginning, of course, American revolutionaries chose as their emblem a rattlesnake with the motto 'Don't tread on me!' They sloughed off the constraining skin of British imperial rule, and the seminal experience for so many Americans was of a frontier where government was inchoate. For Llewellyn H. Rockwell Jr (president of the Ludwig von Mises Institute and one of America's self-proclaimed champions of the free market), the founding ideology of the US was around an idea of liberty where humanity scaled previously unattainable heights in pursuit of their dreams, cooperating and competing with each other as they chose. So for Rockwell, it is 'a profound political paradox' that the US government has become a leviathan – 'larger, more consolidated, more powerful, and more intrusive than it has ever been in its history'. But this view is not confined to right-wing ideologists. Geoffrey Gorer observed in the 1940s, 'With practically no exceptions, Americans regard their own government as alien; they do not identify with it, do not consider themselves involved in its actions, feel free to criticize and despise it.' The contemporary American anthropologist, Peter L. Berger, reflects this view when he writes that public institutions now confront the individual as an immensely powerful and alien world, incomprehensible in its inner workings, anonymous in its human character.

Conspiracy theories are impossible to disprove – that, perhaps, is why they are so prevalent – but what is incontrovertible is the dominant place that patronage holds on the political stage. Anthropologists are familiar with societies – such as those of the Mediterranean – where patron–client relationships underpin political structures: those who enjoy power advance friends and supporters, partly to bring benefit to a mutual interest-group, partly to reward past favours and partly to ensure access to trustworthy allies while navigating the treacherous waters of statecraft.

The surprise is to find patronage playing such an important role in the so-called 'Anglo-Saxon' society of the US, suffused as it is with free-market principles (although, of course, the mosaic of migrant communities creates the perfect conditions for 'Tammany Hall' politics to flourish). It is found at all levels of polity. At the local level, the city mayors and county executives will appoint citizens to serve on boards, committees and commissions. In Texas, the governor is likely to make 3,000 appointments in the course of a four-year term. In California, the governor's office issues periodic announcements of appointments to such varied bodies as the California Air Resources Board, the Building Standards Commission, the Tehama District Fair Board of Directors, and the California Commission on Teacher Credentialing.

In 2006, President George had a larger, more elaborate court around him than that of King George in 1776; and this has not changed with Obama's arrival in the post. Some 9,000 government appointments are made by the president. They are listed in the 'Plum Book' – *The United States Government Policy and Supporting Positions* – which identifies all offices in the legislative and executive branches of the federal government that are subject to non-competitive appointments. It is the norm for the political affiliation of each appointment – especially at state and federal level – to be declared, and although there is an occasional 'independent', the majority will belong to either the 39 million membership of the Democratic Party or the 30 million membership of the Republican Party.

Americans are familiar with periodic revelations about the corruption of local politicians at town, municipal and state level. The nation was shaken, for instance, in December 2008 by news that the governor of Illinois, Rod Blagojevich, had been arrested by the FBI for trying to sell the Senate seat vacated by Barack Obama. Over 1,000 officials and businessmen have been convicted of corruption in Illinois since the 1970s, including three former governors. Illinoisans will point out that surveys show other states – notably Louisiana – are even more corrupt, but they also recognize that the state operates unusual rules for managing the bankrolling of political campaigns, which allow unlimited direct corporate contributions to politicians' campaign funds.

The phenomenon of 'earmarks' – condemned so vociferously by President Bush in his speech at the semiconductor factory – is seen as the ultimate manifestation of political power-broking. At its crudest, a legislator intervenes in the process of distributing federal funds by shoe-horning money into projects that will promote either favoured interest-groups or their own personal standing within their constituency. There is no doubt that earmarks can be used for corrupt purposes: the case of Randall Harold Cunningham, known as Randy 'Duke', represents the most blatant example of this in the first decade of the twenty-first century. He represented California's 50th District (in San Diego) as a Republican member of the House of Representatives from 1991 to 2005. In March 2006, this heroic 'flying ace' from the Vietnam War was sentenced to over eight years in prison after he pleaded guilty to accepting at least $2.4 million in bribes and to federal charges of conspiracy to commit bribery, mail fraud, wire fraud and tax evasion. This is the longest prison sentence ever given to a congressman for bribery.

A notable piece of evidence was the so-called 'bribery menu' where Cunningham had set out – on a sheet of congressional stationery – how much he expected in kickbacks from his co-conspirators in the defence sector for earmarks pushed through Congress: he wanted a yacht worth $140,000 for the first $16 million in government contracts and $50,000 for each additional million thereafter. Cunningham was well placed to influence federal expenditure as a member of the House Appropriations and Intelligence Committees.

The Office of Management and Budget now tries to keep track of earmarks, maintaining a website that allows the 'pork-barrel' element of Bills to be scrutinized. In 2005, for instance, 13,492 earmarks were registered in appropriations bills, totalling almost $19 billion; in 2008, this fell to 11,524 earmarks totalling $16.5 billion. A further 6,335 multi-year earmarks were linked to Authorization Bills at that time, amounting to over $23 billion. Conservatively, the annual 'pork-barrel' expenditure between 2000 and 2009 amounted to $20 billion; the equivalent to the annual Gross Domestic Product of two countries too often associated with wholesale brigandry and corruption – Albania and Georgia.

Public debate in the US focuses on the more absurd or egregious examples of earmarks, such as the 'Iowa Rainforest' (sponsored by Senator Charles Grassley) or Alaska's 'Bridges to Nowhere' (promoted by Senator Ted Stevens and Representative Don Young). However, to the neutral observer, most earmarks appear worthy, even innocuous, with municipal authorities or academic research institutes receiving funds to take forward work that can benefit local communities or society at large. The following list – drawn from the 2005 crop – illustrates the range:

- $400,000 to improve University Drive, Macomb, Illinois;
- $10 million for the reconstruction and rehabilitation of the intersection of K-18 and 12th Street interchange in Riley County, Kansas;
- $200,000 for Streetscape-Cordele, Georgia;
- $15 million for New York Department of Transportation to

purchase three ferries and establish system for ferry service from Rockaway Peninsula to Manhattan;

- Spin Electronics Consortia led by Arizona State University to receive $16.2 million to develop a means to significantly increase the density of solid state magnetic storage using novel packaging, spin momentum transfer and novel spin transport effects;

- Minot Air-Force Base, North Dakota, to receive $8.9 million to add/alter Dock 1 to multi-purpose hangar;

- Southern Methodist University in Texas to receive $990,000 to develop a multi-fabrication manufacturing technology for NASA;

- Balcones Canyonlands National Wildlife Refuge in Texas to receive $487,000 for acquiring land;

- $800,000 for the acquisition of land along CA 86 at the Desert Cahuilla Prehistoric Site, Imperial County, 'for environmental mitigation related to reducing wildlife mortality while maintaining habitat connectivity'.

Only occasionally, an entry might encourage those of a suspicious mien to raise a sceptical eyebrow. However, these are also acts of conspicuous consumption that demonstrate and reinforce the political prowess of their sponsors: they become a source of civic pride and inject funds into the local economy. It is often argued that this is democracy in action, with effective politicians bringing material benefits to their constituency. Nevertheless, interest groups distort local, national and global markets, undermining the image of an efficient, innovative American private sector. Rice production is a good example. The US domestic rice market was saturated long ago, so US rice farmers export around half their output. However, a paper presented to a UN conference in 2004 showed that American rice cost $331 per ton to produce, compared to $70 for Thailand and $79 for Vietnam. In 2002–06, government subsidies made up a remarkable 39 per cent of US rice farmers' total income, thanks – in no small part – to the efforts of the American Farm Bureau that has spent approximately $8 million a year on lobbying in this period.

The 'lobbyist' plays a key role in the process of bargaining between interest-groups and power-blocs – they call it 'pulling and hauling'. There is thought to be a revolving door between Capitol Hill, the Federal Triangle and K Street (where many lobbyists are located): those who have worked as staffers for congressmen, senators and senior figures in the administration take their network and experience to serve new masters in K Street. More than 13,000 lobbyists work in Washington, DC, outnumbering law-makers by 24 to 1; prominent interest-groups involved in hiring their services include the National Rifle Association, the Petroleum Institute, the Aerospace Industries Association, the Association of Realtors, Health Insurance Plans, the Alliance of Automobile Manufacturers and even the Edison Electric Institute. These organizations, and hundreds of others, have substantial resources at their disposal. In July 2005, for instance, the Center for Public Integrity reported that the pharmaceutical industry had spent almost $800 million promoting its interests over the previous seven years ($675 million on lobbying; $87 million on campaign donations to federal candidates and political parties; and $10 million given to advocacy groups). During this same period, congress and government agencies are said to have weakened federal oversight of the industry, strengthening patent protections, granting tax credits and generally protecting the industry's interests at home and abroad.

Many of the country's established companies have their own corporate lobbyists – they are regarded as a forceful source of influence in the capital, working to ensure corporate interests are taken into account by law-makers. League tables of leading lobbyists emerge periodically: on 27 April 2005, for instance, names listed by the congressional newspaper *The Hill* included the representatives of Citigroup, General Motors, Boeing, Microsoft and Ford. Brian Dailey of Lockheed Martin was – in an example of the 'revolving door' – formerly employed on the White House's National Space Council and the Senate Armed Services Committee. During the 2008 presidential election, Barack Obama vowed that 'lobbyists won't find a job in my

White House', but it has been impossible to make good on this promise: by May 2009, 30 out of 267 senior officials in the Obama administration had lobbied in the previous five years, including a Treasury chief of staff who represented Goldman Sachs and a deputy secretary of defense who worked for Raytheon.

Public distaste for lobbyists is a manifestation of a broader disquiet about the potentially corrupting influence of 'big business'. There is a surprising antipathy to the establishment of business dynasties and the incorporation of wealth – as if this in itself represents an echo of the British monarchy that America rejected at the time of the Revolution. As early as the 1840s, Governor Francis R. Shunk of Pennsylvania attacked 'Corporations' for generating wealth by circumventing what he called 'the American law of distributions'. To avoid the creation of an aristocracy, Shunk argued, the founders of the republic had abolished laws of primogeniture and entail, with all descendants receiving an equal portion of any inheritance. Under American intestacy laws, he told his state legislature in 1848, 'all the property of the commonwealth is . . . from time to time divided and put into circulation, the largest accumulations, by the most fortunate men, yield to the resistless influence of our system of distribution'. Corporations, much to his chagrin, had taken on the guise of artificial persons who never died, holding and accumulating property perpetually.

This antipathy to dynastic wealth is aired by contemporary opinion-formers such as Irwin Stelzer (founder and president of National Economic Research Associates) who advocates a 100 per cent inheritance tax: if you believe in affirmative action, he says, you should level the playing field by ensuring that everyone starts from the same line. And Warren Buffett, chairman of Berkshire Hathaway and the second richest man in the world, has memorably argued that the elimination of estate tax leads to the command of the country's resources passing to people who did not earn anything: 'It's like choosing the 2020 Olympic team by picking the children of all the winners at the 2000 Games.'

According to Bernard Gover – an Anglo-American business-man who specializes in acquiring small companies – 'every owner of a mom-and-pop business wants to sell up and retire in Florida'. Unlike their British counterparts, they rarely have an interest in heritage – leaving a business to the next generation. This can reinforce the paradox: while entrepreneurs take their profits in pursuit of happiness in their twilight years, their businesses are acquired by large corporations run by 'company men' who are regarded as the antithesis to entrepreneurialism. The field is dominated – in a society which places immense trust in accreditation – by 'Masters of Business Administration' (MBAs). The MBA has become a rite of passage that initiates the successful graduate into a sort of mandarinate within the US's corporate universe, with 100,000 MBAs graduating each year. This confers grounding in the basics of business – accounting, quantitative analysis, economics, marketing and organizational behaviour. Inevitably, a number of 'Greek' societies exist for students in business, management and administration, including Beta Gamma Sigma (dating back to 1907) and Sigma Beta Delta (1986).

Another generic interest-group – and one dedicated to locking horns with 'management' – is the labour union. Membership has never exceeded 35 per cent of the labour force in the US and it has fallen from the high-tide mark of the 1930s to less than 15 per cent today. There continue to be sectors of the US economy – manufacturing, mining, construction, transportation and government – where organized worker-power is as entrenched as in the most unreconstructed of socialist republics, with tens of millions belonging to one or more unions.

The power of unions is still felt in the country. In the weeks after Labor Day 2007, for instance, there was a strike by 73,000 United Automobile Workers (UAW) union members at General Motors (GM) plants across the country after union leaders and company officials failed to reach an agreement on a new contract. This was the first national strike by the union against GM since 1970. 'It's about time the union stood up against the company and stood for the people,' said Sylvia Hill, who has worked for the company for thirty years and was manning a picket in Detroit. Soon after, the Teamsters – one of the largest unions in the land, with a membership of almost 1.5 million – voiced its support for the UAW strike: its 10,000 members would not cross the picket lines at GM factories. The Teamsters' president, James P. Hoffa, announced, 'Workers should not solely bear the brunt of decades of bad business decisions by GM management. By outsourcing good jobs and creating a growing environment of economic and job insecurity, GM has failed its workers and its customers.' A month later, in November 2007, the country learnt of the first strike in twenty years by the American Screenwriters' Guild, representing 12,000 script-writers. The immediate impact was felt on shows like NBC's *The Tonight Show with Jay Leno*, where comic one-liners are produced by a team of writers.

Neither the financial crisis nor Obama's election has muted the unions' *cris de coeur*. In May 2009, for instance, Los Angeles was facing a strike by teachers, while the American Guild of Musicians was threatening to close down the New York City Opera.

Benefits of union membership are simply summarized by Gina (not her real name), a young Italian-American woman working in a longshoreman's shed on Baltimore Docks. 'It's good money,' she says, 'thanks to unionized labor.' She belongs to Local 333 of the International Longshoremen's Association (ILA). The branch was formed in 1974 when a court ordered the (largely) all-white Local 829 to merge with Local 858 (represen-ting African-American cargo-handlers). She is twenty-two, born in Little Italy and has been working on the docks for three years: she got the job with the help of her father – as common a practice in the first decade of the twenty-first century as it was a century ago. (But Gina's gender and the fact that her foreman, Louis, is an African-American show that some things have changed.) The door over the office where Gina works carries a sign declaring 'Support your union' and once visitors have passed the threshold – looking for help in collecting freight, for instance – it is as if a Dickensian atavism or Kafkaesque dystopia has taken over the Land of the Free. The 'Local' manages the movement of goods on these wharfs and it wields its authority with the aloof indifference of inherited privilege. Louis scrutinizes every page of the sheaf of documents presented by the 'customer' before calling to Gina to take the visitor to fetch his goods. She sits by an electric fire with her feet on the desk pretending to be asleep. When he speaks, she asserts her independence by snoring loudly and melodramatically in the hope that the job will move elsewhere. When the boss persists, Gina stirs and rises slowly, as if out of a deep slumber.

There again, many in the ILA have been in a deep slumber. They have – according to the Department of Justice – allowed organized criminals to dominate the union's activities. Recent scandals have included embezzlement from the union, racketeering, extortion and payoffs, and a $400,000 contract fraud scheme from the ILA healthcare plan. In 2003, *The Wire* (the HBO series about the Baltimore police) gave a fictional account of this world, focusing on Frank Sobotka, secretary of the 'International Brotherhood of Stevedores: Local 1514', who is smuggling contraband to finance his political campaign to rejuvenate the docks.

In the public imagination, corruption is an entrenched feature of American unions. Harry – a financier who has run pension funds for labour unions – says, 'If the workers knew what their executives were up to, they would sack the lot of them!' Union corruption regularly features in the news: in August 2005 and June 2006, for instance, former officials working for the Washington Teachers' Union were found guilty of embezzling millions of dollars for their personal gain. James B. Dworkin, associate dean of Purdue University's Krannert Graduate School of Management and an expert on labour relations, defends the role of the union in US society. It provides a system of checks and balances, he argues, forcing management to act in a more enlightened manner towards employees: 'Without unions, management would enjoy the power to make all decisions on a unilateral basis. In a free society, that type of system won't work very long.'

However, Dworkin accepts that the public has a poor opinion of unions. The cause is not only the disruption caused by walk-outs and the periodic stories of corruption. It is also their restrictive practices that seem the antithesis of America's 'can-do' culture. Dan voices a commonly held opinion. He was raised in a small farming community in Nebraska. He did not go to college, working instead as a carpenter on different building-sites around the country – Colorado, Texas and Tennessee – but the lack of camaraderie among his fellow labourers drove him to leave for New Zealand: 'In the US, union rules kept strict demarcation lines between the trades.' For the aforementioned financier, Harry, the organizations are egoistical:

> My fund was obliged to employ unionized labor in any of its projects. But when developing a property in Chicago, we had two unions – the Carpenters and Painter/Decorators – down tools because they couldn't agree as to which trade had the right to spackle and finish off the interior walls.

Time and time again, we see Americans bridling at the perceived inequity of interest-groups distorting the level surface of the playing field. 'Greek' and secret societies, politicians and lobbyists, big business and unions all come in for criticism. Ultimately, this web of competing interests is judged to corrupt and undermine the competence of government itself – a complaint that is frequently reflected in news headlines: 'Study shows public feels government is inefficient'; 'US health care expensive, inefficient'; 'Critics: US food-aid programs inefficient'; 'GAO criticizes Homeland Security's efforts to fulfill its mission'.

In recent years, a school of political science has emerged to explain why government decisions are so often unsatisfactory. The New Institutionalists argue that public bureaucracy is not designed to be effective given the American democratic process. Terry Moe, professor of political science at the University of

Minnesota, writes, 'Because interest-groups are out for themselves, and because legislators have electoral incentives to do
their bidding, bureaucracy is built in a piecemeal fashion.'

In *Flawed by Design* (1999), Amy B. Zegart extended this
analysis to the evolution of the Central Intelligence Agency, the
Joint Chiefs of Staff, and the National Security Council: 'Anyone
who has ever filed a tax return or stood in line at the
Department of Motor Vehicles will tell you that government
agencies are far from perfect.' She suggests Americans expect
more when it comes to foreign affairs, where the stakes are
higher, but this is not the case. Domestic and foreign policy
agencies differ in fundamental ways, but they all arise from an
American political system that hinders effective design.

Zegart argues that the rational desires of interest-groups,
legislators and presidents lead to irrational agency structures.
Frequent elections focused on districts provide a bias towards
local rather than national interests. The separation of powers
may limit the risk of a despotic president, but effective unilateral
action by the executive is stifled. The president is the only elected
official with an incentive to consider national concerns, but even
the bureaucrats who serve him are likely to resist any executive
order that threatens their own power-base. 'Like their domestic
policy counterparts, American national security agencies are
irrationally designed for rational reasons,' Zegart writes.

Anyone who pays close attention to the nation at dialogue with
itself will discern a tension between the two value systems of
innovation and vested interests. The lionization of the entrepreneur and inventor fits with the philosophy of individualism.
Liberty has got legs and is exploring new frontiers. The current
of opinion favours the innovator and innovation, judging the
'new' to be a distinctive part of the American character. Novelty
is valued.

However, the positive, life-enhancing energy of innovation is
contrasted with the enervating machinations of vested interests
that channel power away from the many to the benefit of the

few. Americans appear shocked to discover that resources and influence are transmitted along power-lines in the United States, no less than they were in the city-states of medieval Italy, the mud palaces of Yemen and the commissariats of the Soviet Union. There is something un-modern and un-American about the rites of Phi Beta Kappa, the pork-barrel antics of Congress, political patronage or the restrictive practices of unions. All of this leaves a sense of disappointment – of utopia deferred – that shows through the heat-haze of optimism that pervades the American Way. There is, in the words of the technicians working the production-line in Manassas, VA, a mismatch in the Lattice Constant.

Those who allow their ideals to be bruised by hard realities overlook the fact that a revolutionary feature of the American political process has been the democratization of power-blocs. Americans are a nation of joiners who have developed the largest collection of associations and corporations in the world. These voluntary groups give the many a chance to enjoy the benefits of a privileged minority. The levers of power are not restricted to the princes, bishops, landed gentry or burghers of the Old World. There are scores of established interest-groups: the farming lobby, labour unions and business corporations, not to mention women's groups, eco-warriors, gay-rights activists, hunting enthusiasts, etc. Each of these can cajole, lobby or pay those in local, state or federal authority in the hope that decisions and resources move in their favour. These opportunities are sustained by the rational, democratic principles of the American Revolution: separation of powers; regular elections; majority rule.

In *The Audacity of Hope* (2006), Barack Obama is clear-sighted about the realities of having – as a politician – to make accommodation with interest-groups who can be a source not only of funds but also of the organization that is needed to win votes and achieve office. He also acknowledges the rich variety of 'special interests' occupying niches in the US's political ecosystem:

to my mind, there's a difference between a corporate lobby whose clout is based on money alone, and a group of like-minded individuals – whether they be textile workers, gun aficionados, veterans, or family farmers – coming together to promote their interests; between those who use their economic power to magnify their political influence far beyond what their numbers might justify, and those who are simply seeking to pool their votes to sway their representatives. The former subvert the very idea of democracy. The latter are its essence.

The strong emphasis on that idealized image of the innovator in the American narrative overlooks certain inconvenient truths: the significant variation of performance between states; a foreign-born bias, where there is greater likelihood that the American Dream is realized by an immigrant than a home-grown citizen; evidence that institutionalized innovation can become a power-play in its own right, with corporate conserva-tism eclipsing the creative impulse; and the crucial role that government plays in laying down both ground-rules and infrastructure to facilitate the free market and to ease the flow of new techniques and technology.

However, it is a contention of *The Cracked Bell* that myth and symbolism carry greater substance and gravity than in-convenient facts and 'realities'. The popular text of virtuous innovator and the vilified power-bloc reveals something profound about America's self-image and aspirations. It ex-presses that irreconcilable gap between the free individual and the wired community.

This theme continues as we stalk the frontier – that mythical preserve not only of the inventor and entrepreneur, but of every pioneering American – to survey the boundaries between wilderness and civilization.

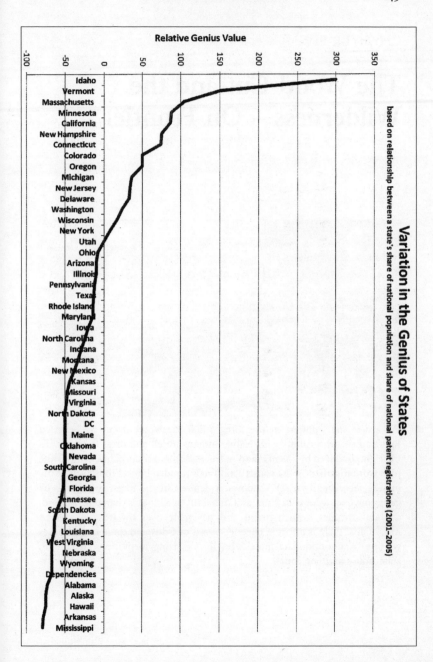

Variation in the Genius of States

based on relationship between a state's share of national population and share of national patent registrations (2001–2005)

CHAPTER FIVE

The Wood-Cut and the Wilderness – On Frontier

We are at the frontier. In the foreground, the wood is cut by behatted Englishmen, who labour with Native Indians to fell and dress the trees. To the right, overseen by a gentleman in frock-coat and tricorn, black and white men work together on the construction of a wooden house. To the left of the picture, obscured by deep shadows, a denizen of the forest appears to be gathering fruit from wild vines as if oblivious to all that is changing. Beyond, a plain stretches from a broad and navigable river towards the distant mountains: there is a fort, a chequer-board of fields and three larger spaces waiting to accommodate, no doubt, the civilizing institutions of church, state-house and law court.

This tiny print appears as a decorative motif above a warrant that advertised, in 1773, a little-known colony called Georgia. It may be almost 250 years old, but it remains powerfully evocative, providing a suitable emblem for another great American paradox: the juxtaposition of Nature and Civilization, the Feral and the Tamed, Freedom and Exploitation.

It is an inconvenient truth that in 1890 the Census Bureau declared the frontier closed. Today, much of the coast and almost all the land-mass of the US is privately owned and commercially exploited. Nature has been packaged into reserves, the open ranges are patrolled by rangers, the birds of the wild forest warble Nokia ring-tones and the frontier spirit has been commoditized into 'Outward Bound'. The hunter and the hiker seek to emulate the nation's progenitors – the trapper and pioneer – overlooking the fact that the pioneers turned the prairies into parcelled conurbations and the trappers decimated their prey. The dream, the ideas and the images of an untarnished frontier persist and Americans still live the myth, regarding engagement with the 'great outdoors' as a process of purification and re-creation.

Walt Whitman argued that the axe was preferable to the American Eagle as the proper emblem of the United States. In his 'Song of the Broad-Axe' (1856) this tool comes to symbolize the clearance of forest, the production of timber for shelter and fuel, and – as an abstraction of American spirit – 'actions that rely on themselves'. His verse grows hypnotic with such simple repetitive tasks as those performed by carpenters who literally domesticate the natural world (and we surely do not need to be a Freudian analyst to recognize an allusive sub-text depicting acts of procreation):

The house-builder at work in cities or anywhere,
The preparatory jointing, squaring, sawing, mortising,
The hoist-up of beams, the push of them in their places,
laying them regular,

Setting the studs by their tenons in the mortises according
as they were prepared,
The blows of mallets and hammers, the attitudes of men,
their curv'd limbs,
Bending, standing, astride the beams, driving in pins,
holding on by posts and braces,
The hook'd arm over the plate, the other arm wielding
the axe,
The floor-men forcing the planks close to be nail'd,
Their postures bringing their weapons downward on the
bearers . . .

This wood-cutting, wood-working trope appears again and
again in American culture. In Benjamin Harding's *Tour through
the Western Country* (1819) – an early guidebook for migrants –
the author expresses surprise not only at the beauty of the
country but also at its rapid growth and improvements,
considering 'how few years have elapsed since was first heard the
axe resound, laying low the sturdy trees, where nothing before
was heard but the yell and whoop of the savage'. George
Washington was memorably reprimanded for using his axe to
chop down a domesticated cherry-tree (the wrong sort of
nature); but this is nothing compared with the damage caused
in L. Frank Baum's book *The Wonderful Wizard of Oz* (1900) –
the source-book for the film – when the Wicked Witch of the
East causes an enchanted axe to cut off the limbs of its owner,
Nick Chopper. (He was to become the Tin Woodman without
a heart.)

The broad-axe truly was essential to the country in its infancy.
It was needed not only to exploit the opportunity of all that
virgin land, but also to repel the threat of the 'heathen wilderness'
– a threat powerfully evoked by Nathaniel Hawthorne when he
wrote of his eponymous anti-hero, 'Young Goodman Brown'
(1835), venturing from a New England village to meet the Devil:

The road grew wilder and drearier, and more faintly traced,
and vanished at length leaving him in the heart of the dark

wilderness . . . The whole forest was peopled with frightful sounds: the creaking of trees, the howling of wild beasts, and the yell of Indians; while sometimes the wind tolled like a distant church-bell, and sometimes gave a broad roar around the traveller, as if all Nature were laughing him to scorn.

The wooden houses that emerged from forest like this are celebrated today in the preservation of log-cabins (e.g. Robert Patterson's late-eighteenth-century cabin in the grounds of Transylvania College, Lexington) and salt-box houses (like those restored in Lewes Beach, Delaware); in the exaltation of the 'balloon-frame' (a technique pioneered in early Chicago to construct strong and efficient structures on the prairies); and in the continuing popularity of clapboard as an exterior detail in modern houses of the East Coast. In Peter Weir's film, *Witness* (1985), the community strength and virtue of Amish society is expressed in a barn-building scene, where thirty to forty men come together in an exercise that recaptures Whitman's imagery.

However, the theodolite was no less important than the broad-axe, transforming chaotic wilderness into rational squares of property, as in the print of colonial Georgia. The vision was that of Sir Robert Montgomery, whose 1717 scheme for the colony specified geometric districts of one square mile. It prefigures the Land Ordinance of 1785 that branded the territory west of the Appalachians with a grid pattern that today covers almost 70 per cent of continental America (excluding Alaska). In an exercise that seems to turn the country into that most homely of American folk-objects – a gigantic quilt – this 'Ordinance for Ascertaining the Mode of Disposing of Lands in the Western Territory' divided the land into square-mile sections (following the lines of longitude and latitude) and then parcelled thirty-six such sections into a 'township' of six square miles, in the New England tradition. A twenty-first-century flight across the Midwest reveals the extent of this fretwork applied to the plains and prairies, where the nap of the land has been rubbed away by human activity. This webbing stretches away in every direction, the squares relieved only by circles created by centre-pivot spray irrigation.

The squaring principle applied to urban development as well, and continues to this day in city 'blocks'. When towns were built out West, they followed the lines and the logic of the Ordinance: at the centre, usually, stood the courthouse – expressing the predominance of the law. Some eight blocks would surround it, with churches at the corners of the central blocks. Section 16 in every township was reserved for the maintenance of public schools and it is said that to this day many schools are to be found located there. The underlying principle was the same throughout, but there would be differences to the template.

There is no better place to see the power of this principle at work than Circleville, Ohio. – the exception that ultimately proved the rule. Circleville was established as the administrative seat of Pickaway County in 1810 and the commissioners who founded the city chose to build it on the ritual earthworks of Indians who had lived 1,500 years ago. The courthouse was placed in the middle of a flattened mound and, although the outlying blocks followed the standard rectangular format, a group of buildings at the centre followed the lines of that sacred circle. However, in 1837, an act was passed that authorized the Circleville Squaring Company to 'replatt' the curvilinear portions of the town. There was some resistance, but the squaring of Circleville was completed by 1856 and is said to be the first example of urban redevelopment in the country.

American cities, then, do not match the haphazard, evolutionary jumble of their European counterparts. Rationality dominates, with an established protocol that runs streets along a grid, identified numerically in one direction and alphabetically in the other. It may be as simple as A Street and First, but the human need for expression will out and the alphabetical sequence often carries the names of national heroes or local worthies.

The enduring character of the code – as well as American partiality for order – is nicely illustrated by Kansas City's

Voluntary Addressing Guidelines that feature as part of its 'Regional 9-1-1 System':

> *1. East–West Street Names* Streets that run primarily east and west should use the numeric street name grid that is commonly used throughout most of the region. The spacing should be based on the current pattern of 8 numeric names per mile.
> *2. North–South Street Names* Whenever possible, streets that run primarily north and south should use a unique acceptable name. The spacing should be based on the current pattern of 16 names per mile.
>
> Since there are 16 named streets and 8 numbered street names per mile, 'hundred block' designations should normally change every 330 feet on an east–west street and every 660 feet on a north–south street.

The introduction of Zoning Improvement Plan (ZIP) Codes in 1963 applied a new layer of regimentation by placing every address in the land within a coded domain. It was instigated by the US Postal Service as a rising tide of business mail flooded their network, with 80 per cent of the post containing such items as utility bills, bank deposits, advertisements, insurance premiums, dividends and department store catalogues. A five-digit code was assigned to every address in the land: the first number designates a broad geographical area ranging from '0' for the northeast to '9' for the far west (the scale tracking the progress of that mythical frontier); subsequent digits pinpoint areas of concentrated population and zoom in on small post offices or postal zones in larger cities. In 1983, a further four numbers were added to the zip code: the sixth and seventh denoting a delivery sector (e.g. a group of streets or a single high-rise office building); the last two denoting a segment, such as a single floor of an office building or a clutch of Post Office boxes.

The nation is inured to the zip code and can be anatomized and analysed by reference to it. The word 'zip' has become common currency in commercial, political and public-sector discourse. The US Census Bureau provides information on 'Zip Code Business Patterns', detailing the number of establishments, the size of the workforce and the weight of the payroll in more than 40,000 zip code areas. Citizens can find their congressman by zip code search; learn about the consumer lifestyle of their neighbourhood through PRIZM ('The new Evolution in Market Segment Analysis'); or be entertained by memory-artist David Rosdeitcher, who has absolute recall of all the codes in the country and can recommend – for every one of them – the best restaurants in town! The Los Angeles poet, Peter J. Harris, evokes – and kicks against – the grip of the zip in his poem 'The Ocean Is Ours', which starts its three stanzas with the lines: 'don't be foiled or fooled by the zip code', 'don't be tempted or trapped by the zip code' and 'don't be stamped or seduced by the zip code'.

Despite Harris' efforts to 'dis' the system, this ordered, rational topography must inevitably influence the manner in which Americans comprehend their universe. In *Wilderness and the American Mind* (1967), Roderick Nash quotes Henry David Thoreau's lamentation at his inability to buy a blank notebook for recording thoughts: the only ones the merchants in Concord offered were ledgers ruled for dollars and cents! So we should not be surprised that when the US Census Bureau reported the top twenty street names in the country (based on the 1993 Census) the results were:

1. Second (10,866)
2. Third (10,131)
3. First (9,898)
4. Fourth (9,190)
5. Park (8,926)
6. Fifth (8,186)
7. Main (7,644)
8. Sixth (7,283)
9. Oak (6,946)
10. Seventh (6,377)
11. Pine (6,170)
12. Maple (6,103)

13. Cedar (5,644)
14. Eighth (5,524)
15. Elm (5,233)
16. View (5,202)
17. Washington (4,974)
18. Ninth (4,908)
19. Lake (4,901)
20. Hill (4,877)

The omission of 'First' from pole position, incidentally, is explained by the incidence of so many 'Center', 'State' and 'Main' streets. It is significant that (with the exception of Washington himself) all alphabetical street names in this list refer to nature (especially trees – Oak, Pine, Maple, Cedar, Elm – in this arboreal society), although the high score achieved by 'Park' is also noteworthy, given the word's allusion to domesticated wilderness.

For those involved in pursuing the commercial rewards promised by the American Dream, there is nothing sentimental or enlightening about confronting nature in its raw and savage state. Alaska represents the closest thing to frontier territory within the United States today. Indeed, its car licence plates carry the tagline 'The last frontier' and its erstwhile governor, Sarah Palin – who had once been a reporter with the *Mat-Su Valley Frontiersman* – made much of her ability to kill, field-dress and cook a moose when she was campaigning as running-mate to John McCain in the 2008 presidential election. When statehood was granted in 1959, more than 95 per cent of the land could be called wilderness; the total white population of an area twice the size of Texas was under 150,000 (it stands at 700,000 today). However, there is some antipathy from the residents to those who regard Alaska as an endangered wilderness. Joe Vogler, founder of the Alaskan Independence Party, argued:

Anybody who says the ecology is fragile is an ignoramus or a goddam liar. Our climate protects the ecology; our

geography protects it. It's a struggle up here, all the way!
. . . Anybody who tells me this land was not put here to use
is a socialist enemy of mine! Anybody who tells me trees
shouldn't be cut, I'd use the axe on him.

Ironically, Vogler himself was cut down prematurely. He
disappeared on Memorial Day 1993. A year later, a vagrant
called Manfried 'Cartoon Freddy' West led police to where he
had buried the politician's bullet-riddled body.

In this Temple of Trade, it should come as no surprise that
private property is an important feature in the process of taming
the wild. When the vast territories of the frontier were opened
up, almost 1.5 billion acres of public land were disposed of
through the Land Ordinance, with 50 per cent of the new
townships sold by auction to companies formed to develop the
land and the rest sold directly to white men over twenty-one
years old. The Homestead Act of 1862 continued the process,
granting title to a quarter-section (160 acres) of public domain
to any settler for as little as $30, provided a house was
constructed and land was cultivated. This engendered the
overwhelming sense of ownership that permeates the American
landscape today. Outside the relatively small swathes of public
land, the traveller cannot escape signs – installed at frequent
intervals – that stipulate: 'Posted'; 'Private property'; 'No
trespassing'; 'No hunting. No fishing'; 'Violators will be
prosecuted'.

This phenomenon recurs again and again, even in places
seeking to draw in the public. For instance, visitors approaching
Storm King Arts Center, in Mountainville, New York – a
sculpture park in 500 acres of lush, gently rolling meadows –
encounter notices nailed to trees every fifty yards, warning them:
'Town Road ends here. Private. Do not enter.' Adventurers
rafting the Arkansas River in Colorado are warned to avoid
touching the ground while fishing, in case this invokes
litigation from an incensed landowner: so river-guide Dan
sings (to the tune of the Woody Guthrie classic, 'This Land is
Your Land'):

This land is my land,
It isn't your land,
If you don't clear off,
I'll blow your head off.

The signs even appear in Marquette County, Wisconsin, where America's greatest champion of wilderness conservation – the Scottish-born John Muir (1838–1914) – spent his formative years. Now commuter homes, hobby farms and vacation cottages are starting to change the traditional landscape of the county, as interstate highways make the area accessible to the inhabitants of Madison, Milwaukee and Chicago. New log homes are being built, but the prefabricated 'mobile' home is also prevalent. There is little sign of land-use regulation: people are free, it seems, to develop their property as they see fit.

Enter the suburb. Today, 80 per cent of the US population resides in metropolitan areas that occupy less than 20 per cent of the nation's land-mass – the majority in suburbs where they find some respite from the four-square universe that dominates so much of their realm. The suburb is a form of self-delusion: trees, streams and lawns lull the inhabitants into the false sense of solitude. Traditionally, the boundaries between homes are unmarked and there is an absence of fences. Many generations of Americans recall a childhood where kids would run wild, gathering from different households to play a game of baseball on the open grass. In the suburbs, the grid pattern is eroded by 'eyebrows', as town planners call these curved streets. The Kansas City authorities acknowledge this threat to their gridiron universe when they write – with tight-lipped tolerance – in their standards: 'the curvilinear streets and cul-de-sacs found in newer subdivisions create situations which are far harder to address than the traditional rectangular grid pattern of streets'. Such streets tend to be assigned 'secondary' names, such as 'Way' or 'Close', as if this demotion in the ranks maintains order and accommodates the anomalous.

The suburbs represent a refuge for a growing number of Americans who long for quieter, less hectic lives away from the congestion, noise, pollution, multi-family residences and high prices typically found in the heart of the city. Furthermore, since many of the nation's citizens are only a generation or two removed from farm or small-town living, the suburbs provide a way of bridging rural and urban life, the wild and the tame. The appearance of the suburban home contributes to the ambiguity. In the Midwest, it is likely to emulate the little house on the prairie, in New Mexico an adobe dwelling, in California a Spanish *hacienda*, while clapboard predominates on the East Coast.

In the new suburbs of Greater Phoenix, Arizona – the fastest-growing community in the US – there is a fashion for 'xeric' gardens, planted with species that replicate the desert that has been destroyed by development. However, there is much to remind us that this is an invasive form of occupation that gives little quarter to the spirit of place: the emerald-green golf courses and over 300,000 blue swimming pools show up like luminous scabs on the desert's dun skin; there is a reliance on air-conditioning for survival (where even the poorest household survives with a 'swamp cooler'); and there is the relentless and unsustainable draw-down of water from the snow-fed Colorado.

'Beddin' Down', a bed and breakfast outside Salida, Colorado, exemplifies the mixed message of the suburban home. It has the appearance of a modern pine-log cabin: the central room opens up to a pitched roof and the walls are honey-coloured logs. There are cowboy and pioneer memorabilia fixed to the walls: an old pistol and holster, rifles, animal skins and a beaver hat. Downstairs there's the 'Hideout' that sleeps ten or more – perfect for sorority sleepovers. Another bedroom is called 'Soiled Doves' (after the term used in the old days by the miners of Leadville for the whores of Salida). But the effect is counterbalanced by notices that appear throughout the house: 'Take off your shoes or clean the floor!'; 'Please do not use the pillow shams as pillows'; 'If you're smoking you must be on fire and we'll take appropriate action.'

* * *

The suburb goes some way towards blurring the categories of outside and inside, wild and tame, but this does not eliminate the sense of regret felt by many at the pace of real-estate development in the country. Artist Carole Bolsey watched suburbs engulf the isolated farms and orchards of Westchester County, New York, turning the landscape into a world of 'mock colonial houses with asphalt tiles, filled with people without any soul'. She hates the suburbs, she says: 'density without community, isolation without the solitude'. She describes her work as – 'The Sovereignty of Self-Definition': is about being alone in isolation.

It is not uncommon to encounter a sense of poignant regret, even an uncharacteristic melancholy, over the loss of something 'natural' in the land. Partly, it is concern that one facet of the American Dream (the drive to prosper, profit and exploit the land) is outstripping and erasing another (the sentimental attachment to frontier and wilderness). Partly, this is a concern that Americans are breaking the tap-root that connects them to the earth as they stay indoors and plug into broadband. Stephanie, mother of three teenagers living beside the Patuxent River in Maryland, says:

> If you take away the wilderness from our lives, well it's like Delilah chopping off Samson's hair. We lose that source of inner strength. Children need to be exposed to nature: I worry about a world where everything is technological. They need to be able to get out into the open, to play with sticks and stones and mud.

In 'The Historical Roots of Our Ecological Crisis' (1967), historian Lynn White blamed the Christian notion that God gave the earth to people for their use and dominion; but environmentalist church groups have subsequently promoted the opposite view – that God made humanity stewards of the earth. The Evangelical Environmental Network, based in Suwanee, Georgia, has been publishing the quarterly *Creation Care Magazine* since 1998, with articles like 'Serve God, Save the

Planet'; and in 2004, evangelical leaders including senior representatives from the National Association of Evangelicals and the Southern Baptist Convention, gathered in Sandy Cove, Maryland, for a three-day session of prayer and discussion on the issues, leading to the 'Sandy Cove Covenant', with its commitment to the principles of creation care:

> We invite our brothers and sisters in Christ to engage with us the most pressing environmental questions of our day, such as health threats to families and the unborn, the negative effects of environmental degradation on the poor, God's endangered creatures, and the important current debate about human-induced climate change. We covenant together to engage the evangelical community in a discussion about the question of climate change with the goal of reaching a consensus statement on the subject in twelve months.

Coral (a retired school-teacher) avoids reference to religious doctrine, but there is something explicitly spiritual in her reaction to the loss of wilderness. She has incorporated into her quilt-work a commemoration of the swamp in Pasco County, South Carolina, where she spent her childhood in the 1950s:

> Me and my sister loved that place. We played with the alligators and knew the names of all the plants and all. We knew so much that when we went on a nature tour the other day, the guide called us 'Flora' and 'Fauna'!

However, according to Coral, a neighbouring county acquired rights to the land, sank wells and extracted the water, draining the swamp. So her quilt is to be viewed from both sides: here, you see all that water supporting fish and birds, surrounded by green trees and vegetation; but turn it over, and you see that the stitched outline on a black backing depicts the same creatures as corpses. She adds:

We loved that swamp so much because it was a part of who we were. We were a long way from any other children so that's where we played. We have to learn to love nature, to develop responsibility for it, because it's all very well kids playing with their electronic gadgets and their software games, but when the electronics is rusted it's the land that is left to sustain us.

This use of art to communicate a sense of dislocation between nature and civilization is not a new phenomenon. When George Inness painted *The Lackawanna Valley* in 1855, he exaggerated the features of the railroad at the request of the railroad company who commissioned him, but he also displayed a field of tree stumps in the foreground. 'Ambiguous in tone, the landscape can be read as a glorification of development or as a reminder of the price of progress,' notes a commentary by the National Gallery of Art.

More recently, the cinema has provided a modern medium for expressing the sense of displacement felt by modern society in its relationship with the natural world. In John Boorman's *Deliverance* (1972), four city-dwellers test their manhood and courage against the wild as they venture on rafts down a river and through a valley that is condemned by a dam construction project that will flood the area. The driving force behind this adventure is Lewis Medlock (Burt Reynolds), a bow-hunter and macho outdoorsman, who responds to the whines of the portly, unfit insurance salesman, Bobby Trippe, who wants to know the point of it all:

They're gonna flood a whole valley, Bobby, that's why. Dammit, they're drownin' the river . . . Just about the last wild, untamed, unpolluted, unfucked up river in the South. Don't you understand what I'm sayin'? . . . They're gonna stop the river up. There ain't gonna be no more river. There's just gonna be a big, dead lake . . . You just push a little more power into Atlanta, a little more air-conditioners for your smug little suburb, and you know

what's gonna happen? We're gonna rape this whole
god-damned landscape. We're gonna rape it.

Bobby Trippe will, of course, himself be raped by one of the
jungle's degenerate, inbred backwoodsmen (an interesting
commentary on the long-held American view of the salubrious
influence of exposure to the wild), and the civilized standards of
decency and logic give way to Medlock's laws of the jungle.

Francis Ford Coppola addressed a similar theme in *Apocalypse
Now!* (1979), which follows Special Forces assassin Willard
(Martin Sheen) on his mission through the literal (and moral)
wilderness of Indo-China to kill the rogue American general,
Kurtz (Marlon Brando). He fulfils his mission, but not before
we realize that he and Kurtz share the same outlook –
that America, lacking a frontier in which to be tested and
tempered, has become weak and soft when compared to the
jungle-hardened Vietcong.

Medlock, Kurtz and Willard are examples of the marginal
men that anthropologists find in the mythology of many
societies around the world: they operate on the boundary
between the feral and the tamed and, like the mythical pioneers
of the past (Daniel Boone, for instance), they are close – perhaps
too close – to the 'savage'. The ultimate archetype, here, is the
cowboy in the Wild West – an icon that flourishes even though
the number of people working as cowboys today is no more
than a few thousand. The idea of 'The West' provides an arena
where America explores those tensions that emerge elsewhere in
the culture, between the free-ranging individual and the orderly
demands of community. Recent 'westerns' that have addressed
the issues of lawfulness and lawlessness – raising questions of
justice, crime, punishment, vengeance and violence – include
Unforgiven (1992), *The Quick and the Dead* (1995), set
appropriately in a town called Redemption, and *3.10 to Yuma*
(2007). But a sustained exploration of these themes is to be
found in HBO's television drama, *Deadwood* (2004–06) about
the 1870s growth of a makeshift camp for gold prospectors into
a town, before and after its incorporation into Dakota Territory.

Notable performances include that of Ian McShane as the amoral saloon-owner, Al Swearengen (who experiences bouts of existential angst as his victims are fed to the ravenous pigs of Mr Wu the Chinaman), and Timothy Olyphant as Seth Bullock – a man trying to escape the onus of a sheriff's duties. The creator of the series, David Milch, has said he wanted to illustrate progress from chaos to civilization; in the process, he observes the replacement of the rugged individualism of the old West with corporate capitalism and corrupt government.

Arthur Miller wrote a particularly poignant memento mori for the West in his screenplay for *The Misfits*, a 1961 film directed by John Huston (and starring Miller's wife, Marilyn Monroe). Featuring such memorable lines as, 'If I'm going to be alone, I want to be by myself,' it is set in Reno, Nevada, and observes a newly divorced beauty mixing with a trio of cowboys who compete for her attention. The film reaches a sort of anti-climax in the pursuit and capture of wild mustang in the mountains. The world has changed, we learn, and now horse-traders will sell these horses for dog-meat rather than for mounts: the poetry has gone out of the chase, and – as an act of defiance against this new world – the horses are set free. This tale of anomie is a moving, regretful story of America in flux.

As Miller divined, the image of the cowboy was under stress, and it has shifted and been reinvented in recent years. In *Midnight Cowboy* (1969), for instance, Joe Buck's rodeo outfit – boots, hat and fringed suede jacket – has become associated with rent-boys in New York's 42nd Street; in *Blazing Saddles* (1974), Mel Brooks satirized *Dodge City* (1939) – and, indeed, the whole 'western' genre – by sending a black sheriff into a lawless frontier town (Brooks himself plays the Yiddish-speaking Indian chief). More recently, *Brokeback Mountain* (2005) has challenged another stereotype, exploring gay love between cowboys.

Yet still, across the land, the cowboy remains an icon for the spirit of the frontier. Western ranches have given greenhorn Easterners the chance to experience 'outdoors' work since the late nineteenth century and this continues to be a flourishing – if niche – business. Bayard Fox, owner of the Bitterroot Ranch in a remote valley at the base of the Absaroka Mountains, Wyoming, has views on the benefits of this way of life:

> Over the last hundred years dude ranches have done much to preserve and foster the spirit of self-reliance, personal freedom, love of wild nature and commitment to family which have been so important in making America the great place it is today. At its best, a dude ranch is the antithesis of watching TV or playing computer games. At a dude ranch, riding a horse through wild country, people are experiencing the real rather than the virtual; they are active participants in charge of their own fates rather than passive watchers having vicarious thrills.

However, those saddled to the couch in 2007 can still get their thrills by watching *Texas Ranch House*, a reality TV programme that shows a group of twenty-first-century Americans experiencing life as nineteenth-century cowboys working on a ranch with all manner of hardships including food deprivation. Or it is possible to leave the world-class shops, restaurants and summer concerts of Aspen, Colorado, to go to the Snowmass Rodeo, which welcomes visitors to:

> an American tradition that goes back decades to the days when ranch cowboys got together to show off their skills, honed by daily hard work riding horses and tending cattle. And boys being boys, some of their contests got pretty wild and woolly.

There is bareback riding on horses and bulls, cowgirls racing small, powerful mounts against the clock and various competitions to lasso calves and bullocks. There is even a cowboy clown, in mauve top with purple-and-white grease paint on his face, who aims to distract the bulls once they have thrown their riders by moving in front, dodging and running. Afterwards, children crowd around a camp fire cooking marshmallows as a cowboy guitarist sings 'Home, home on the range' where – those free spirits looking to escape the harsh world of office politics will be relieved to learn – seldom is heard a discouraging word.

Brian – author of the 'Goin' RV boondocking' blog – regards himself as a cowboy at heart. He says he always seems to be drifting into ranch work but it is hard, he admits, to keep the lights on and beans on the table with a cowboy's wages. His real passion is for dry-camping deep in the far country where the silence soaks into your soul: 'You won't see me back east too awful much. I just need more room than they have back there.' There is no better way to connect with the enduring power and spirit of the 'cowboy's way' than to listen to the views expressed by men like Brian, or his blog-buddy 'Pat at the Cabin' who in May 2009 was offering comfort and support in the face of adversity, using language that is rooted in the American ideal of freedom:

> Cowboy, you're heading out of the storm into the sunshine for the rest of your life. It may take awhile for you to realize it and look ahead, not behind. Bet when you're on your motor cycle you are always enjoying just the ride and looking ahead, not behind. That's what your life is now and you're FREE to go down the road and enjoy YOURSELF for a change. Give yourself permission to have some fun and be a little selfish for a change. It's a great big world out there just waiting to embrace you with sunrises and the wind in your face.

This is the spirit evinced in that most enduring of frontier songs – Cole Porter's 'Don't Fence Me In'. Most Americans will be familiar with what has become an anthem to the national spirit, which was adapted from a poem entitled 'Open Range' written by Bob Fletcher (the self-styled 'Poet Lariat'). It was first sung by Roy Rogers in *Hollywood Canteen* (1944). A version by Bing Crosby and the Andrews Sisters sold over a million copies in 1944–45 and the song reached a new audience in what some might regard as a postmodern production in Episode 221 of *The Muppet Show* (February 1978) when an aged Bob Hope crooned away while riding a gangly muppet mount called 'Paul Revere'. But the true irony is that Fletcher, who penned the lyrics, was an engineer with the Department of Highways in Helena, Montana, who was building the roads that gave access to, and diminished, the wilderness he was extolling.

This search for irony represents a very un-American, Old World mentality that contaminates the pure expression of the Western spirit. We should resist these thoughts, just as we should avoid telling 'Pat at the Cabin' that if Brian rides with sunrises in his face he's going to end up back East, where no cowboy wants to be.

Joni Mitchell sang in 1970's 'Big Yellow Taxi', about all the trees being continued in a museum. Perhaps she had in mind the Wilderness Act of 1964, which legitimized and domesticated wilderness by drawing boundaries around it. Congress made its decision surrounded by vast canvases of American wilderness, such as Thomas Moran's paintings of the Grand Canyon from c.1871, which hangs in the Senate Lobby. The Act is clear in its purpose: 'to assure that an increasing population, accompanied by expanding settlement and growing mechanization, does not occupy and modify all areas within the United States'. It contrasts a wilderness with those areas where man and his own works dominate the landscape; it is 'an area where the earth and its community of life are untrammelled by man, where man himself is a visitor who does not remain'. Through this legislation, Congress sustained favourable conditions for the cult of the frontier to endure.

You can still experience the idea of wilderness, even if these days it costs $20 to enter a park to view it. Clayton R. Koppes (Dean of Arts and Sciences at Oberlin College, Ohio) has written of:

the rush you get standing at the edge of the Grand Canyon and seeing aeons spread before you, the spiritual commu- nion you experience as you walk among the towering, fog-shrouded redwoods, and the sense of liberation you feel as you discern a panorama of mountain peaks.

Sally, a banker and head-hunter who takes holidays hiking and rafting in the wild, expresses similar views:

> It defines what it is to be an American. To have that wilderness to explore is what we are about. It emphasizes the size of the country, as well, and some of the landscape we've got is truly spectacular: that makes me feel *what a great country!* Whether it's true or not, when I was small my teacher told us that America was self-sufficient in every way. And having that wilderness there seems to confirm that: it's as if we've got more than enough space, land, for our needs and can afford to have land lying free. We can own our own home, have our own property, without having people tramping by it or through it: they can go into the national parks if they want that.

'My need for the great outdoors to recharge batteries and to find peace and tranquillity is certainly in the American tradition,' says Frank, executive secretary of the North Virginia Hiking Club, who leads walks through the Appalachians. 'It's kind of a back to basics to satisfy a yearning for simplicity and authenticity.' Frank's reference to wandering reminds us – in a society that expects its citizens to be focused on so much of what they do – that the aimless journey carries particular significance. The very words 'Oklahoma Trail' and 'Route 66' evoke a sense of liberation and one is reminded of Whitman's poem 'Song of the Open Road':

> Here on dark earth – before we all
> go to heaven, visions of America –
> All that hitchhikin', all that
> Railroadin', all that comin' back to America . . .
> A hat is on my head, a bundle
> on my back, and my staff, the

Refreshing breeze and the full moon.
Afoot and light-hearted I take to
the open road, Healthy, free, the
world before me. The long brown
path before me leading wherever I choose.

   The yearning for the road is associated with youth (although in this nation 'youthful exuberance' is a concept as elastic as chewing gum and is often a defining characteristic of the superannuated). It is taken as given that the young will be driven into the wilderness by unbridled, inchoate dreams, searching – as the children's writer E.B. White expressed it – for a longer route to somewhere they don't want to be. In 2007 the nation commemorated the fiftieth anniversary of Jack Kerouac's *On the Road*, the novel that is hailed as the ultimate expression of this American wanderlust. Special editions were published and the iconic 'roll' – that single scroll of teletype paper on which Kerouac drafted his book – went on display at the New York Public Library as part of a four-year national tour of museums and libraries.

   Kerouac explores the theme of travel in many of his works, including *The Town and the City*, *Dharma Bums* and *Big Sur*, but *On the Road* is his masterpiece and continues to achieve worldwide sales of 100,000 per year. Fans of all ages, habitually wearing backpacks, will make a pilgrimage to Lowell, Massachusetts, where Kerouac grew up and is now buried. The champion of the restless spirit would hardly approve of the fact that the City Fathers have established a 'Kerouac Park' – truly a monument to the American oxymoron – shaded by weeping willow trees and embellished with a circle of granite columns bearing excerpts from his works. A few miles south, at the Edson Cemetery, his grave has become a shrine around which worshippers scatter their tributes – cigarettes, a bandanna, black flip-flops and a note (pinned to the earth with a pencil) that reads, 'The only people for me are the mad ones. Here's to you Jack!'

   In his book, Kerouac's narrator and alter-ego, Sal Paradise, attaches himself to the coat-tails of Dean Moriarty – one of those Huck Finn characters who exist on the margins of society and for whom the journey is more important than the destination. He tells Sal, 'Nobody bothers you and you cut along and make it your own way. What's your road, man? – holyboy road, madman road, rainbow road, guppy road, any road. It's an anywhere road for anybody anyhow. Where body how?' The characters in *On the Road* seem to be on a spiritual quest, testing the American Dream by trying to secure its promise of unlimited freedom. Sal loses himself in the process: in a gloomy old Plains hostel in Des Moines, Sal wakes up and for fifteen seconds does not know who he is.

The road is life, we are told, but this novel is also a celebration of the car. There are descriptions of Dean at the wheel going ninety miles per hour, the car flying straight as an arrow, the white line of the road hugging the left wheel of the car. This could almost be a commercial and it remains the case today that the frontier is used repeatedly to sell cars. The 'Sports Utility Vehicle' (SUV) is the archetype. This off-road car is driven by thousands who do not even use it to climb the kerb, but this does not diminish the magnetic attraction of the frontier trope that is expressed in those names: Land Cruiser; Wagoneer; Bronco; Explorer; Mountaineer. One TV ad shows a Jeep driving through forests, fording rivers, and racing free across plains with mountains in the distance, to the pop tune 'There's a time for us to let go'. An almost identical series of shots – of car and forest, rocky streams, plains and mountains – advertised the Ford Escape.

It may be the case that the most common car in the US is the self-effacing Toyota Camry. (How many of these citizens of the Republic know the word means 'little crown' in Japanese?) It may also be true that the trail that Americans most commonly take is not Kerouac's Route 6, but the road to work. However, car ownership has almost become a citizen's right, with the latest statistics showing there are more registered vehicles in the average household than registered drivers; and millions of car-owners experience the vicarious pleasure, through these commercials, of ranging free across an inaccessible landscape in an SUV they could never afford.

Nevertheless, their cars will also carry them on an occasional recreational retreat away from the suburbs and here the myth truly comes into its own. It is this enduring philosophy that compels Americans to take commercial packages such as those offered by Outward Bound USA which advertises its wilderness programmes by conjuring up an encounter with the raw elements: 'Scale a wind-swept mountain peak. Ride a surging white-water river. Hike into a remote glen. Sail to an offshore island.'

The mountains and canyons in particular offer balm for millions, drawn to the primitive beauty of the National Parks. Some 4 million visits are made each year to the Grand Canyon and Yosemite respectively, over 3 million to Olympic, Yellowstone and Rocky Mountain, and visits to Acadia, the Grand Tetons, Zion, Glacier, the Hawaii Volcanoes, Mount Rainer, Badlands, Death Valley and Everglades are all numbered in six figures. Equipped with the latest kit from companies like Backcountry Gear or Hudson Trail Outfitters ('Wilderness Outfitting Specialists'), hikers venture in their thousands into the National Parks to escape their urban or suburban environment and connect with the elements.

Ed and Natalie, who are typical of the breed, were encountered on a trail through the spectacular scenery of Rocky Mountain National Park in Colorado. They had moved from San Diego to Boulder, cashing in the huge growth in the price of their Californian home and trying to get – Ed said – somewhere 'closer to reality'. He is a software developer; Natalie works in property development. They can afford a Friday out in the mountains because Ed has been head-hunted and is between jobs. They are following one of thirty-three routes in the Park's *Dayhiker's Guide* and they are prepared for any eventuality – so much so that one would be forgiven for believing they were surveying an uncharted wilderness for a year rather than a taking an afternoon stroll in the park. They wear the finest state-of-the-art boots. They wield Leki 'Super Makalu Ergometric

Antishock' walking poles. They carry lightweight Acrux packs (complete with 'hydration bladder pocket'). And their belts are loaded with an arsenal of colourful spray cans, designed to repel – respectively – black bear, brown bear and mountain lion.

Ed and Natalie have come to get away from it all and they feel they have chosen well. There again, the whole landscape seems to have been designed to challenge anyone set in their ways – it appears, indeed, to be in need of therapy itself. The distant summit of Front Range is seriously bipolar, with water flowing to the Atlantic on one side and to the Pacific on the other. 'Quaking' aspens wave their leaves in neurotic fashion, as if incapable of containing some inner excitement. A grove of ponderosa pine are – by contrast – solemn, introverted and depressed. And the trail leads to a field of eccentric granite monoliths, resembling sculptures from Henry Moore's oeuvre, which seem to present a catalogue of personality disorders. No wonder Americans come here to find themselves.

The reality is, of course, that complete solitude – while not a fruitless quest – is difficult to find. At the busiest times of the year, the place teems with thousands of people all seeking the quietude that will help them to re-create themselves (just as a seaside retreat like the Chesapeake Bay – which once held explorer Captain John Smith's solitary boat – now supports a flapping flotilla of sailing craft and a buzzing swarm of motor-vessels). Some 750,000 visitors came to Rocky Mountain Park in July 2002. Hikers are taken to the start of the most popular walk (that trails evocatively past Bear, Nymph, Dream and Haiyaha Lakes) in convoys of buses that leave the Park Reception Center every thirty minutes. This press of humanity threatens some of Rocky Mountain's more fragile ecosystems, such as the tundra found at the higher altitudes.

Hunting is regarded as a national pastime. Indeed, the rivers and slopes of the mountains around Estes Park (where the National Park is based) had been stripped of their trout and elk by the time F.O. Stanley built his hotel in 1909. Hunting is an expression of the self-reliance that is a defining quality of the American spirit – even though fewer than 6 per cent of the population actually venture after game. In *The Winning of the West* (1889), and through establishing the Boone and Crockett Club, future president Teddy Roosevelt not only advanced his love of shooting and fishing but also, in the words of Roderick Nash (leading historian of America's relationship with wilderness), encouraged 'a vigorous, masterful people, sound and firm of mind, with energy, resolution, manliness, self-reliance and a capacity for self-help'.

Those of us who tend towards the plump, bookish and myopic take comfort from the fact that in Roosevelt we have a leading advocate of nature as a crucible for tempering character who was full-faced, short-sighted and literary. He contributed valiantly to the narrative of American masculinity fostered in wilderness. There is, of course, an inevitable gender bias in this genre, but there has also been an ethnic bias – this notion of individual re-creation belongs, predominantly, to a white narrative tradition. The Indian is set in opposition to the 'hero' and the black man is typically excluded from the cast of primary characters (the comic impact of Cleavon Little's black sheriff in *Blazing Saddles* derives from the dissonance of this image). For students of cultural fissures, there is even a class element to this analysis: when Roosevelt's friends in the Boone and Crockett Club established the New York Zoological Society Park, they did so with the aim of creating a place where the masses – especially immigrants and the poor who were confined to urban quarters – could learn the lessons of nature and how those lessons should be applied to everyday life. Littering, cutting trees for firewood and bird shooting were strictly prohibited and these rules were enforced through signs, guards and newspaper articles.

However, Michael K. Johnson has demonstrated in *Black Masculinity and the Frontier Myth in American Literature* (2002) that African-American writers have harnessed the utopian narrative of frontier, adapting the tradition to suit their circumstances: the frontier, for instance, becomes an idealized place devoid of racism and discrimination. Furthermore, in 1918 Willa Cather was able to conjure up a heroine of the frontier in *My Antonia* (a sort of Sarah Palin without the lipstick); and the woman's connection with wilderness is broadly emblemized by the Girl Scouts of the USA (founded by Juliette Gordon Low in 1912, and now boasting 3.2 million members).

The tradition of African-American Boy Scouts is even older, dating back to the first 'Negro' troop in Elizabeth City, North Carolina, in 1911. The invidious rule of segregation predominated in the early years of black scouting, with 248 all-black troops in the country in 1926. However, over time the tables have been turned and there has been some cultural adaptation to suit an African-American narrative. In Baltimore, for instance, a group called Roots of Scouting was created in 1980 to cater for the needs of African-American scouts, resurrecting the 'Corroboree' – a camp that resembles 'festive Aborigine tribal gatherings', first established by black scout leaders in the 1930s. In 1992, the annual Kwanzaa Fellowship was set up to celebrate America's Pan-African holiday and the seven principles of 'Nguzo Saba' – Unity, Self-Determination, Collective Responsibility, Cooperation, Purpose, Creativity and Faith.

African-Americans are linked back, through scouting, to an institution that seems to derive from an Anglo-Saxon 'forest romance'. At the turn of the twentieth century, a number of boys' organizations were formed by men inspired by the belief that time spent in the company of Mother Nature, rather than mother, would do wonders for the inner man. Daniel Carter Beard established the Sons of Daniel Boone and the Boy Pioneers; and Ernest Thompson Seton set up a youth organization called the Woodcraft Indians. In 1910 they joined forces with Chicago publisher William D. Boyce to establish the Boy Scouts of America (BSA).

The National Scouting Museum in Irving, Texas, salutes the contributions of Beard, Seton and Boyce, as well as James E. West, BSA's first chief scout executive. West – and how fortuitous it is that he bore that name, for someone promoting the frontier spirit – is credited with turning the BSA into the largest and most effective youth organization in the world. It claims to have 3.4 million scouts formed into 142,587 units, and to this day it upholds the notion that young people learn to be good citizens and effective leaders through time spent 'outdoors'. Its museum features full-size replicas of campsites from 1910, the 1950s and today; and it runs 'high-adventure areas' in Minnesota, the Philmont Scout Ranch in New Mexico and the Florida National High Adventure Sea Base in the Florida Keys. Scouting, the BSA website explains, is designed to take place outdoors:

> It is in the outdoor setting that Scouts share responsibilities and learn to live with one another. In the outdoors the skills and activities practiced at troop meetings come alive with purpose. Being close to nature helps Boy Scouts gain an appreciation for the beauty of the world around us. The outdoors is the laboratory in which Boy Scouts learn ecology and practice conservation of nature's resources.

The BSA makes a point of underscoring the links that exist between scouting and the US space programme, with eleven out of a dozen men who walked on the moon's surface involved in scouting. This is apt, with space travel serving as another emblem of the nation's frontier spirit. In an article published on NASA's website in January 2007, the organization's administrator, Michael Griffin, asked 'Why Explore Space?' He referred to the Pilgrim Fathers, and evoked the idea of the American journey continuing into outer space:

> If humans are indeed going to go to Mars, if we're going to go beyond, we have to learn how to live on other planetary surfaces, to use what we find there and bend it to our will, just as the Pilgrims did when they came to what is now New England – where half of them died during that first frigid winter in 1620. There was a reason their celebration was called 'Thanksgiving.' The Pilgrims were only a few thousand miles from home, and they were accomplished farmers and artisans. And yet, when they came to an unfamiliar land, they didn't know how to survive in its harsh environment. They didn't know what food would

grow and what wouldn't. They didn't know what they could eat and what they couldn't.

However, there is a disconnection between the traditional image of the bewhiskered backwoodsman – driven to lunacy through solitude and extended exposure to the wilderness – and the massive bureaucratic exercise behind the first lunar landing in the 1960s: it cost $20 billion (the equivalent to $100 billion today) and – according to Catherine Thimmesh, author of *Team Moon* (2006) – the effort of 400,000 men and women. The nation's interest in space exploration may have declined since then (although there was a surge of interest in July 2009 as the fortieth anniversary of the moon landing was commemorated), but in every year since 2000 some $15 billion has been committed to the space programme, rising to $17.6 billion in 2009.

There are critics – like the Space Frontier Foundation – who disapprove of the exploration of outer space becoming the preserve of the public sector. The Foundation stipulates that its mission is to 'unleash the power of free enterprise and lead a united humanity permanently into the Solar System'. Justifications for venturing into outer space often echo the arguments of the British adventurer companies who promoted the thrust into the New World – to reap profits. Even the 1958 Space Act – which created NASA – whistles this tune, tasking the agency 'to seek and encourage, to the maximum extent possible, the fullest commercial use of space'. The future of America's mythical frontier may, then, be sustained through the launch-pads of Cape Canaveral and the Kennedy Space Center.

For those who lack the patience to wait for the cryogenic torpor of inter-planetary travel, there is the *terra incognita* of inner space available through computer programs such as 'There', 'EverQuest', 'Active Worlds', 'Second Life' and 'World of Warcraft'. There are few reliable figures on numbers, but Second Life claims to have over 15 million registered users logging nearly 400 million hours in 2008; and in that year, the 'occupied' land-mass of Second Life increased 82 per cent to 1.76 billion square metres of virtual land. (Incidentally, those who have become owners of a 'Full Region' can go on to acquire their very own wilderness: 'Openspace' property comprises forest, countryside or ocean.)

Each player takes the identity of an avatar to explore these virtual worlds. In EverQuest, with two million players in 2004, their adventures take them to the planet of 'Norrath', its moon Luclin and alternative planes of reality such as those of Hate and Growth; they fight monsters and enemies for treasure and 'experience points', gaining power, prestige, spells and abilities along the way. In a reflection of how things are back home, the main forms of activity are adventuring, trading and social interaction.

There is a special thrill experienced by those who – seemingly confined in the cubic space of a bedroom or snug – venture through the Fifth Wall of the computer screen to lose themselves in a cyber-universe. In one sense this experience is not profoundly different from that felt by an audience viewing the Grand Canyon in 3-D at an IMAX cinema ten years ago; or those who have reflected in past centuries upon the pictures of Winslow Homer, Frederic Edwin Church, John James Audubon, Thomas Cole and Albert Bierstadt – artists who invested the American landscape with moral sentiment and psychological meaning.

Literature has also served as a portal to the frontier – not only in the poetry of Whitman and the novels of Kerouac, but also in the hugely popular 'Leatherstocking Tales' of James Fenimore Cooper and the works of Melville, Hawthorne and Jack London. A century ago, adolescents were enthralled by dime novels whose brightly coloured covers depicted scenes of bloodshed and courage at the frontier: stories published in *Rough Rider Weekly*, *Log Cabin Library* and *Wild West Weekly*, a periodical dedicated to the adventures of a young hero called 'Wild' West, told of encounters between Indians and settlers or dramatized the life of outlaws such as Jesse James. But there again, the role-player in computer games experiences something different from the mind-shift achieved through literature, film or canvas. The game-player's avatar interacts with the outside-in world of the program: he exacts cause and effect, discovers new landscapes and experiences reward and retribution for his actions. Like the pioneer of old, character is tested and self-interest is pursued.

It would be ironic, indeed, if the frontier for twenty-first-century Americans became the ridge of the plasma screen and if chip and broadband replaced the chop of the broad-axe. However, events of the early twenty-first century (9/11, Katrina, H1N1) seemed to affirm that the United States faces real, not just metaphorical, frontier-challenges. There is a sense that the wilderness – once lost – has been unexpectedly recovered.

It has been said that the UK has spent the last fifty years struggling to come to terms with the loss of an empire. It could be said that the US has spent a hundred years coming to terms with a frontier that no longer exists. Terms like 'Wild West', 'wilderness' and 'frontier' are no longer topographical: they are mythical, moral, psychological, emotional and poetical. The notion of uncharted terrain lying beyond the next ridge emblemized the American challenge and its reality – encountered at the watershed – gave substance to the guarantee of freedom contained in the American Dream. However, it also encapsulated a conundrum: if American destiny is fulfilled through outgunning the savage and absorbing the wild, what happens when the wilderness is gone?

It would appear that those who buy into the myth of the enduring frontier receive counterfeit goods. Almost every square inch of the United States has been rationalized, commercialized, optimized and industrialized. The rule of law is in the ascendant, the savage scalp-hunter has been tamed. Water flows into the desert and out of the flood-plains, air-con tames the fiercest heat and insulation keeps the frost at bay.

But still the belief, the illusion, is sustained, as if each American stood still with one foot in the wild Eden of their dreams. 'The West' is a stage-set where – through a willing suspension of disbelief – Americans play out an enduring drama in two acts. In Act I, the individual travels through limitless solitude in pursuit of the pipedream of self-expression, self-discovery and self-fulfilment. In Act II, the American community is built through the conquest of that wilderness and the citizen finds his moral compass recalibrated through encounters with the wild. Americans pursue a rite-of-passage – whether through summer camp or outward bound – where neophytes abandon the world, immerse themselves in nature and return having conquered their fear of the wild by mastering it.

The American imagination is sustained, here, through literature and the arts, in advertisements, in public discourse and in private dreams. It is even apparent in the dress code: the cowboy hat and boots remain *de rigueur* in Texas, of course, but elsewhere we find a choice of informal dress that sustains the cult of the frontier. It is common to see adults wearing shorts (evocative of scouting in the forest), T-shirts (from the battlefield), lumberjack shirts, Timberland boots and, above all, jeans – deriving from the denim 'waist overalls' that were first created by Loeb (Levi) Strauss for prospectors in the Gold Rush and then worn by cow-hands on western ranches.

The dramatization of weather is another example of this phenomenon. A whole sub-culture – indeed, a theatre – has formed around the delivery of weather news, quite apart from the campaign of violence against authority started by the militant 'Weathermen' in 1969.

American meteorologists can point to a heritage stretching back to the Founding Fathers: Benjamin Franklin is reputed to have been the first man to track a hurricane in 1743 and in June 1752 he researched the electrical qualities of lightning using a kite. (In an exercise worthy of the attention of Jonathan Swift, English authorities took it as evidence of republican revolutionary sentiments when Americans subsequently started to protect their buildings with pointed lightning rods – on the advice of Franklin – as opposed to the blunted rods favoured by King George. One such revolutionary rod protected the Philadelphia State House and the Liberty Bell.)

The TV meteorologists broadcasting today have established a

distinctive profile for themselves, as popular – often sensation-
alist – personalities typically delivering the forecast in front of a
regional map linked to radar images that show up the 'storm
cells'. They have been the subject of two romantic comedies in
recent years: *The Weather Man* (2005), set in Chicago and
starring Nicholas Cage, and *Weather Girl* (2009), set in Seattle
and starring Tricia O'Kelley (with the memorable tagline 'partly
cloudy with a 90 per cent chance of total meltdown'). There have
even been 'Weather Wars' with local news stations competing to
win over viewers through the alleged superiority of their radar
systems. One station – WTWO in Terre Haute, Indiana –
broadcast commercials attacking the competition (WTHI). And
on the national stage, CNN's weatherman, Chad Myers,
resembles *Die Hard* hero Bruce Willis and when he delivers his
updates he has the knowing assurance and contained aggression
of a Special Forces commando operating behind enemy lines.

In a nation where most news channels concentrate on the
parochial, coverage of natural dramas can be extensive. News
channels across the nation will report on the wild-fires that rage
in the Midwest, such as the one in July 2002 when over
2.5 million acres burned, or the incident in May 2009 when
30,000 people were evacuated from homes near Santa Barbara,
California. Every hurricane heralds the statutory camera shot of
a reporter clinging to a lamp-post (preferably with a nearby
palm tree bent horizontal) and the most urbane of governors
will don a lumberjack's shirt and jeans as they 'get down to
business'. Tornado alerts sound in the smallest Midwest towns,
the siren summoning up an orderly procession to the communal
shelter or 'root cellar'. Snow warnings strike in the Eastern
Seaboard, leaving schools and city offices deserted. Most people
living between Boston and Washington, DC, sit – hobbit-like –
beneath a green forest canopy, and falling branches and
uprooted trees cause excessive damage when hurricanes blow
through or an ice storm descends. Households in some of the
most expensive zip codes in the land can be without electricity
for a week or more after a storm because of the damage done to
power cables. Films like *The Day After Tomorrow* (2004) and *The*

Perfect Storm (2000) pit men against the elements. The latter is based on 'The Storm of the Century' when, on 6–7 February 1978, fifteen-foot waves and hurricane-force winds rearranged the shoreline of Cape Cod, cutting Monomoy Island in two, breaching the dune line at Eastham's Coast Guard Beach, where it flattened 90 per cent of the dunes, and carrying off most beach cottages including the house Henry Beston built, occupied and described in *The Outermost House* (1925).

The nation's fascination with the power of nature is exemplified by a recent book published by American science writer, Alan Weisman: *The World Without Us* (2007) imagines what would happen to the Earth if humans were taken out of the equation tomorrow. We see nature reclaim Manhattan: water, weed and wolf appear in the streets and in time the waterlogged foundations of the city's great skyscrapers cause the buildings to topple, given an extra nudge by passing hurricanes.

We must not dismiss this melodrama as pure hype – a piece of artifice designed to preserve the idea of the wild. The US does face real threats from earthquake, hurricane and drought: there is sound science, for instance, behind the Redoubt Volcano alerts published by *Mat-Su Valley Frontiersman* in Alaska and the great cities along the San Andreas Fault have experienced devastation in the past, and will again. Meanwhile, New Orleans struggles to restore itself after the ravages of Katrina. Ken Knevel is an architect in the city working to rebuild the hospitals. In June 2007, he spoke with passion about the challenges he is facing: 'New Orleans is our frontier now. It's tough. It's hard. The city is struggling. Don't get me wrong. We say the disaster was man-made: the levees failed us. But it was started by Nature and we're fighting Nature.' He adds: 'Everyone is getting nervous now that the season is approaching. They worry another one is going to come through and finish the city off.'

In a further twist to the trope of the American frontier, the Wild West of open plains and forest-cloaked mountain ranges has morphed into a new form of social wilderness. There are new frontier zones represented by derelict neighbourhoods whose denizens are neither lions, bears nor sharks but Uzi-toting gangs of the dispossessed. Every city of America seems to contain those zones where the gangs have the upper hand. The language of the frontier is frequently applied to these places: in 2004, for instance, guests invited to smart parties in northwest Washington, DC, would be warned against parking their cars east of 15th Street because this was 'The Wild West': vehicles were broken into and drug-dealers living in apartment blocks would get into fire-fights.

Of course, by then the nation knew that there was no impregnable barrier around any of its hard-won territory: the asymmetric warfare waged by Al-Qaeda had shattered any sense of security. It is unsurprising that a few days after the shock of 9/11, the *Washington Post* carried the following headline: '"Dead or Alive" – Bush Unveils Wild West Rhetoric'. In an address to the Pentagon, the paper explained, the commander-in-chief had described his military as standing ready to defend freedom at any cost. However, President Bush also wanted justice: 'There's an old poster out West that said, *Wanted, dead or alive.*' Three years later, in 2004, the 'Global War on Terror' still evoked the rhetoric of frontier. Troops fighting the campaign in Afghanistan and Iraq were – according to Robert D. Kaplan, writing in the *Wall Street Journal* – operating in Indian Country, with the American military back to the days of fighting Indians.

Indian Country has been expanding in recent years because of the security vacuum created by the collapse of traditional dictatorships and the emergence of new democracies, whose short-term institutional weaknesses provide whole new oxygen systems for terrorists. Iraq is but a microcosm of the Earth in this regard.

The US Army itself had failed to vanquish the Plains Indians, according to Kaplan, because it had never adapted to the challenge of an unconventional enemy; ultimately, it was the deluge of settlers aided by the railroad that brought security to the Old West. In the absence of any Middle Eastern counterpart to those settlers, Kaplan concludes, as Kurtz and Willard might have done before him, American ground troops were going to have to learn to be more like Apaches if the goal of a liberal global environment is to be secured. Kaplan claimed that army and marine field officers themselves embraced the image of Indian Country 'because it captures perfectly the combat challenge of the early twenty-first century'.

No one who has witnessed America's sons and daughters going off to fight some far-off campaign can doubt that the Wild West spirit endures. Young men and women assemble, in desert boots and khaki uniform, in ports like Baltimore Washington International to travel to the conflict zone. They display none of the giddy bravado of the teenage tribe. Their nervousness is palpable. Some sit quietly, alone with their thoughts, or with a cell-phone pressed to an ear in what must feel like the last intimate exchange with loved ones. Others pace a concourse where the food outlets on parade symbolize the land of *e pluribus unum* that most are leaving for the first time: Phillips Seafood, McDonald's, Arby's, California Tortilla, Mamma Ilardo's, Quiznos Sub, Charlie Chiang's Kwai.

These young soldiers are crossing a boundary between the known and the unknown, and – they must feel – between the domesticated and the wild. In doing so, they sustain an American myth and enact a distinctive American rite of passage. They are also participating in the American paradox – of War *and* Peace, taking lives and occupying land in the name of freedom.

CHAPTER SIX

The Cicada's Wing – On War, Peace and Empire

In the summer of 2021, crab-like aliens invade the capital of the free world. They emerge from the ground and shape-shift into airborne creatures that plunge into an orgy of gluttony, procreation and death.

This is not the treatment of a Hollywood sci-fi blockbuster. This will happen, just as it happened in the summer of 2004. In fact, Washington, DC, experiences 'The Curse of the Periodic Cicada' every seventeen years, like clockwork. These wonders of nature spend over 99 per cent of their life suckling the sap of tree roots. Then a hormonal switch is tripped – in millions, almost simultaneously – and they are compelled to leave the darkness they have known for over sixteen years and climb out into the open. This drama grips the capital for six weeks. Pedestrians, cyclists, car-drivers, even tennis-players, learn to navigate around the creatures that flutter about with ungainly grace. The air fills with a mating call that is part gurgle, part hiss, resembling air trapped in water-pipes. At the end, their corpses cover the ground and are hoovered up by predators. All that remains are their transparent, inedible wings.

There is a tale about these fragile wings that grandmothers tell. Look closely, and you will see marks of oracular significance: one of two letters will be visible on the waxy surface. 'W' augurs seventeen years of war; 'P', seventeen years of peace. In 2004, these wings littered the streets of Washington. At first glance, there was nothing other than the tracery of thin veins you might find on the surface of a leaf; but on closer inspection a small 'w' was present there, as if drawn in bold ink, and every wing carried this Mark of Mars.

The Legend of the Cicada's Wing may be fanciful, but it points to a feature of the American condition that deserves deeper scrutiny and reflection. The paradox of war and peace is emblemized in the nation's official seal, where the eagle clutches arrows in its right claw and an olive branch in its left. There is a tension between the high-minded values of a peace-loving nation and a high-quality, well-equipped military that has projected American power around the globe.

The America glimpsed from afar in the 1960s seemed to be involved in a tug-of-war-and-peace. On one side, there were the combat uniforms and napalm of Indo-China; on the other, the cheesecloth and incense of the college campus.

When Saigon fell, it felt like a victory not just for the Vietcong but also for the peaceniks, and the output from Hollywood (*Bilko*, *M.A.S.H.*, *Catch-22*, *Dr Strangelove*) showed up the defence establishment to be an object of ridicule. Hippies set up an alternative American colony around 'Freak Street' in Kathmandu, and the closest thing to an American military deployment in the Third World was the Peace Corps (created by President John F. Kennedy in March 1961 and affirmed by the Peace Corps Act). More than 185,000 Americans have served in the Corps, working in 139 countries to promote – in the words of the Act – 'world peace and friendship'.

Peace has a pedigree in America. William Penn's Quaker ideals led him to eschew violence when establishing his colony in Pennsylvania in the seventeenth century, and his 'Great Treaty' with the Indians at Shackamaxon – when he paid them £1,200 for their land – has acquired iconic status. The Penn treaty is commemorated in a frieze on the US Capitol, and the depiction of the event in folk art was the subject of an exhibition – entitled *An Image of Peace* – at the State Museum of

Pennsylvania in 1996. 'Within everyone lives a desire for peace,' declared the show's strapline.

Penn wanted his real estate to be a colony of heaven for the Children of Light. Sadly, the natives had other ideas: unschooled in the rules of European warfare, they resisted the white man's advance by attacking from nowhere and making no distinction between war-fighter and non-combatant. In *The Americans: The Colonial Experience*, historian Daniel Boorstin described how men, women and children were all fair game to the Redskin; even foetuses were ripped from the womb and displayed on spears as a deterrent. Yet for decades, those running Pennsylvania's affairs clung to Quakerism's pacifist ideals; in the face of heathen violence and brutality they opted for inner effulgence over the outward spark of flintlock or flash of cannon.

As late as 1745, the governor – a non-Quaker – could only equip his garrison at Louisburg through deception: he secured the funds for 'Bread, Beef, Port, Flour, Wheat or other Grain', without admitting that the last item referred to gunpowder. This could not last. In June 1756, after the governor declared war against the Delaware and Shawnee Indians, Quakers withdrew from the Assembly, writing that they could not comply with the public call for military action: 'we conclude it most conducive to the Peace of our own Minds, and the Reputation of our Profession, to permit in our Resolutions of resigning our Seats'. So ended this grand experiment in pacifist governance.

There was, paradoxically, an antipathy to belligerence among those who fought for liberty from Britain. After all, the Declaration of Independence in 1776 complained that King George 'affected to render the Military independent of and superior to the Civil Power'. George Washington took his inspiration from Cincinnatus, and he followed the example of this home-loving, fifth-century BC Roman farmer and general when in 1783 he resigned his commission and hurried back to his estate and family for Christmas. A statue by Jean-Antoine Houdon in Virginia's Capitol Building depicts Washington as Cincinnatus: he has unbuckled and hung up his sword, wields a walking stick in his right hand and covers the axe-heads of the Roman fasces to indicate his nation is at peace. (It is worthy of note that four men elected to the office of President have been awarded the Nobel Peace Prize since its inception in 1901: Teddy Roosevelt, Woodrow Wilson, Jimmy Carter and – in October 2009 – Barack Obama.)

To this day, Washington's Monument in Washington, DC, provides a focal point for those calling for peace. Susan and Mike are typical of the tens of thousands of citizens who set off from the obelisk in 2002, marching through the streets of the nation's capital to demonstrate against military action in Iraq. The couple – who live close to Old Rag Mountain in Virginia's Rappahannock County – expressed their concerns about the levels of 'violent negative energy' building up in the country. The government was pressing for war with Iraq; Washington, DC, was suffering indiscriminate attacks from a sniper; and Senator Paul Wellstone of Minnesota – a vocal opponent of war – had just died in a plane crash. Susan bewailed the lack of coverage of her cause in the media, but described a peace movement that was flourishing on the web: 'There's moveon.com, and we are proud of what we've got in Rappahannock County: there's a website with chat rooms where those committed to peace engage in extensive discussion here.' (MoveOn was persevering in 2008, when it launched its 'Not Alex' advertisement: a mother – resting her first-born, Alex, on her knee – looks into the camera and speaks to Republican presidential candidate John McCain, who had entertained the idea of American troops being stationed in Iraq for 100 years: 'Were you counting on Alex?' she asks. 'If you were . . . you can't have him.')

The internet provides an environment where advocates for peace air and amplify their views (although the silo-like cells of the world wide web are filled with practitioners of free speech who interpret the hollow reverberation of their own views as evidence of victory in a debating-chamber rather than what they really are: reflections in an echo-chamber). They find justification for their position in the founding principles of the nation: bloggers, for instance, denounce the loss of constitutional powers to constrain war-making that were established by the Founding Fathers. The Continental Congress had indeed expressed its aversion to standing armies in peacetime, since these were 'dangerous to the liberties of a free people and generally converted into a destructive engine for establishing despotism'. The authors of the Constitution regarded such armies to be inconsistent with the principles of republican government and they deliberately gave Congress control over the initiation and authorization of war. They wanted to separate, in their words, the purse from the sword: 'Those who are to conduct a war cannot in the nature of things be proper or safe judges whether a war ought to be commenced, continued or concluded,' wrote James Madison. Thomas Jefferson praised the transfer of war power 'from those who are to spend to those who are to pay', and George Mason was for 'clogging' war and 'facilitating' peace. Congress passed the first Neutrality Act in 1794, after Washington had been persuaded by Alexander Hamilton to proclaim the country neutral with regard to the war between France and Great Britain.

There is a view that trade has itself been a force for peace. According to historian Robert Kagan, American statesmen of the late eighteenth and early nineteenth centuries voiced the rhetoric of the Enlightenment when, albeit from a position of weakness, they 'extolled the virtues of commerce as the soothing balm of international strife', appealing to international law and opinion over brute force. Tocqueville recognized this feature of nineteenth-century American society when he wrote that, 'Trade is the natural enemy of all violent passions.' Even in the middle of the First World War, President Woodrow Wilson could speak of America's businessmen leading the struggle 'for the peaceful conquest of the world' when he addressed the Salesmanship Congress in Detroit.

The Louisiana Purchase (1803) is credited, of course, with doubling the size of the nation's footprint without the twitching of a single military muscle. Jefferson bought 900,000 square miles from Napoleon for $15 million (the equivalent to $300 million in 2008, using the GDP deflator), and Americans boast of this as the greatest real estate deal in history, at 4 cents an acre. This tradition continued with the work of the American Colonization Society, founded in 1816 to buy an African homeland for American slaves: Liberia emerged from a tract of land sold to the society by the native rulers on Cape Mesurado in 1822. (This is also the guiding principle in the acquisition of territory in the computer game Second Life, where land is acquired through auctions.)

Accounts of the great transcontinental expedition that followed the Louisiana Purchase – with the 'Corps of Discovery' led by Meriwether Lewis and William Clark – emphasize the message of peace relayed to the native inhabitants of Jefferson's newly acquired territory. They told the Otoe Indians, 'The great chief has sent us out to clear the road, remove every obstruction, and to make it the road of peace between himself and his red children.' The Peace Pipe and Peace Medal became tokens of the contract between American and Indian. Up to 367 peace treaties were drawn up between the US government and individual tribes in the ensuing decades (the last in 1871) and the peace emblem appears in the strangest places – for instance on the medallion on Strawbridge & Clothier's Department Store in Philadelphia, where the words 'Commitment and Trust' en-wreathe the image of an Indian, with a peace pipe and feathered head-dress, shaking the hand of an Anglo in tricorn and frock-coat.

A number of advocacy groups were formed in the twentieth century to uphold the principles of peaceful co-existence. In the First World War, the American Union against Militarism opposed the establishment of a 400,000-man army and a navy equal to the British on the grounds that this drained resources from civilian needs. A similar surge of anti-war activity preceded the Second World War, with the Emergency Peace Campaign organizing committees in 2,000 cities and towns and 500 campuses. Congress passed a rash of Neutrality Acts in this era.

Active pacifism reached a new intensity with opposition to the atom bomb after the Second World War. A Quaker Action Group (AQAG) spawned the Movement for a New Society which in turn sponsored anti-nuclear groups like the Clamshell Alliance. Antipathy to nuclear weapons eventually led to what has been described as 'ten million citizen activists' campaigning to change US policy.

In the following decades – until the 'Global War on Terror' – the administration periodically became engaged in what it called 'peace-keeping' campaigns. Sometimes this involved the deployment of the US's considerable diplomatic and financial clout to promote the cause of peace (as in the Middle East and Northern Ireland); but on other occasions troops have been sent to 'keep the peace' (as part of NATO's deployment in the Balkans, for instance).

But everything changed in the months after 9/11. The United States was then decidedly a warrior nation.

The flag, the uniform and the war-fighter were – in spring 2002 – subjects of respect, honour, veneration, even adulation. Troops were deployed to Afghanistan on 'Operation Enduring Freedom' in what was to become the first front to be opened up in the 'Global War on Terror'. Seven years later, they were still on active service in that country – having overthrown Saddam Hussein's regime in Iraq – campaigning against Taliban insurgents in Helmand Province in 'Operation Panther's Claw'.

A revised National Security Strategy emerged in September 2002. It conjured up a dystopian world where the United States is threatened by failed states and weapons of mass destruction in the hands of an embittered few: if these ingredients came together, the argument went, the mixture could destroy the American way of life. In response to these threats, the strategy reserved the 'right of pre-emption'. It also asserted that the US would allow no peer competitors: the country stood alone in a unipolar world order and would keep its forces strong enough to dissuade all potential adversaries. The strategy declared:

It is time to reaffirm the essential role of American military strength. We must build and maintain our defences beyond challenge. Our military's highest priority is to defend the United States. To do so effectively, our military must assure our allies and friends; dissuade future military competition; deter threats against US interests, allies and friends; and decisively defeat any adversary if deterrence fails.

This is stirring stuff – encapsulating the vision, language and purpose of a powerful, militaristic society. But this was not just posturing. There has been a substantial expansion in the Pentagon's budget to support this strategy: the initial proposal was for a 2003 defence budget of $396 billion – 27.5 per cent greater than that for 2001. By 2009 the budget had reached $662 billion, and the Obama administration has lodged a request with Congress for a record $663.8 billion for 2010. These figures exclude expenditure on military operations, which were met in each of the middle years of the decade by supplemental bills of $50–$87 billion. In 2009, President Obama asked for $130 billion for Overseas Contingency Operations. (We are approaching the point when the US's military expenditure exceeds the combined defence budgets of all other nations of the world. In 2007, the most recent year for which accurate comparative data are available, the United States accounted for 43 per cent of the world's total defence spending, investing five times more than China, eight times more than Russia, eighty-five times more than Iran, and a hundred times more than North Korea.)

On 21 May 2009 – in a speech at the National Archives, standing in front of the US Constitution, Barack Obama spelled out his support for the American soldier:

For the first time since 2002, we're providing the necessary resources and strategic direction to take the fight to the extremists who attacked us on 9/11 in Afghanistan and Pakistan. We're investing in the twenty-first-century military and intelligence capabilities that will allow us to stay one step ahead of a nimble enemy. We have re-energized a global non-proliferation regime to deny the world's most dangerous people access to the world's deadliest weapons.

And we've launched an effort to secure all loose nuclear materials within four years. We're better protecting our border, and increasing our preparedness for any future attack or natural disaster. We're building new partnerships around the world to disrupt, dismantle, and defeat al-Qaeda and its affiliates.

It seems plausible to argue that the size of military expenditure in this decade reflects a post-traumatic reaction to 9/11, with the US going through a temporary, uncharacteristic period of belligerence. However, there is no evidence that the US had previously starved its forces of materiel. Indeed, the current draw-down from GDP (at about 3.7 per cent) is nothing compared to the 7 per cent figure that dominated the Cold War years. Even during the Bill Clinton years – when the country was celebrating 'the end of history' with the fall of the Iron Curtain, the US's military budget strengthened in comparison with the combined military budgets of France, Germany, UK, Russia, Japan and China; by 2001, the funds directed to defence in all these countries represented a mere 75 per cent of the US budget.

President Clinton's view of his right to use force overseas would have shocked the framers of the Constitution and was cited by commentators at the time as evidence for a continuing drift of war power from Congress to the president. In June 1993, he launched twenty-three Tomahawk cruise missiles against the Iraqi Intelligence Service in Baghdad. In October 1993, he sent troops to Somalia and Haiti. In February 1994, he authorized air strikes in Bosnia.

The reality is that 9/11 did not change very much. The nation was already well versed in the ways of war and a historical perspective shows that the military have been engaged in campaigns for at least 124 of the country's 234 years. In *The Warrior State* (2004), Everett Carl Dolman (professor of comparative military studies at the US Air Force School of

Advanced Air and Space Studies) has drawn links between the United States and ancient Athens and Sparta, arguing that disciplined military service makes a contribution to the development of liberal democratic institutions, promoting communal loyalties and trust.

The National Museum of American History tells visitors to the permanent exhibition, called *The Price of Freedom*, 'Americans have gone to war to win their independence, expand their national boundaries, define their freedoms, and defend their interests around the globe.' This is a society where fighting men and women are held in high esteem. You can sense this from sampling the tens of thousands of messages 'To Our Soldiers' on the US Army website. Heather, from Georgia, captures the feeling in her text:

> I know a lot of people take their freedoms for granted. They don't realize someone is in another country, or on a base where someone is working to protect us, the country, and our freedom. If it wasn't for you soldiers, all of you, we would have nothing that we do now. I will never forget my rights, and I will never forget the people that fight, and die for us so we can have those rights. More people need to appreciate the sacrifices and hardships our soldiers go through! Thank you just doesn't say enough.

However, the warrior class is not representative of the whole nation. Those who sun themselves on Venice Beach, or work in a beef-feed lot in Nebraska or a trading-room in Wall Street, are not overwhelmed by the sense of a nation at war. Rural Republicans are over-represented in the casualty lists; East Coast Democrats less so. Patriotic sentiment runs high in those communities which have seen their National Guard deployed to Iraq or Afghanistan: one Humvee destroyed by an IED (improvised explosive device) can have a serious impact on a town's high-school class. Hence there is a yearning – from some congressmen – for the draft, to ensure that the sacrifice is more evenly spread.

One gets an impression of the high regard paid to the armed services by observing the treatment and behaviour of their chiefs during the ritual display and theatre surrounding the State of the Union Address. The joint chiefs of staff sit to attention, in their pressed and garlanded uniforms, in reserved seats in the front row when the president – their commander-in-chief – addresses Congress. Their body language demonstrates acute lack of interest in the partisan responses of the politicians behind them, who will regularly rise to their feet to clap and cheer whenever a statement meets their approval. Periodically the president will produce a paean of praise for the military: then, and only then, the chiefs will join in the clapping with gusto.

These senior officers are housed in conditions of splendour. Anyone sailing out of the Washington Marina will pass the handsome federal-style mansions lining the waterfront at Fort McNair. These are the *ex-officio* homes of generals serving at the Pentagon. They and their families have access to an officers' mess with a fine-pillared portico, swimming pools, tennis courts and manicured grounds, and helicopters will whisk them to and from work. An old Soviet hand observed, 'If this was Russia, we would look at the occupants of these places with disapproval and call them *nomenklatura* [the beneficiaries of the patronage system in the Soviet bureaucracy, controlled by the Communist Party].'

This honoured status is shared by the men who run operations around the world. They sit at the apex of Joint Unified Commands created by the Goldwater Nichols Act of 1986. Some of these administer key operational functions: TRANSCOM for transport; SOCOM for special operations. Others cover segments of the globe: SOUTHCOM, South America; EUCOM, Europe; PACOM, Asia; CENTCOM, the Middle East and Afghanistan; NORTHCOM, North America. These generals are likened to the pro-consuls of the Roman Empire. There have been versions of this command structure since the Second World War, when the generals and admirals became known as CINCs (commanders-in-chief). In 2002,

Secretary of Defense Donald Rumsfeld reminded the military that 'POTUS' (President of the United States) was the one and only CINC. The title has now changed to 'Combatant Commander', but this has not diminished the power and authority associated with the post: the Goldwater Act gave the CINCs total responsibility for operations in their region, reporting directly through the secretary for defense to the president.

A career in the armed services offers young men and women far more than access to networks of power and influence. It can represent an escape from the stifling parochialism that dominates the lives of many, especially in the American heartland. Rickey exemplifies this, holding a senior position in the Pentagon, in 2003. He has travelled a long way from his birth-place – a small town near Nashville, Tennessee. His father was a sharecropper whose big 'step-up', Rickey said, was to get a job as a factory hand. Rickey joined an artillery regiment: 'This got me an education at college. It got me out of Tennessee. But my father could never understand why I should want to move away: he never saw me in uniform.'

The military community, and its influence in American society, extends far beyond the sphere of the active war-fighter. Veterans are honoured with their own public holiday (on 11 November) and their heft is recognized by the fact that the secretary for veterans' affairs sits on the president's cabinet. He describes himself as serving 25 million veterans and their 45 million relatives – 25 per cent of the population who are eligible for benefits and services provided by his department. In 2003, his budget rose by 11 per cent at a time when education – a presidential priority – grew by only 6 per cent. In 2009, President Barack Obama was seeking a record $112.8 billion for the department, with over $47 billion directed towards healthcare and with entitlement benefits increasing by over 20 per cent. An entire health service is dedicated to the wellbeing of veterans and they can make use of sports and social clubs on military bases across the country.

Max Cleland personifies the drive to honour the veteran. He was severely wounded in Vietnam in April 1968, losing both legs and one arm. He turned to politics once he had recuperated and was elected to the Georgia State Senate before progressing to the US Senate (1997–2003). In 1975 (aged thirty-four) he had been asked by President Jimmy Carter to lead the Veterans' Administration. The timing was significant: this was two years after the end of the Vietnam War, in which US forces had suffered 58,000 deaths, in addition to over 304,000 wounded in action. Cleland instituted a revolutionary 'Vets' Center' programme offering psychological counselling as well as physical care for combat veterans. He served, briefly, on the 9/11 Commission (resigning in the face of what he believed to be stonewalling) and in May 2009 he was appointed secretary of the American Battle Monuments Commission by the president, responsible for establishing shrines to America's war-dead overseas.

It is telling that a Vietnam veteran has been tasked with this solemn duty. One must never underestimate the profound effect that the Indo-China conflict has had on the US. The American people blamed returning draftees for the disastrous conduct of the war – draftees who had been sent into a battle they neither wanted nor endorsed. The 'Ride to the Wall' on Memorial Day, also known as 'Rolling Thunder', was initiated by these wretched veterans who felt the government was not doing enough to recover the prisoners-of-war and the remains of the dead abandoned in Indo-China. This protest has now been absorbed into the mainstream – on the Sunday before Memorial Day, the highways into Washington, DC, become choked with convoys of Harley-Davidsons, silencers removed, heading for the Mall and the Vietnam Memorial, where one is likely to encounter a huge, wild-eyed vet in grey ponytail, studs, tattoos and leather biker's gear being embraced by a young, uniformed, close-shaven Marine. The Gold Star Mums are there to heal the wounds as well – as one put it, 'to give these poor outcasts the hugs they never had when they returned home'.

The Vietnam War returned to the limelight in 2008: Senator John McCain, the Republican candidate in presidential elections, bears the scars of torture from his time as a POW. But men like John McCain and Max Cleland demonstrate that it is wrong to think of America's veterans as forming part of a dependency culture. It is career-enhancing to have served under arms and the British visitor will be surprised at the number of retired generals holding positions of authority in the government. In the months after 9/11, General Wayne Downing, Admiral Steve Abbott and General John Gordon took up positions in the White House on the staff of the National Security Adviser. Generals Frank Libutti and Patrick Hughes and Admiral James Loy filled key positions in the new Department of Homeland Security. General Michael Hayden moved from running the National Security Agency to become deputy director of National Intelligence before being nominated CIA director in 2006. Barack Obama has continued this tradition in the appointments he made in 2009: for instance, Admiral Dennis Blair is his director of National Intelligence, and his national security advisor is General James L. Jones, a former EUCOM combatant commander and commandant of the US Marine Corps.

A particular mystique surrounds the US Marines, which serves them well in pursuing employment after their return to civilian life. The Marines are renowned not only for their courage and camaraderie but also for their innovative and lateral thinking. One Marine (James) – who studied philosophy at Cambridge before joining the Corps – has spoken of the monk-like quality of his fellow officers as they promote a strong sense of brotherhood. Marines quote the motto 'Semper fidelis' ('Always faithful') to one another the whole time, and they mean it!

The flourishing careers of ex-Marines, it is said, stem from this culture. Frank Libutti and William Parrish (respectively under- and assistant-secretary at the Department of Homeland Security) extolled that Marine tradition of caring for their men. Libutti said:

> What gets me up in the morning is the fine body of men and women I am going to work with each day. People don't

understand the tradition Bill and I come from. When we say our two priorities are *the mission and the men* it's not mission first and men second . . . they are both top priority, because you can't achieve the mission without the commitment and motivation of your men.

General Libutti was the product of a private military college near Charleston called the Citadel. He wears his class ring (complete with palmetto and star motif) to prove it.

To the critical eye, there is something vulgar about these class rings: they have the crocketed surface of a Gothic finial and the golden sheen of costume jewellery. However, to military officers, this is a badge of distinction and the class ring is a common feature in the club rooms, courtrooms and corridors of the capital. Its significance was decoded by Jack, a distinguished Washington lawyer and an army graduate from West Point, who sports his ring, as custom dictates, on his wedding finger: the college crest is engraved on one side of the ring; on the other is the crest for his year, specially designed for the class. Jack's has the number 66 and an eagle.

The military cadet is allowed to wear the ring in his last year at college: it goes on the second finger of the left hand with the class device closest to the heart. On graduating, this is switched so that the college crest is shown to be higher in one's affections. There is a code associated with the class ring when an officer comes to marry: if his proposal is accepted, his fiancée will be presented with a small replica of the class ring; on marriage, the wedding band is fashioned to fit beside the class ring that overlaps it. Jack said, 'My class-year is very close to me. Five hundred and fifty graduated out of 700 who began the course.' He claims he can recognize the class ring of a brother officer from a hundred paces.

There is a second public holiday that is wired into America's martial traditions, carrying greater symbolic import than Veterans' Day. Memorial Day became a federal holiday in 1971, when Congress passed the National Holiday Act. Over two dozen towns and cities claim to be the birth-place of Memorial Day, citing stories of graves of the war-dead being decorated in an annual mourning ceremony. According to the website of the Department of Veteran Affairs, its roots go back to a proclamation in May 1868 by General John Logan, the head of an organization of Union veterans – the Grand Army of the Republic. He established 30 May as 'Decoration Day', a time for the nation to decorate the graves of the war-dead with flowers. By 1890, the day was recognized by all Northern states, but Southern states insisted on going their own way, lest they become contaminated by Unionist ways. Today, there seems to be a grudging acceptance of a common date for the whole nation – the last Monday in May. In 2009, President Obama used the occasion to address the nation on the theme of 'Sacrifice', referring to the sacred trust that exists between America and all who wear the uniform of the armed services.

Memorial Day also represents a seasonal milestone in the US calendar: it marks the start of summer. This is a well-established protocol (although some features of the code – such as the convention preventing women from wearing white before Memorial Day – have been eroded). Regardless of the weather, swimming pools open and householders change their seasonal décor on this day. There is an almost ritual pilgrimage to the seaside (at least for those on the East Coast). In one very local custom, Alaskans get the go-ahead to bury their dead after Memorial Day, because only then is the ground judged to be accessible to the spade (with the winter frost dispelled and frozen ground softened). Meanwhile, all across the country the day is observed with parades, ceremonies, speeches and prayers led by city officials and county commissioners, posts of the 'VFW' ('Veterans of Foreign Wars') and units of the United War Veterans' Association, high-school bands and boy scout troops. Typically, these rites centre on war memorials and military cemeteries.

The preponderance of military burial-sites in the US points to the number of engagements fought inside the national borders. For two centuries (the eighteenth and nineteenth) the country was not so much punctuated as eviscerated by bloody rivalries between competing forces who struggled for ascendancy. Many conflicts, of course, involved the Native American tribes and nations: 'wars' – and history describes them as such – were fought against the Creek, Seminole, Sioux, Arikara, Cayuse, Nez Perce, Cheyenne, Yakima, Apache, Navajo, Modoc and Kiowa. Others involved battles between competing 'Anglo' interests, such as the Utah (or Mormon) War and the Wakarusa skirmish in Kansas in 1855, when escalating violence between Free-Staters and pro-slavery activists led to an army of Missourians invading Kansas.

This last episode was, of course, a precursor to the Civil War and it is this conflict that weighs most heavily on the American conscience and consciousness: more than 3 million Americans saw battle in the Civil War – in a population of 31 million, it is reasonable to assume that this amounted to at least 30 per cent of adult males. Some 620,000 soldiers lost their lives, a further 400,000 were wounded or disabled and, as James M. McPherson points out in *Battle Cry of Freedom* (1988), innumerable Southern citizens died as a direct or indirect consequence of the war. This wretched experience impacted on most families in the country and it has engendered a powerful urge to honour and remember the dead that continues to this day.

The battlefields of the Civil War have come to hold a particular, haunting fascination for the American people. Many of these sites are now designated National Parks, equipped with visitor centres, film-shows, bookshops and maps. Uniformed rangers describe the battles in vivid detail and there are self-guided tours on foot, bicycle, car and horseback. The American public shows a level of interest in these places that the British might reserve for archaeological sites or country houses. Antietam is a popular destination for visitors looking to witness the scene of the bloodiest day's battle in the Civil War. Forty thousand Southern troops (General Robert E. Lee's Army of Northern Virginia) faced 87,000 in General George McClellan's Army of the Potomac. During some phases of the battle, men died at a rate of over one per second and there were 23,000 casualties on 17 September 1862. Early photographs show the extent of the sacrifice, with a sunken lane, for instance, brimming with bodies. These images, unique at the time, had a profound influence on the American people: they could reflect in tranquillity on the consequences of war. One of Virginia's leading contemporary artists, Sally Mann, continues to photograph this landscape, using the nineteenth-century technique of collodion salts to create a ghostly, vaporous effect.

However, it is Gettysburg which holds particular sway over the American imagination, drawing 1.8 million visitors each year. The battle-site has taken on mystical and mythical dimensions, largely because of the mortal remains resting there. In a ceremony far removed from the ritual decorum of Acoma's cemetery, 8,000 corpses were planted into ground ploughed up by the industrial instruments of war, and there are accounts of the rise and swell of decaying humanity in the weeks that followed the battle. The earth gave as visitors walked across it and these were uneasy graves, harvested by desperate relatives looking for their loved ones. Within a few weeks, according to one account, 'arms, legs and heads began to protrude from the ground like some vile crop, and hogs grubbed up corpses to eat'. It is not surprising that today there is a flourishing trade in ghost walks in Gettysburg or that rangers will point to the white butterflies that hover above the ground in the summer and refer to them as the spirits of the fallen.

In time, at least the unsettled terrain was stabilized, with the dead re-interred in orderly fashion in parcels of land dedicated to each state. President Lincoln came to dedicate this official cemetery for the dead, and the address that he delivered that day – in a voice so *pianissimo* that it went unheard by most of the people present – has become celebrated as a masterpiece, distilling and amplifying the vision of the Founding Fathers.

Battlefields like Gettysburg, Manassas and Antietam are studded with statues, cast-iron plaques and copper cannons (turned symbolically nose-down into the ground) commemorating the dead, and across the nation war memorials and military cemeteries have become sacred, or semi-sacred, sites of great significance, visited by millions of people a year. In this way, America's warrior past is honoured and an enduring martial spirit is celebrated and sustained.

The public spaces of cities are likely to celebrate war heroes, typically generals shown mounted on their chargers. Monument Avenue in Richmond (capital of Virginia and, formerly, of the Confederacy) is a notable example, with its sculptures of Robert E. Lee, J.E.B. Stuart, Jefferson Davis and Thomas 'Stonewall' Jackson. Folklore has developed around the iconography of these sculptures: the number of hoofs in the air indicates how the subject died; the position of the hat shows whether the subject was victorious or defeated in battle, and so on. However, there are also images and memorials to ordinary soldiers to be found punctuating the landscape of the Civil War conflict. Go to a tiny rural township like Crawford in New York State and there you will find a cemetery, set by the roadside and surrounded by fields, containing the bodies of two soldiers who fell in the Civil War. Each year, on Memorial Day, a contingent comes to honour them: they play 'Taps' (the bugle call for 'lights out' at the close of day, always played at a military funeral), fire a rifle volley, salute and place American flags on the graves. Then the honour-guard moves on and the site is left to its vegetal stillness.

The figure of a Confederate soldier in Oxford, Mississippi, exemplifies the symbolic freight carried by a number of seemingly insignificant statues dotted around the towns and cities of the South. It stands on a graceful pillar in front of the 1873 courthouse (built over the remains of an earlier court razed to the ground by Union forces) and it plays a walk-on part in the closing sequence of William Faulkner's Southern Gothic masterpiece, *The Sound and the Fury* (1929): the castrated idiot, Benjy Compson, weeps when his black carer (Luster) walks him past the soldier the wrong way. Benjy and Luster both understood about the rites of respect for this symbol of sacrifice and service that should be observed but could be flouted. Through Benjy's tears at Luster's actions, we sense the pent-up emotions of a defeated yet defiant, impotent yet self-important South.

Another tribute to military prowess is found in the band of decorative panels running around the old Department of Pensions in Washington, DC (now the Museum of Buildings). In a cross-reference to those Greek friezes that display warriors caught in frozen motion, the artist – Casper Buberl – depicted Union soldiers, sailors and Marines marching off to war with pack-horses and cannon. But there is deeper significance, here. The building that carries this frieze was designed by Montgomery Meigs, quartermaster-general of the Union Army and a man who had suffered the loss of his son in the Battle of Swift Run Gap. This young soldier was initially buried in the family plot in Oak Hill, but in 1864 his body was disinterred and carried South across the Potomac to be buried, together with twenty-five of his compatriots, in the vegetable garden of Confederate General Lee's home at Arlington. Meigs, it is said, looked on with 'grim satisfaction' as the bodies were lowered into the land belonging to his nemesis. The symbolism is powerful and profound, here. It connects to a primeval wellspring and might have emerged from the pages of anthropologist James Frazer's *The Golden Bough: A Study in Magic and Religion* (1890). The corpses of an ascendant North are planted in Southern soil, specifically in the vegetable patch of an enemy general.

The seeds sown in that plot germinated into the crop of military graves – including that of the former Commander-in-Chief, President John F. Kennedy – known as Arlington Cemetery. Its green flanks dominate the southern vista of Washington, DC, rising up across the Potomac from the Lincoln Memorial, beyond the measured spans of Memorial Bridge. Tens of thousands visit the grounds each year and a tour through the cemetery typically ends at the Tomb of the Unknowns where a military guard performs its immaculate clockwork march. The right to burial in Arlington falls to those who die in active service; those who retire after a lifetime career in the armed services; reservists honoured with a medal; and the spouses and children of all of the above. Projections indicate, at the current rate, that the cemetery will run out of space in sixty years. Small ceremonies of remembrance and despatch are being performed at Arlington throughout the year, but the greatest begins on the Thursday before Memorial Day, when 1,200 soldiers of the Third US Infantry place small American flags by each of the 260,000 gravestones and guard these with patrols throughout the weekend.

War memorials have also become a major feature in Washington, DC. In addition to the Korean and Vietnam War Memorials, there is now the World War II Memorial, dedicated on Memorial Weekend, 2004. After a service in the National Cathedral, a huge crowd – including many veterans in uniform – gathered in the National Mall to participate in what was termed a 'Salute to Heroes'. President Bush received the monument on behalf of the American people. He spoke of the 'modest sons of a peaceful country' who went to war, making special reference to 462 men who received Medals of Honor. He then described one soldier in the 58th Armored Field Artillery who had the best-kept rifle in the unit but who wanted to cover it with salt when the war ended, hang it on the wall and watch it rust.

A cynic might argue that any gesture that leads to the disposal of old stocks of weapons will be welcomed by the 'military-industrial complex' – that colossus that shadows the Defense Department and the armed services. President Dwight D. Eisenhower initiated the term, in his 'Farewell Address' in January 1961, at a time when 3.5 million people were directly engaged in defence-related work:

> We have been compelled to create a permanent armaments industry of vast proportions. This conjunction of an immense military establishment and a large arms industry is new in the American experience. The total influence – economic, political, even spiritual – is felt in every city,

every State House, every office of the Federal Government. Our toil, resources and livelihood are all involved; so is the very structure of our society.

His great fear was that the US's defence industry could gain unwarranted influence in government, bringing about what he termed the disastrous rise of misplaced power.

The military-industrial complex remains substantial, despite presumptions – through the 1990s – of a peace dividend following the end of the Cold War. *Defense News* publishes its league table of the 'Top 100' defence companies in the world, and US companies consistently dominate this: forty-three companies feature in the latest table (published in 2008), earning $226.3 billion. The top five US companies are Lockheed Martin, Boeing, Northrop Grumman, General Dynamics and Raytheon; between them, defence-related revenues in 2007 amounted to $136.4 billion and they employ almost 600,000 people around the world.

Let us provide some context. The annual revenue of these top five companies is a close approximation – after inflation – to the ten-year budget to put a man on the Moon and it is 450 times the cost (again after inflation) of the Louisiana Purchase that doubled the size of the American land-mass. This illustrates the extraordinary traction enjoyed by companies dedicated to equipping the American war-fighter. It comes as no surprise, therefore, that these companies contribute hundreds of thousands of dollars to the Democratic and Republican parties or that they employ an army of lobbyists, publicists and lawyers to represent their interests on 'The Hill'.

Of course, in the free-market atmosphere of the US, these companies are susceptible to the shifting currents of opinion within the Pentagon: one gains a sense of this from a speech given by Secretary of Defense Robert Gates, on 6 April 2009, when he set out his recommendations for his 2010 budget. He identified plans to trim or even abandon some equipment programmes (e.g. the 'Multiple Kill Vehicle' and the 'Airborne Laser' aircraft), but his shopping list included: fifty Predator-class unmanned aerial vehicle orbits by FY11 (a 62 per cent increase); spending $500 million more on helicopters – a capability that is in urgent demand in Afghanistan; buying more Littoral Combat Ships (LCS), increasing the order from two to three ships in FY 2010, but with the goal of eventually acquiring fifty-five LCS; increasing the procurement of F-35 Joint Strike Fighters from fourteen in 2009 to thirty in FY10, with the aim to buy 513 F-35s over the five-year defence plan, and, ultimately, 2,443.

As we saw in 'The Lattice Constant', the merchant, the manufacturer and the entrepreneur have benefited from the warrior state for centuries: profit motive, can-do, and know-how make a potent mixture. It is said that Eli Whitney invented the American system of mass production when supplying 10,000 muskets to the young American army. Whitney is lauded in the American Precision Museum at Windsor, Vermont – suitably housed in the original Robbins and Lawrence Armory – alongside Simeon North, the scythe-maker who signed a contract with the War Department in 1800 for 500 horse pistols to be delivered within one year.

The connection between scientific research, technology and war reached a milestone with the Manhattan Project – the development of the atom bomb in the Second World War. In 1939, the government's total budget for research and development was $1 billion (much of it dedicated to agriculture); but the Manhattan Project cost $2 billion (the equivalent to $25 billion today – still a fraction of what the defence sector now earns) and it was delivered through an unprecedented melding of science, industry and engineering. Just as the first nuclear blast created a new mineral – trinitite – at the White Sands test site, so it is that three extraordinary research institutions emerged from the Manhattan Project: Los Alamos, Sandia and Lawrence Livermore National Laboratories. The US military continues to pride itself on being research-minded and hundreds of thousands of men and women are involved in this work.

Los Alamos is the largest employer in New Mexico, with 10,000 personnel and 1,600 PhDs, located among the isolated canyons and mountain ridges where J. Robert Oppenheimer developed the nuclear bomb under conditions of utmost secrecy. The staff claim, with the braggadocio that Americans cannot resist, that their computers are so powerful that they work out a calculation in one second which it would take a man 10 million years to complete. Sandia designs all the non-nuclear parts of nuclear weapons, but its portfolio extends to such wonders as the Synthetic Aperture Radar that enables US warplanes to see through cloud cover. Gerry Yonas typifies the sort of scientist-entrepreneur who flourishes in the US's defence realm. This expert in particle beam fusion weapons would fit in an Oxbridge seminar-room: a rather conservative, bearded and grizzled gentleman in his late fifties, shooting out ideas like a Catherine wheel spouting sparks.

Yonas will happily enunciate Sandia's vision statement, which opens with the words, 'Securing a peaceful and free world through technology'. This chimes with the language used repeatedly by the American administration and the military establishment. But does this talk of 'peace' and 'freedom' provide cover for an American programme of external predation designed to further US influence and interests? As American troops deploy themselves and their high-tech equipment around the world, are they spearheading – as some fear – the creation of an American Empire?

The question of American imperialism has come to preoccupy a host of intellectuals and political scientists in the country's universities and think-tanks. A survey of recent publications on the subject reveals a long list of books (see Bibliography) bearing the word 'empire' in their title. Interest in this issue was exemplified by the debate held at the American Enterprise Institute in Washington, DC, in 2003: 'The United States Is, and Should Be, an Empire'. At this event, Niall Ferguson (at the time, professor of financial history at New York University) argued that 'empire' had less to do with territory – the US possesses only fourteen dependencies – and more to do with power.

America is a military, economic and cultural 'colossus' in the world, making it an empire despite so many of its citizens refusing to acknowledge the fact.

Robert Kagan (of the Carnegie Endowment for International Peace) disagreed. The US is, indeed, powerful – in fact, it is the most successful global power in history – but this does not make it an empire because it fails to exhibit predatory, territorial ambitions. The American tendency, when intervening in any place around the world, is to commit to an early departure. It is, Kagan argued, precisely because everyone knows that the US will not exercise imperial control that its rising hegemony has been so widely accepted and so little feared.

The nature of this debate rightly reflected the fact that there is little consensus about whether or not an American Empire exists. The battle between opposing camps is usually conducted with decorum – the high-brow equivalent to aerial manoeuvres – but sometimes descends to hand-to-hand combat. Weapons can be interchangeable and references to the 'Monroe Doctrine', the 'Roosevelt Corollary' (see below), the American occupation of the Philippines, or the US military bases around the globe float back and forth between combatants like frisbees on a campus lawn. The arguments – if word-play is appropriate here – are as much non-empirical (based on value judgments and interpretation) as empirical (verified by means of observation or experiment).

Debate over empire is not focused exclusively on the exercise of military muscle. For instance, in *Irresistible Empire* (2005) Victoria de Grazia has charted the infectious spread of America's consumer culture through Europe, spearheaded by such brands as Coca-Cola, Kellogg's Corn Flakes and Wrigley's Chewing Gum. The powerful Bureau of Foreign and Domestic Commerce supported the process, tasking consular attachés to produce detailed intelligence reports on foreign markets. American values, products and technology can be seen to embody a 'soft' power that achieves a cultural hegemony: in this vision of a Mickey Mouse Empire, the US holds a predominant position of influence in the world through the promised delivery of gratification rather than through the threatened delivery of shock and awe. The coke has trumped the nuke.

Nor is the debate confined to the overseas dimension. Historian Charles Maier reminds us that a nation does not need to have an empire: it can simply be one (Tsarist Russia is one example; eighteenth-century Britain might be another). With the odd exception – Hawaii, Alaska – the blocks of real estate that have gone into forming the US have been adjacent to, or lie within, the country's borders. The US has most frequently exercised military authority not in some distant province but in and around its own borders, or to strengthen the wider security blanket. It subjugated the Native Americans. It annexed the Hispanic southwest through military force. Some enthusiasts wanted to add Canada to the bag in the war of 1812, and subsequently to take over Cuba. It acquired a Polynesian kingdom called Hawaii – bearing neither geographic nor cultural links to the North American continent – as a valuable base for its navy in the mid-Pacific.

Today, Puerto Rico and the US Virgin Islands are colonies in all but name. The former, which fell into American hands after the war with Spain in 1898, receives $17 billion in aid each year and is said to supply a greater ratio of fighting men and women than any full-grown state of the Union. The US Virgin Islands were bought in 1917 from the Danish as a defence against the Kaiser's navy, which was thought to threaten US shipping in the Panama Canal. There are those in Puerto Rico and the Virgin Islands who are clamouring to become the 51st State, but Puerto Rico had its own, violent, independence movement, and in many cases (such as the southwestern states, the Indian territories), the populace was pressed into union by an unwelcome, iron embrace. Is this empire- or nation-building?

One can throw into the mix that extraordinary culture war that erupted between North and South in 1861. The different names for the American Civil War are themselves indicative of different narratives: – 'War of Southern Independence', 'War Between the States', 'War of the Rebellion' and 'War of Northern Aggression'. The origins of the American Civil War lie in a complex set of competing issues around concepts of slavery, federalism, identity, innovation and morality, fuelled by party politics, expansionism, sectionalism and economics. Ultimately, a Northern hegemony bore down on the South, imposing its preferred value-system and banishing slavery. There is, in this context, something familiar about these lines from Maier's *Among Empires*:

> Empires are about civilizing missions, the diffusion of cultural styles . . . The suppression of practices perceived as barbaric – such as human sacrifice and suttee. Occasionally they are about bringing peace and the rule of law or defending what we have defined as freedom. But they are also about violence and bloodshed.

Notwithstanding these questions of commercial empires abroad and an internal empire at home, the focus of debate returns to military ascendancy overseas. Robert Kagan may believe the US to be 'a behemoth with a conscience', whose intentions are entirely worthy, but he has identified a philosophical outlook informing the undeniable projection of massive force into the global arena. In *Paradise and Power* (2003) he acknowledges that while the Old World appears to subscribe to Immanuel Kant's notion of 'perpetual peace', the US sees itself operating in an anarchic, Hobbesian world where true security – and the defence and promotion of a liberal order – depend on the use of military might.

There is substance to this analysis, although it may be biased by the experience of George W. Bush's Manichaean worldview. When he took presidential office for the second time in January 2005, the main theme of his inaugural speech was liberty overcoming tyranny; he quoted Abraham Lincoln – 'Those who deny freedom to others deserve it not for themselves; and under the rule of a just God cannot retain it.' Nevertheless, this theme has emerged frequently in foreign policy since the Civil War. Theodore Roosevelt, for instance, espoused 'Big Stick Diplomacy' through his 'Corollary' to the Monroe Doctrine, declaring a willingness to intervene in countries that failed to show 'reasonable efficiency and decency in social and political matters'.

A spate of military deployments in the Caribbean and Central America followed Roosevelt's corollary. From 1909 to 1933, the US was rarely out of Nicaragua and it played a policeman's role in protecting lives and property in Santa Domingo, Cuba, Haiti and the Dominican Republic. In these cases, the dough of self-interest was leavened with the yeast of missionary zeal – to protect the freedoms or ordinary people denied the benefits of democratic institutions and/or to compel foreigners to accept the indisputable benefits of the American way of democracy. If this meant the exercise of violence for a good cause, then so be it. Nowhere is this attitude better expressed than in an exchange in 1913 between Walter Hines Page, US ambassador to the Court of St James, and Sir Edward Grey, British foreign secretary. At the time, Mexico was proving a thorn in the American flank and the US was sizing up for a fight:

Grey: 'Suppose you have to intervene, what then?'
Page: 'Make 'em vote and live by their decision.'
Grey: 'Suppose they will not so live?'
Page: 'We'll go in again and make 'em vote again.'
Grey: 'And keep this up for two hundred years?'
Page: 'Yes. The US will be here two hundred years and it can continue to shoot men for that little space of time till they learn to vote and rule themselves.'

Woodrow Wilson used more mellow tones when sending his troops to Europe to fight in the First World War and his words were pointedly anti-imperialistic:

The world must be safe for democracy. Its peace must be planted on the tested foundations of political liberty. We have no selfish ends to serve. We desire no conquest, no dominion ... We are but one of the champions of the rights of mankind.

Much confusion about the question of American imperialism stems from this combination of right and might. Belief in the rectitude of the American Way, backed with superior military force, demonstrates for some the fact that the US is imperialistic while others see this tradition as evidence to the contrary. The argument can easily distil into a sterile debate about semantics: is the US 'hegemonic' (enjoying a paramount influence over other countries, but not the will to compel obedience), 'imperial' (displaying its power to overawe others) or 'imperialist' (territorially expansionist and/or bent on controlling the policies of weaker states)?

The answer is probably all of the above, some of the time, differently, in different situations. However, for the anthropologist intent on surveying the American Way, the answer is less important than the nation's preoccupation with the question. This would appear to indicate a pressing need to make sense of America's place in the world. To be an American, it is said, is to be a champion of all those who yearn for liberation. A substantial armed force has been established, therefore, not only to defend the republic but also to bring freedom to the oppressed around the globe. This mission is articulated in different ways, in keeping with the tenor of the times. It may be in the uncompromising language of Walter Hines Page or in the more naive and benign tones of Arthur Schlesinger, who has said of the early years of the Kennedy administration, 'We thought for a moment that the world was plastic and the future unlimited.' This is how the National Security Strategy puts it today:

> The presence of American forces overseas is one of the most profound symbols of [our] commitments to allies and friends. Through our willingness to use force in our own defense and in defense of others, the US demonstrates its resolve to maintain a balance of power that favors freedom.

There is, of course, a significant minority in the country who argue against this projection of power overseas. On 7 March

2002, an open letter was published by the 'Not In Our Name' project:

> The US has commenced a series of wars, beginning with Afghanistan where they killed thousands of innocent civilians ... The government has targeted Arab and Muslim immigrants, rounding up over 1,000 and still holding hundreds in indefinite detention, refusing even to release their names. They have gutted longstanding civil liberties and unleashed police spying. The executive branch of government has seized vast new powers, unchecked by either the legislature or the judiciary. They have attempted to intimidate all dissenting voices, and tried to make critical thought itself suspect.

Seven months later, a young Illinois state senator called Barack Obama addressed an anti-war rally in Chicago's Federal Plaza, where he told them that he was not opposed to all wars, but that he could not support the use of military force against Saddam Hussein because this would be 'a dumb war, a rash war, a war based not on reason but on passion, not on principle but on politics'. For Obama, now Forty-Fourth President, the US's challenge is to move the world in the direction of greater equity, justice and prosperity without assuming that the country can single-handedly liberate other people from tyranny. He joins his predecessor in believing that there is a universal desire to be free but he has acknowledged the problems that occur when freedom is delivered through outside intervention.

This has not stopped Obama from deploying an additional 17,000 troops to Afghanistan, assessing that the Taliban pose a threat not only to that country's fragile democracy but also to US national security. In doing so, on 27 March 2009, he reminded the world that 'the United States of America stands for peace and security, justice and opportunity: that is who we are, and that is what history calls on us to do once more'. Four weeks later, in Arlington Cemetery on Memorial Day, he asked his fellow citizens to 'advance around the world' the enduring ideals of justice, equality and opportunity, for which so many American soldiers have died.

But the ideal of the honoured and honourable warrior fighting to make the world a better place – an ideal dramatized in films like *Saving Private Ryan* (1998) and in the TV mini-series *Band of Brothers* (2001) – has been challenged by accounts of the Global War on Terrorism. US troops are seen by some observers to be operating abroad with ignorance, indifference, and even soulless cruelty. For instance:

- Evan Wright's experience as a *Rolling Stone* journalist with a Marine battalion in Iraq, led him to describe the young soldiers as *Generation Kill*; they have been raised on computer games where they shoot first and ask questions later: they are, he believes, incapable of applying any ethical judgment about the targets in their scopes;
- Charles Clover was a journalist embedded with the 1st Battalion, 505th Parachute Infantry during operations in Falluja; this resort town of 300,000 on the banks of the Euphrates, west of Baghdad, became a centre of resistance after American troops fired indiscriminately on a largely peaceful demonstration against their presence on 29 April 2003; Clover has described the alienating impact of these 'Kevlar-plated stewards of a modern-day manifest destiny' as they conduct raids on Iraqi homes.

Here's the paradox. The champion of liberty is compelled to develop an engine of war to safeguard cherished freedoms at home. In response to complex events in an unstable and globalized world, arguments can be made – some principled, some tendentious and self-serving – for taking the fight overseas to crush the oppressive enemies of freedom. But even with the best of intentions, the deployment of 'boots on the ground' and 'kinetic force' can be seen to repudiate the values that inspired the mission. This moral confusion has been reinforced, for Americans in the opening decade of the new millennium, by images of Iraqis tortured in Abu Ghraib; stories of atrocities against prisoners-of-war in Bagram; revelations about extra-judicial renditions and the extra-territorial concentration camp at Guantánamo; and the corpses of innocents counted as collateral damage in air-strikes against the Taliban in Afghanistan.

These are not new dilemmas, although America's impassioned advocacy of freedom adds an edge to the issue. The moral philosopher Immanuel Kant wrestled with this riddle when, in the eighteenth century, he envisaged a global government charged with instituting a 'state of universal peace': this could only be achieved, he concluded, by a level of despotism that would destroy human freedom. And Shakespeare expressed the dilemma mordantly when – in *Julius Caesar* – Brutus commands Caesar's assassins to go out into the streets of Rome, having washed their hands in the dead dictator's blood: 'and waving our red weapons o'er our heads, Let's all cry *Peace, freedom and liberty!*'

We have found that a substantial investment of physical and emotional capital is dedicated to America's martial institutions. The war-fighter is highly regarded as a guardian and protector of the American Way. The reaction to the 'Fort Hood Massacre' (in November 2009) bears testament to this: the nation was shocked when Major Nidal Malik Hasan – an army psychiatrist and Arab-American – turned on his fellow-soldiers, killing thirteen and wounding many more in a shooting spree at the largest military base in the world, in Texas.

One has to conclude that America's commitment to liberty is greater than its commitment to peace. Everett Carl Dolman encapsulates this when he opens *The Warrior State* (2004) with the sentence, 'Political freedom begins with military service'. Self-belief in the righteousness of the American narrative, coupled with the conviction that American values are universal, has led the richest nation in the world to maintain a military force of unprecedented power. Its mission is explicitly and simplistically benign: to protect the Land of the Free and to liberate those suffering oppression (although realism frequently prevails, cautioning that this should apply only where there is good reason and justification for doing so).

America has become, determinedly, a unipolar power in the world in response to the chimes and knells of Liberty's cracked bell. It has pushed out its virtual frontier through long-range radar, armed encampments abroad, the threat of intercontinental ballistic missiles and the reality of Tomahawk strikes in distant lands (with the 'Red' Indian's weapon of choice now transformed into the American weapon against today's 'Injuns').

But the message of 9/11 is not reassuring. Military might projected overseas to preserve national security can be powerless against acts of 'asymmetric warfare' that strike America within its borders. The innocuous, inconspicuous, besuited passenger sitting on an internal flight to Los Angeles is capable of destroying the nation's sense of self-confidence, optimism and invulnerability with a box-cutter and an unfinished flying course. The frontier 'out there' is breached 'in here', evoking a sense of instability similar to that generated by those Escher images – the Impossible Torus or the Klein Bottle – whose surfaces should not exist in three-dimensional space.

Citizens of the Republic are frequently reminded of the blood shed in historical conflicts within their own borders. Some fear that the United States could turn on itself yet again: in a society prone to conspiracy theories, they look with trepidation at internal security measures such as the Homeland Security Department, the Patriot Act, and the creation of a new military command (NORTHCOM) responsible for the North American continent. These measures themselves add to the levels of insecurity, emblemized not only in movements that protest against the erosion of civil liberties but also in national scares about hostile alien fauna – Africanized killer bees, South American fire ants, Burmese pythons and Korean snakehead fish – that invade and overwhelm peace-loving American species.

In the face of instability and threats abroad, and with fear of terrorist attacks and civic strife at home, Americans may well look anxiously towards 2021. When the Periodic Cicada next invades, there can be no certainty that its wing will bring any respite by bearing an imprinted 'P' with its portent of peace.

CHAPTER SEVEN

Liberty Under the Law – On Freedom and Conformity

On the second anniversary of 9/11, US television channels ran a series of advertisements promoting a commodity close to the heart of every American.

Viewers saw victims of totalitarian regimes (Cambodia, Ukraine, Soviet Armenia) talk about their redemption through escape to the US. As they spoke, symbols of imprisonment were intercut with images of Abraham Lincoln and the Statue of Liberty. The soundtrack suggested metal shutters rolling back, perhaps, or a sword drawn from its sheath. Finally, words flashed by at speed: 'Freedom'; 'Appreciate it'; 'Cherish it'; 'Protect it'.

This was the second stage in a 'Campaign for Freedom' by the Advertising Council to inform, involve and inspire all Americans to celebrate their freedoms. Ads in 2002 had pictured an imagined American dystopia, where a citizen could be arrested for requesting the wrong book in a public library. Now the 'Inspire' phase, with its focus on refugees from political imprisonment, wanted the viewer to reflect upon the underlying freedoms that define the American way of life.

Liberty is, indeed, the defining motif in American society. Barack Obama was the latest in a long line of leaders to extol the importance of this value for his people, when – in his inaugural address in January 2009 – he described freedom as the permanent hope of mankind, the hunger in dark places, the longing of the soul. In obeisance to the Divine, he said, 'History

has a visible direction, set by liberty and the Author of Liberty.'
He went on to refer to the Liberty Bell sounding out when the
Declaration of Independence was declaimed. It meant something then, he said, and it still means something today: 'America,
in this young century, proclaims liberty throughout all the
world, and to all the inhabitants thereof.'

However, there is an errant side to this spirit of liberty. The
germ of 'freedom' has been glimpsed behind each paradox
encountered in our survey of twenty-first-century America: the
image of the citizen wrestling to be free of an ethnic heritage that
will not always let go; the intoxicating drive to consume,
whatever the cost in unintended consequences; the clash and
confusion of unshackled creeds; the tradition of innovation
tangling with unreconstructed interest-groups; the myth of the
liberating wilderness in a land whose frontiers closed long ago;
and the warrior state marshalling its arsenal to defend and
extend the American Way of peaceful opportunity.

This chapter will now survey the domain of 'freedom' but will
also explore liberty's hinterland – the American spheres of
crime, punishment and intolerance. We will keep company with
lawyers as they patrol the porous, irregular, elusive boundary
between the two – always remembering the poet Robert Frost's
words: 'Something there is that does not love a wall.' This, then,
is the heart of the matter: the ultimate American paradox of
Liberty under the Law.

According to poll data, 'personal freedom' – defined as the
opportunity to make one's own choices and priorities in life –
features second only to religion as the overriding personal value
in the United States – ahead of family, job security and financial
success. 'Freedom' is identified with archetypal American heroes
like George Washington, Abraham Lincoln, Martin Luther King
and Thomas Jefferson. Freedom is expressed in the most
commonplace of objects: in the nineteenth century, coins
showed a seated female figure representing Liberty, and today
the one-cent coin bears the word in large letters. The licence

plate FR33DOM is highly prized by car-drivers and the 'eternal' first-class postage stamp shows the Liberty Bell and the word 'Forever'. The greatest national icons are, of course, the Statue of Liberty and that Bell with its inscription from Leviticus.

In a tradition dating back to 1988, the Declaration of Independence is read aloud every 4th of July by presenters (notably the mellifluous Carl Kasell) on National Public Radio's *Morning Edition*. In the nation at large, the most quoted clause from this document represents a mission statement for many Americans: 'We hold these truths to be self-evident, that all men are created equal, that they are endowed by their Creator with certain inalienable Rights, that among these are Life, Liberty and the pursuit of Happiness.' The declaration goes on to list the 'oppressions' imposed on these American colonies by the King before asserting that the 'United Colonies' are now free and independent states. Jefferson, the author of these words, had been inspired by an ethnographic fantasy of pre-feudal, pre-Norman, Saxon tribes who had lived in the dark forests of Germany without the encumbrance of rulers. The Constitution itself is more nuanced in its references to freedom, with the Preamble looking to 'secure the Blessings of Liberty to ourselves and our Posterity'. The only other reference to freedom is in the sub-section on taxation, where a distinction is drawn between 'free Persons', Indians and 'all other Persons' (i.e. slaves, who, for fiscal and other purposes, counted as three-fifths of a free man). It was only in the amendments to the Constitution that the Declaration's commitment to liberty came to life.

The 'Charters of Freedom' described above are enshrined in the Rotunda of the National Archives and have gained an emblematic or totemic status. The Declaration of Independence, Constitution and Bill of Rights are barely legible, but the faded script on fragile parchment has the symbolic allure of holy relics. Visitors walk reverentially past dim-lit cabinets containing the documents, pressing their noses to the armour-plated glass to pay their respects before buying reproductions of the texts for their walls at home. It seems fitting that when, in May 2009, President Obama spoke about the values that underpin his foreign and national security policies, he did so in front of these charters saying, 'I stand here today as someone whose own life was made possible by these documents.'

Those interested in a more idiosyncratic expression of this national faith in liberty should travel to the Lilly Library at Wabash College, Crawfordsville, Indiana. Here, in 1957, businessman Pierre F. Goodrich designed and built a chamber to help students understand the evolution of individual liberty. Limestone slabs mark milestones in the history of freedom with the names of key people and events; the west wall, facing the entrance, carries a vacant space corresponding to the Dark Ages. The sequence opens with the cuneiform inscription from a clay document dating from 2300 BC in the Sumerian city-state of Lagash – it represents the word *amagi* ('liberty'); the journey ends with the Declaration of Independence as if this represented the culmination of some evolutionary process leaving the US at its apogee. The shelves beneath contain books of relevance to each step along the path to freedom, with works extending through to the twentieth century.

The evolution of the ideas underpinning the US's dominant focus on freedom has been charted by Michael Kammen (in the Curti Lectures, given to the University of Wisconsin in October 1985) and by Yehoshua Arieli in a 1964 work published, appropriately, by Harvard's Center for the Study of the History of Liberty in America. They demonstrate the link to a vibrant tradition sustained for centuries in the British Isles, described in a speech by Virginia's Governor, Patrick Henry, in the aftermath of the Revolution:

> We are descended from a people whose government was founded on liberty; our glorious forefathers of Great Britain made liberty the foundation of everything . . . We drew the spirit of liberty from our British ancestors; by that spirit we have triumphed over every difficulty.

Arieli – who died in 2002 – plotted the subsequent development in America of a distinctive attitude towards the individual and the community, generating deeply engrained beliefs that persist to this day. Notions about mankind's innate morality and sociability, advanced by British eighteenth-century philosophers like Lord Shaftesbury, Francis Hutcheson and Adam Smith, formed the ingredients of a Utopian confection that would – it was believed – sweeten any bitterness between the rights of the individual and the needs of society. Hutcheson coined the aphorism 'the greatest happiness of the greatest number' in 1725 and his *System of Moral Philosophy* (1755) was the principal text-book of America's colleges on the eve of the Revolution. These enlightened ideas inspired the Founding Fathers to create a nation that would demonstrate the perfectibility of man and the progressive nature of voluntary social cooperation.

There was also a belief from the early days of the republic in the merits of *laissez-faire* ('Let do!') – a slogan of economic liberalism that upholds the value of private initiative and production over state interventionism and taxation. The phrase was introduced into the English language by Benjamin Franklin and George Whatley in *Principles of Trade* (1774), and *laissez-faire* sentiment shines out from the writings of J. Hector St John de Crèvecoeur, who argued that the US had become the most perfect society in the world in his letter entitled 'What Is an American?' (1782): 'We are all animated with the spirit of industry which is unfettered and unrestrained, because each person works for himself . . . Here man is free as he ought to be.'

The view took root that *laissez-faire* would dissolve economic, social and political privileges, leading to the liberation of all forms of labour and enterprise in a free society where there was equal opportunity for all. This theory was doubtless reinforced by unbounded horizons to the west and ready access to sea-passages offering sea-captains and merchants of the eastern ports the chance to make their fortune. Over time, the benevolent vision of the Scottish Enlightenment hardened into an American model, where the capitalist and the entrepreneur became standard-bearers of the revolution and the Utopian dream.

The social philosopher, Senator John Taylor of Caroline, was an early advocate for change, replacing the pursuit of happiness in Jefferson's list of basic rights with property. Then, in the nineteenth century, Edwin L. Godkin started arguing for the primacy of the individual as a free agent, unencumbered by the compulsion of status or privilege, conducting his affairs exclusively on the basis of contract. Less emphasis was given to social justice and improvement, although balm was applied with the assurance that justice was a natural adjunct to these freedoms. By the start of the twentieth century, a philosophy of rugged individualism had become embedded in the national narrative, reinforced by notions of a Chosen People in a Chosen Land.

The English philosopher Herbert Spencer – often described as a Social Darwinist, with his passionate advocacy of the rights of the individual – fuelled the debate: his influence is apparent in the controversial Supreme Court judgment *Lochner v New York* (1905) which found that New York's regulation of the working hours of bakers (to protect their health) was not a justifiable restriction of the right to contract freely under the Fourteenth Amendment. Over the next three decades, the court – led by a quartet of conservative justices nicknamed 'The Four Horsemen of the Apocalypse' would strike down, in the name of liberty, numerous attempts by state governments to improve working conditions or protect consumers.

Today, the cause of freedom is most frequently espoused by reference to a small number of political tracts – Lincoln's 'Gettysburg Address', for instance, and Martin Luther King's memorable 'I Have a Dream' speech with its coda 'Free at Last!' The arts also play their part: before Jack Kerouac took to the road, one fictional outcast seemed to represent the spirit of freedom – Mark Twain described Huckleberry Finn as someone dreaded by all the mothers of the town because he came and went of his own free will: 'Everything that goes to make life precious that boy had.'

The spirit of Huckleberry Finn is be found in another American icon – the free-wheeling, free-thinking, boundary-breaking artist who has appeared in different incarnations over the years. Walt Whitman, the great American poet of the nineteenth century, was an outspoken advocate of freedom: 'I have allowed the stress of my poems from beginning to end to bear upon American individuality and assist it,' he wrote in 'A Backward Glance' (1888). Moondog is a more recent example: this blind composer, renowned for his minimalist music and innovative instruments (such as the 'Oo' and 'Trimba'), spent twenty years living on the streets of Manhattan and became known as 'The Viking of 6th Avenue'.

America's libertarian credentials gain lustre from the sanctuary offered to artists evading dogma and totalitarianism. Composers such as Béla Bartók, Paul Hindemith, Kurt Weill and Igor Stravinsky; artists like Josef Albers, Max Ernst, Roberto Matta, Yves Tanguy, and André Masson, fled Europe to push the boundaries of artistic expression in the Land of the Free. Albers taught at Black Mountain College in North Carolina – a beacon of experimentation in the visual, literary and performing arts. Other teachers there included Walter Gropius (the German architect and founder of the Bauhaus movement that aroused the ire of the Nazi Party), Merce Cunningham (dancer and choreographer), Buckminster Fuller (architect and designer) and John Cage (composer), connecting the college to the revolutionary compositional structures of Abstract Expressionism and the radical music of the New York School.

The American cult of freedom is seen in the spontaneity and energy of Jackson Pollock's 'action' paintings, and heard in the licks and phrases of improvised riffs that represent America's greatest contribution to world culture – jazz. Meanwhile, Cage's pupil, Christian Wolff, applied the concept of indeterminacy to his music: in Wolff's oeuvre, the performer makes choices about pitch, duration, timbre and rhythm. His works are impossible to reproduce, since each performance creates a unique constellation of sound. The score of *Edges* (1968) exemplifies this: it looks like a map dotted with symbols denoting aural limits (loudness, clarity, softness, etc.), with each instrumentalist picking his own path.

In the same year that Wolff composed *Edges*, his namesake – Tom Wolfe – published *The Electric Kool-Aid Acid Test*. This chronicled the adventures of Californian Ken Kesey and the Merry Pranksters as they crossed the US in a school bus called 'Further' (painted in the colours of the rainbow), distributing marijuana and LSD to people as they went. A cultural revolution was sweeping the country, exemplified by the Free Speech Movement on the campus at Berkeley, California, and Ken Kesey's hippies. Eldridge Cleaver (the radical writer and Black Panther acitivist) saluted these rebels from his cell in Folsom Prison:

> What do they care if their old baldheaded and crew-cut elders don't dig their caveman mops? They couldn't care less about the old, stiffassed honkies who don't like their new dances: Frug, Monkey, Jerk, Swim, Watusi. All they know is that it feels good to swing to way-out body-rhythms instead of dragassing across the dance floor like zombies to the dead beat of mind-smothered Mickey Mouse music.

On the East Coast, Timothy Leary was dismissed from Harvard for promoting the use of psychedelic drugs and moved to Millbrook Big House to pick the locks of the subconscious and tweak the nose of the establishment. In 1966 he founded a new religion – the League for Spiritual Development – that incorporated the consumption of LSD into the Catholic mass. The hippie movement sought to uncover the Huck in a generation of Americans who wanted to dismantle the barriers of 'square' order and authority. Leary wanted his followers to break free from the bonds of human nature, to achieve the status of a deity – as described in an article he wrote in 1966 for an East Village underground newspaper, introducing his 'Do-It-Yourself-God-Kit Program'. Although he died in 1996, Leary remains an iconic figure in American society; on 19 April 2007, *Time* magazine asked the question 'Was Timothy Leary Right?', as it reported that

Harvard was conducting its first research into therapeutic uses of psychedelic drugs since firing Leary for the practice in 1963.

Travellers through the US still encounter the stay-behinds from that era. The Age of Aquarius is now superannuated and sheltering in redoubts like Boulder, Taos and Haight-Ashbury, where spaced-out, grey-haired hippies read the Sixth Canto of the *Srimad Bhagavatam* and Carlos Castaneda's *The Teachings of Don Juan* (1968). Some commentators uphold these texts as far more than joss-stick-scented novelties: it has been argued that the revolution in cyberspace, the spread of the PC and the liberating power of the world wide web stems from the hippie counter-culture rather than the goal-oriented demands of the military-industrial complex.

There is also a connection between the spaced-out dopeheads and grasshoppers of the hippie era and the political activists who battled against racial segregation. The Freedom Riders were the precursors to the Merry Pranksters: in 1961 these black and white students travelled together on interstate buses into the South to test the impact of the Supreme Court's judgment (in *Boynton v Virginia*) to outlaw racial segregation. They suffered attacks from the Ku Klux Klan under the disregarding stewardship of Eugene 'Bull' Connor (commissioner of public safety in Birmingham, Alabama), but their passive resistance was an inspiration to others. In November 2001, the Freedom Riders Foundation celebrated their fortieth anniversary with a four-day event at Jackson, Mississippi: the gathering was overshadowed by the events of 9/11, but in their newsletter they resolved to carry on, announcing in block capitals: 'TERRORISM DID NOT STOP US THEN, WILL NOT STOP US NOW'.

Americans remind themselves, with narratives like these, that their allegiance to the cause of liberty is a defining feature of their society and something fundamentally noble, enlightened and courageous. This American creed of freedom would lead one to believe there is a national commitment to human liberty in all its varieties. In fact, many issues divide along party-political lines.

Census data show, for instance, that Republicans align themselves in particular with the right to bear arms. The first Congress sought to ensure that each state had a militia equipped to defend the republic, and this requirement, embodied in the Second Amendment, has been turned into a benchmark of personal freedom for one tranche of society. The National Rifle Association (NRA), founded in 1871, has a membership of almost 3 million who read *The American Hunter, The American Rifleman* and *America's 1st Freedom* and subscribe to the slogan 'I'll give up my gun when they pry it from my cold, dead hands.'

Democrats are more likely to support the efforts of the American Civil Liberties Union (ACLU) than the NRA. Its membership is a tenth that of the NRA, but its declared aims are not dissimilar – to Keep America Safe and Free. It has been championing liberty since 1920 and its list of issues include criminal justice, the death penalty, drug policy, free speech, immigrants' rights, lesbian and gay rights, prisoners' rights, racial justice, the rights of the poor and reproductive freedom.

Abortion is a divisive subject for Americans, as demonstrated in the 2008 presidential campaign by the 'pro-choice' position of the Democrats' Obama and the 'pro-life' position of the Republicans' McCain. Five years earlier, the country had commemorated the thirtieth anniversary of the Supreme Court ruling in *Roe v Wade* that overturned many laws against abortion since these breached the right to privacy under the liberty clause of the Fourteenth Amendment. The court considered the rights of the child, but concluded that those who framed the Constitution and its Amendments had never intended their rules to extend to the unborn. As a result, there were over 33 million legal abortions between 1973 and 2003; the trend is declining, but there were still 820,000 legal terminations in 2005.

The Supreme Court ruling sparked a sustained anti-abortion campaign led by right-wing Christians: this has included the picketing of abortion clinics, the intimidation of their clients and violent attacks. In 2003, the State of Florida executed Paul Hill, a former Presbyterian minister who murdered a doctor who ran an abortion clinic. Six years later, on 31 May 2009, Dr George Tiller – whose clinic specialized in late-term abortions – was shot dead outside the Reformation Lutheran Church in Wichita, Kansas, where he was serving as an usher at the Sunday service. Scott Roeder, a fifty-one-year-old man who was later arrested, drove off from the scene in a car embellished with the 'Jesus Fish'. Newspaper reports linked him to 'The Freemen' – a group of anti-government 'Christian Patriots' that kept the FBI at bay in an armed standoff at Jordan, Montana, for almost three months in 1995–96.

Debates over gun laws and abortion demonstrate the paradox facing any society that takes liberty as its dominant ideology. A 'pro-choice' doctor who terminates foetuses to enhance the quality-of-life – freedom? – of young, unmarried, white girls (over 50 per cent of abortions fall into this category) has his life taken by a 'pro-life' Christian using a hand-gun whose ready availability is taken as testament to America's commitment to liberty. There is enough syzygy here to win the World Scrabble Championship.

It is self-evident that no nation can grant its citizens unbounded freedom without creating conditions where some become less free than others. Sidney Hook put it this way in *The Paradoxes of Freedom* (1962):

> All too often the meaning and associations of the specific historical freedoms won by the American Revolution have become absorbed in the penumbral emotive overtones of the words, which then function as slogans and thus get in the way of clear thought. The term becomes a fetish, and is invoked by groups who want diametrically opposite things.

Those, then, who claim to govern a land where liberty prevails must introduce measures that operate to bind the free. In United States they call this 'justice'. The paradox is openly expressed in inscriptions engraved into the stonework of many public buildings. The walls of the National Archives carry the message that 'Eternal vigilance is the price of freedom'. The Supreme Court Building captures the theme in the allegorical sculptures over the front door, with a group entitled *Liberty Enthroned Guarded by Order and Authority*. The rear entrance reinforces the point, with an architrave bearing the legend 'Justice the guardian of liberty'.

There is an affinity between these inscriptions and the memorable speech – entitled 'Liberty under the Law' – proclaimed by Warren G. Harding in August 1920 when campaigning for the presidency. He warned against throttling liberty in response to the threat from communism. Freedom of speech, press and assembly, he said, were as sacred and inviolable as the freedom of religious belief, the rights of life and the pursuit of happiness. However, in almost the next breath he asserted that government had the right to defend liberty by crushing sedition and stamping out threats to the republic.

Security and the majesty of the law are the first essentials of liberty . . . Men have a right to question our system in fullest freedom, but they must always remember that the right to freedom impose [*sic*] the obligations which maintain it.

He who shows contempt for authority, Harding argued, ceases to be a loyal citizen and forfeits his rights to American freedoms.

This harsh articulation of the *realpolitik* values of American freedom contrasts with idealistic exponents of libertarian views, who are frequently portrayed as marginal figures – lunatics, cult-members, outcasts – as in this passage from Hugh Henry Brackenridge's quixotic *Modern Chivalry* (first published in 1792):

In the next apartment was an insane person, who stiled himself the Lay Preacher, and who took his text as usual; and began to preach. Book of Judges, 21.25. 'In those days there was no king in Israel; and every man did what was right in his own eyes.' That was right, said a mad democrat, who was confined in a cell across the passage. When we got quit of a king, the same thing was expected here, 'that every man should do that which was right in his own eyes' but behold we are made to do that which is right in the eyes of others. The law governs, and this law is made up of acts of assembly, and the decisions of the courts; and a kind of law they call the common law . . . We see honest men knocked down with the jaw bones of lawyers.

This reminds us of a tradition of anarchic libertarianism – far removed from the communist ideology that so troubled President Harding – that is vehemently opposed to the idea of government and judicial interference. In recent years, there have been armed groups like the Montana Freemen, while movements like the Free State Project (FSP) and Free State Wyoming (FSW) seek to achieve their goals democratically. FSP, founded in 2001 by Jason Sorens, aims to create a libertarian stronghold in the nation and targeted New Hampshire in October 2003. This led Kenneth W. Royce (a.k.a. 'Boston T. Party') to form FSW – opting for a west-coast site rather than an east-coast one: he wants to liberate the Cowboy State, establishing 'a haven for Americans who desire not to live as, or under, government supremacists'. The dream, according to their website, is 'truly to enjoy our rights of gun ownership, privacy, schooling, health and diet, unrestricted travel, and property' – although counter-intuitively these freedom-lovers require you to register before participating in their virtual Wyoming community.

We can sense, here, that same impulse that led the Pilgrims to cross the Atlantic, pioneers to cross the prairies, migrants to cocoon themselves in ethnic island-communities and individuals to seek an unencumbered wilderness. But if the bounty of seemingly endless tracts of virgin land helped to create the wealthiest nation in the world, and the illusion of independence, so it has engendered the dark matter of prejudice and bigotry that weighs on the condition of liberty in the US.

* * *

The Southern lynch-mob is the most abominable manifestation of intolerance in the Land of the Free. A recent estimate suggests up to 20,000 African-Americans were killed by the Ku Klux Klan between 1868 and 1871, and a further 3,417 were lynched between 1882 and 1944 (over one a week on average); in *The End of Blackness* (2004), Debra Dickerson has raised that total to approximately 4,742 between 1882 and 1968. This grim episode in America's history is captured in the Allen-Littlefield Collection of photographs and postcards held today by Emory University in Atlanta, Georgia. (Some of these were exhibited at the Martin Luther King Jr National Historic Site – under the title *Without Sanctuary* – from May to November 2002.) The images are harrowing. They show corpses – mostly of African-American males – hanging by the neck from tree branches, bridges, lamp-posts and other makeshift scaffolds; some are dismembered and burnt beyond recognition. A record of faculty discussions at Emory about the aptness of exhibiting these images includes the following observations:

> The perpetrators and spectators (including children) in the photos often appear proud, even gleeful. Their faces suggest a festive, carnivalesque atmosphere. Adding to the brutality are the messages scrawled on the cards: 'This is the Barbecue we had last night'; 'The answer of the Anglo-Saxon race to black brutes who would attack the Womanhood of the South'.

The nature of this gruesome ritual is illustrated in a contemporary account in *The Springfield Weekly Republican* of the justice meted out to Sam Holt of Newman, Georgia, in 1889, who was accused of raping a white woman. A crowd of 2,000 took him and tied him to a tree: he was stripped and a heavy chain wound round his body:

> Before the torch was applied to the pyre, the Negro was deprived of his ears, fingers and genital parts of his body. He pleaded pitifully for his life while the mutilation was

going on, but stood the ordeal of the fire with surprising fortitude. Before the body was cool, it was cut into pieces, the bones were crushed into small bits, and even the tree on which the wretch met his fate was torn up and disposed of as 'souvenirs'. The negro's heart was cut into several pieces, as was also his liver.

This macabre theatre goes beyond what Michel Foucault has described as the poetics of jurisprudence. There is a political and psychological dimension to the spectacle: the liberated ('uppity') black man is emasculated by white men who have themselves been culturally neutered in military defeat. The power of the impotent is ritually and brutally reasserted.

However, the illiberal culture has deep and extensive roots. Students of American literature are taught that the continent's first book of satire was *The Simple Cobbler of Aggawam* (1647). The witty work, full of word-play and extended conceits, is by Nathaniel Ward, who studied law at Emmanuel College, Cambridge, before becoming a Calvinist minister. In 1633, Ward was effectively gagged for non-conformity by Archbishop Laud and he sailed to join the Puritans of the Massachusetts Bay Colony. Here, he helped to compile the first code of laws for the colony – 'The Body of Liberties' – and Ward was living in Boston when he wrote *The Simple Cobbler*. Humour is used both as a shield and a weapon, and it is salted with passages of dyspeptic prejudice that give an ironic twist to the principles of freedom (and, indeed, to the idea of laws called 'Liberties'):

I dare take upon me, to be the Herauld of New-England so farre, as to proclaime to the world, in the name of our Colony, that all Familists, Antinomians, Anabaptists and other Enthusiasts, shall have free Liberty to keep away from us, and such as will come to be gone as fast as they can, the sooner the better.

You still find Americans who express twenty-first-century versions of the Cobbler's worldview. Dennis McCroskey is a case in point. He fulminates on his blog about the political correctness of judges and politicians: 'This idea of America being a multicultural community has served only to dilute our sovereignty and our national identity. As Americans we have our own culture, our own society, our own language and our own lifestyle.' He concludes this particular entry with his variant of the Cobbler's diatribe, directed towards immigrants:

If Stars and Stripes offend you, or you don't like Uncle Sam, then you should seriously consider a move to another part of this planet. We are happy with our culture and have no desire to change, and we really don't care how you did things where you came from. This is OUR COUNTRY, our land, and our lifestyle. Our First Amendment gives every citizen the right to express his opinion and we will allow you every opportunity to do so! But once you are done complaining . . . whining . . . and griping . . . about our flag . . . our pledge . . . our national motto . . . or our way of life . . . I highly encourage you to take advantage of one other Great American Freedom . . . THE RIGHT TO LEAVE.

McCroskey may be exhibiting unreconstructed intolerance, but he highlights a particular conundrum associated with the American brand of liberalism. The mores of political correctness have arisen in an attempt to counter the excesses of racism, sexism and homophobia that have scarred America's liberal ideal. However, the phenomenon tends to reinforce these varieties of intolerance and introduces a new form of illiberal behaviour that suppresses the public expression of views that are deemed beyond the pale.

There are tricky dilemmas generated by contrasting views over freedom, which regularly receive a public airing in the courts and opinion/editorial pages of newspapers: Is cross-burning an act of intimidation and harassment or an act of free expression? Does a free man's right to bear arms include semi-automatic assault rifles? Is government's collection of intercept material to identify terrorists an unjustifiable invasion of privacy of free citizens? Can the Law School at the University of Michigan use race as a factor in the selection of students (when 40 out of 100 points go to minorities)?

College students studying American history learn about illiberal right-wingers who have accused socialists, Catholics, Jews, Germans and Japanese of being 'un-American'. There are the twentieth-century 'witch hunts' associated with Senator Joseph McCarthy of Wisconsin and, in the previous century, 'Nativism' resisted the influx of foreign migrants through 'fraternities' like the Loyal Men of Liberty, the Order of the Little Red Schoolhouse, the Order of the Mystic Brotherhood and the American Knights.

We have already seen, in earlier chapters, that racial tension and xenophobia are not restricted to America's past. Fear swept the nation after 9/11, with 20 per cent of those polled believing that they personally will be the victims of a terrorist attack, but mercifully this did not erupt into the persecution of Muslims or Arabs within the domestic space. However, there are hidden fears, illustrated in the popularity of the party game called 'Mafia': players act the role of villagers, some of whom are secret members of the Mafia, others are their prospective victims; villagers periodically make accusations against suspected Mafia members and execute them, although the accused will defend themselves and point the finger at others. The game is said to have originated in Soviet Russia where fears of the secret police and informants were rife, but American commentators link its popularity to fears about hidden Al-Qaeda cells.

It is wrong, however, to assume intolerance is exclusively a right-wing phenomenon. In June 2006 the liberal president of Harvard University – Larry Summers, a former treasury secretary in the Clinton administration who is now economic adviser to President Obama – was obliged to resign for challenging the PC hegemony at the university. Summers had become sceptical about what he regarded as a number of dubious courses – on women's studies, for instance, and black history; he is also reported to have confronted the performance of a black professor, Cornel West, who had allegedly produced more rap music in recent years than academic books or papers. Summers opposed an effort to block university investment in Israel and condemned attempts to ban the US Armed Forces from recruiting on campus. The final straw came when he asked whether a dearth of women professors in mathematics and engineering might reflect not only sexual discrimination, but also gender-specific aptitudes in different disciplines. Summers faced outrage from his academic community for the impertinence of such intellectual curiosity. He had to go.

Nor is aggressive prejudice the preserve of Caucasians, despite white racists setting the benchmark for so many decades. Byron Hurt has shown in his 2007 documentary, *Hip-Hop: Beyond Beats and Rhymes*, that the rap music emerging from the urban African-American communities of the East Coast is largely defined by misogyny, violence and homophobia. These sentiments predominate in the lyrics of artists like 50 Cent, Fat Joe, Talib Kweli and Chuck D. In an interview with Movies on MTV.com, published in January 2006, Hurt cites the musical campaign that 50 Cent has waged against fellow artist Ja Rule:

> 50 Cent called Ja Rule a 'bitch-ass nigga,' right? The way that you go for the jugular, if you really wanna emasculate somebody, you call 'em a bitch, a faggot or a girlie man. You see the same kind of hyper-masculine violence in movie after movie after movie, in sports culture, video games, military culture. I mean, America is a hyper-aggressive nation. So it stands to reason that a rap artist like 50 Cent would be palatable to a nation that perpetuates cultural violence.

The attitude to violence described above needs to be seen in the context of a deeply engrained American attitude to crime and punishment. In Puritan New England, excessive violence was habitually meted out to those who threatened or challenged the established order. Rebellious servants were burned. Political dissenters were maimed. Quakers were hanged. Witches were executed. The body of the victim-culprit became a canvas upon which society recorded its displeasure, with nostrils slit, ears amputated and faces branded.

The mummified face of *The Visible Man* is linked to this phenomenon. Visitors to www.nlm.nih.gov can e-anatomise his corpse – described as the record of a perfect physical specimen – stripping away skin, flesh and musculature to reveal the skeleton beneath, or scanning wafers of body from skull-cap to foot-sole. Packing it together again, they gaze on the face of an executed killer – Joseph Paul Jernigan, a Texan put to death in 1993. There is something profoundly symbolic about the transition of Jernigan to *Visible Man* – reportedly the first corpse to be digitally salami-sliced and repackaged for the benefit of society.

However, in popular culture the law-breaker is frequently idolized. It is surely no coincidence that the United States' (and the world's) first narrative feature film was *The Great Train Robbery* (1903), featuring the hold-up of a train by Butch Cassidy's 'Hole in the Wall' gang. This tradition continues with films like *Reservoir Dogs* (1992), *The Usual Suspects* (1995), *Ocean's Eleven* (2001), *Catch Me If You Can* (2002) and *Inside Man* (2006), all celebrating the autonomy of their criminal heroes. Gangsta rap has become a popular form of music among white middle-class teenagers; and the successful computer game *Grand Theft Auto* engages the player in the felonious adventures of Niko Bellic, an illegal Serbian migrant who makes his violent way through 'Liberty City' – a mordant re-creation of New York with a beaming 'Statue of Happiness'. The mischievous trickster is, of course, a folklore figure who has flourished around the world and throughout history. American Indians have their own version in *Winnebago* – the shape-changer who moves through the world in search of wealth, power and sex.

The exploration of the amoral – in these stories – can also work to define and affirm the proper values needed to sustain community wellbeing. But there is an intensity to America's interest in, even admiration for, the criminal. This may link back to the anti-authoritarian roots of so many migrants who fled repression in the Old World. It is also no coincidence that the thief enacts a corrupted version of the dominant political philosophy centred on liberty and wealth creation.

Today, the US is said to have the highest crime rate in the world and the nation is unique among Western democracies for its use of the death penalty – applied by thirty-eight states. In 2008, there were forty-two executions (compared with sixty-five in 2003) – typically by lethal injection – and there are currently over 3,500 convicts on 'death row'. In recent years the Supreme Court has taken world opinion into account when abolishing the death penalty for juveniles and the mentally retarded, but the right-wing Justice Antonin Scalia has jibbed at this foreign influence: 'We must never forget that it is a Constitution for the US that we are expounding. The views of other nations ... cannot be imposed on Americans.'

The US also incarcerates more of its law-breakers than any other Western nation – the number has quadrupled in the past twenty-five years. At the beginning of 2008 the Pew Center reported that for the first time in history more than 1 in 100 adults were in prison – 2,319,258 adults or 1 in every 99.1 men and women. A detailed scrutiny of the figures reveals that while 1 in 30 men aged 20–34 is incarcerated, the figure is 1 in 9 for black males in that age group. California – much-vaunted for its liberal culture – operates a surprisingly repressive regime where a villain can be sent to prison for life as a 'three strike' felon for three misdemeanours (even if the last crime is as minor as shoplifting). Three thousand people were said to be serving life sentences under this regime in 2009.

American prisons have traditionally been places designed to remind the inmates of the loss of their citizens' rights – not just through incarceration, but also through repression and ill-treatment. The severity of the punishment plays its part in emphasizing the privileges of freedom – a point that Tocqueville recognized in 1833.

American prisons were reformed in the last century under the influence of superintendents such as Clinton Truman Duffy and Kenyon J. Scudder; and there are many other men whose work to improve the lot of prisoners has largely gone unsung – see, for instance, Eldridge Cleaver's adulatory account of the teacher, Chris Lovdjieff, known as 'The Christ' by the prisoners who studied under him in Folsom. However, there are penitentiaries in living memory that included forced labour, lock step, silent rules, beatings, shackling and long-term segregation. An investigation at Soledad Prison in California in 1970 by state legislators revealed that guards were fostering racial fights among inmates and passing weapons to favourites. They encouraged white prisoners to throw excreta into black prisoners' cells and to mix their food with urine, glass or cleansing powder while they, as a matter of course, provoked prisoners with racial slurs.

Prisons appear as a microcosm of the intolerance and division that exists in American society today. When documentary-maker Louis Theroux visited San Quentin jail (outside San Francisco) in 2007 he found the 3,000 inmates gathered in the prison yard with whites in one corner and blacks, Hispanics and Indians in the others. His film, *Behind Bars*, shows the prevalence of gang culture in the penitentiary and that these gangs also divided on racial lines (white, black, Hispanic – although there is deep enmity between the northern and southern Hispanic groups). Theroux spoke to members of white supremacist groups Bavarian Brotherhood and Northern Structure whose bodies are covered in tattoos with words like 'Skinhead' engraved in Gothic script. They explain that you join the gang for protection and support – to have 'brothers' who will watch out for you, and stop, for instance, your food being stolen. Violence is endemic: one skinhead had abandoned his gang when the leadership ordered him to stab a white cellmate for borrowing dominoes from a black man.

If most Americans prefer to avert their gaze from the harsh realities of prison life, they received a shock in April 2004 when photographs emerged of Iraqi prisoners humiliated and mentally tormented by their American keepers in Abu Ghraib. One image has become iconic: a hooded figure standing on a crate before a wall that is smeared with ordure; his hands are held out at his sides with electric wires attached to them: he had been told he would be electrocuted if he moved. A second image shows a pyramid of naked men, piled on one another as if engaged in some bath-house orgy, with Private Lynndie England crouched beside them, grinning at the camera. Specialist Charles Graner, army reservist, posed behind another group of seven naked detainees stacked in a human pyramid, in a photograph taken on what has been dubbed the 'Night of the Seven Riders'. He is quoted as saying: 'The Christian in me knows it is wrong, but the corrections officer in me can't help enjoy seeing a grown man piss himself.'

Military campaigns in Afghanistan and Iraq, and operations in the so-called 'Global War on Terror', have resulted in renditions of terrorist suspects overseas and their detention in facilities such as Guantánamo Bay that almost lie out of reach of the US judicial system. Military commissions were established there, but these were subsequently described by the US National Association of Criminal Defense Lawyers as 'unethical' – it advised its 11,000 members to turn down any request to represent detainees. It is telling that the first presidential order signed by Barack Obama, on his first day in office, was to suspend Guantánamo's military courts for 120 days; not long afterwards, he signed another order initiating a process to plan for the closure of the detention facility at Guantánamo within a year. However, in November 2009 Obama appeared to acknowledge that this pledge was not going to be met. There was no obvious place to send more than 200 detainees languishing in Guantánamo.

References to the Supreme Court, whether in relation to enemy combatants or aborted foetuses, remind us of the critical role that the judiciary performs in patrolling the shadow-line between freedom and intolerance. As with other liminal zones of human endeavour, those seeking to promote the American Way have formed cadres of ritual specialists to manage the margins. In other societies, this role might be performed by a priest, shaman or witch-doctor; in the United States the function falls to the lawyer.

The US has more lawyers per head of population than any other country in the world. One out of every 365 citizens is a lawyer and the trend is for more: in 1951, the ratio was 1 out of every 695. Altogether, 1.3 million – almost exactly 1 per cent of the workforce – work in legal services. Of these, 651,000 are lawyers and 39,000 are judges. The latter oversee 17,000 law courts operating in fifty-one separate and distinct legal systems.

The US does not only have an abundance of lawyers and jurisdictions. It also has an abundance of laws. In addition to the US Constitution and federal statutes enacted by Congress, every state has its own constitution, laws passed by its own legislature and municipal ordinances established by governing bodies such as city councils (all the way down to a public swimming-pool that enforces twenty-seven rules including 'Only One Bounce Per Dive on Diving Board').

Then there are administrative regulations made by the agencies, boards, bureaus, administrations, commissions, departments and authorities that federal and state legislators have spawned to create more laws. For instance, the Inland Revenue Service sets rules for payment of taxes; state boards set standards for nursing homes; local zoning boards rule on where restaurants and malls can be built. Some 7,000 federal administrative regulations are issued a year: after twenty-five years, they occupied more shelf-space than all the laws of Congress over 200 years. Citizens are also susceptible to a multitude of minor violations: in 2008, for instance, the New York Police Department issued over half a million summonses for minor criminal violations (such as urinating in the street); but this is a fraction of the number of tickets that they issued in 2003, when shopkeepers like Jin Yi of Flatbush Avenue were fined $400 for that most flagrant of anti-social acts – having too many words on a shop-sign. (The canopy in front of the Jin and Xia store, violated a 1961 by-law stipulating that awnings could carry only the shop-name and address.)

Those who breach these petty regulations are dealt with in the lower courts. These have been described as 'sausage fac-tories' where cases are mass-processed rather than individually adjudicated. Instead of advising individual defendants of their rights, for instance, judges are prone to start the day with an announcement to the whole courtroom, making little effort to establish whether defendants – including those like Jin Yi, whose grasp of English is limited – have heard or understood. Law professor Malcolm M. Feeley has scrutinized the system and described the experience for defendants:

> Jammed every morning with a new mass of arrestees who have been picked up the night before, lower courts rapidly process what the police consider 'routine' problems – barroom brawls, neighborhood squabbles, domestic disputes, welfare cheating, shoplifting, drug possession, and prostitution – not 'real' crimes. These courts are chaotic and confusing; officials communicate in a verbal shorthand wholly unintelligible to accused and accuser alike, and they seem to make arbitrary decisions, sending one person to jail and freeing the next. But for the most part they are lenient; they sentence few people to jail and impose few large fines.

Under circumstances like these, it is no surprise to find that in and around New Orleans there is a rich tradition of voodoo court spells designed to protect the practitioner from a distant and incomprehensible judicial process. Chewing the root known as 'High John the Conqueror' while dealing with a judge or the police is said to influence them to your advantage; or you could rely on 'Law Turning Powder', 'Get Away Powder' and 'Law Stay Away Sprinkle' (available in the best voodoo retailers). Those caught up with a lawsuit might also try washing their face with 'Old Indian Clear Water' while burning 'Fast Success & Compelling Power' incense.

At least these charms and potions are available to the man in the street, which is more than can be said for the supply of attorneys. Only a small percentage of America's lawyers are actively involved in representing a client before a judge or negotiating to settle out of court. Most lawyers work for companies that write off the cost of legal services as a business expense, or for wealthy individuals who can afford the best legal advice. The majority are drafting contracts, counselling clients and presenting cases before regulatory agencies. Since 70 per cent of lawyers work in private practice, it is unsurprising that market mechanisms influence their business decisions. The distribution of lawyers around the country is, furthermore, distorted: 25 per cent are located in two states (California and New York), with another 30 per cent in Florida, Illinois, Ohio, Pennsylvania, Texas and Washington, DC.

The fact is that few citizens get represented in a lower court despite their constitutional rights. Low fees do little to attract attorneys who ultimately have their eyes on more lucrative pickings. The experience of Jeff, working in a Californian town near Los Angeles, illustrates the point. While studying for his bar exams, he worked as a para-legal in a firm specializing in employment law. His job was to filter potential clients, selecting those who offered the practice a handsome return. A caller might complain of racial or sexual harassment but these are difficult violations to prove: Jeff was under instruction from his bosses to move the conversation on in search of a more productive 'class action' (a lawsuit brought by one or more plaintiffs on behalf of a larger group who are said to share a common grievance). For instance, employers who breach California's statutory half-hour lunch-break can be fined $1,000 per day of transgression; this amounts to over $1 million for a worker who has been five years in the job. 'Do the math!' as Americans say. If the company employs a workforce of 250 staff who are on the payroll for an average of thirty months, the fine would be $140 million, before past employees join the party. Jeff's law firm would aim to negotiate an out-of-court settlement for a fraction of that fine, with senior partners taking 10 per cent of any proceeds. Ironically, Jeff was sacked when he asked if he could have a lunch-break of only ten minutes, leaving work twenty minutes early to see his new-born baby at bath time. 'You're joking,' came the reply. 'You could sue us!'

Jay occupies a higher position in the food chain. He is a judge on the California State Court Circuit, covering both civil and criminal cases. He describes the process of selection, ultimately designed to ensure that judgments connect with popular sentiment: he was nominated by the governor, but then had to be vetted by two commissions in a process that includes up to seventy-five lawyers being invited to comment on the candidate's qualities. Once this ordeal is over, and survived, a judge can sit for six years before others can challenge the incumbent in an election. Jay acknowledges the central role that justice plays in American life, but he is critical of the media obsession with court cases – especially murder trials, which provide a source of melodrama for the public. TV programmes like *Judge Judy* fuel people's interest – this is a 'syndi-court' show in which former family court judge, Judith Sheindlin, arbitrates small claims cases.

The US Supreme Court stands at the polar opposite to the lower courts of the state system. It claims to be the final arbiter on questions of liberty, giving the American people the promise of equal justice under the law and functioning as guardian and interpreter of the Constitution. It is conventionally regarded as the 'court of last resort', but once more the myth diverges from reality. With few exceptions, the Supreme Court hears a selection of cases of its choosing, taking 150 appeals a year from 8,000 petitions. It aims to focus on the most pressing policy issues of the day, looking to strike a balance – in its own words – 'between society's need for order and the individual's right to freedom'. The court has developed the judicial review to invalidate legislation or executive actions which conflict with the Constitution. It is a sobering thought that this responsibility has rested in the hands of a small cadre of individuals: since the formation of the court in 1790, there have been only nineteen chief justices and 111 associate justices (including Sonia Sotomayor, nominated by Barack Obama in May 2009). The combined ranks would fit into one carriage of the Washington Metro.

The decisions of these nine men and women encapsulate 'liberty under the law'. Over the years they have made crucial rulings that relate to freedom of speech, freedom of religion and racial segregation – indeed, it has been said that the history of liberty in the United States has emerged from judicial responses to practical problems and the observance of procedural safeguards. Americans are surprisingly knowledgeable about these acts of justice and historic judgments feature prominently in public discourse, made available not only through teaching and text-books at law schools, but also through Wikipedia, FindLaw, organizations like the First Amendment Center that works 'as a forum for the study and exploration of free-expression issues', and the records of the Supreme Court itself.

A key right enshrined in the First Amendment relates to freedom of worship. Given the 'culture war' that rage between systems of belief today, and given the evidence for religious bigotry and antipathy in the early years of colonial America, it is surprising that the Supreme Court did not wrestle with the question until 1878. In the case of *Reynolds v. United States* the justices were invited to rule on the practice of polygamy by Mormons in what was then the Territory of Utah. George Reynolds had been found guilty of bigamy but he appealed, claiming this violated his constitutional rights. Chief Justice Morrison Waite drafted the court's opinion, and the substance of his finding shows the benefit that anthropologists can derive from court records, extracting cultural values that are preserved like insects in amber. The practice of polygamy, Chief Justice Waite pronounced, was 'always odious among the northern and western nations, and, until the establishment of the Mormon Church, a feature of the life of Asiatic and African people'. He found, furthermore, that laws were made to govern action and while the court could not interfere with religious belief, they could with religious practice:

> Suppose one believed that human sacrifices were a necessary part of religious worship, would it be seriously contended that the civil government under which he lived could not interfere to prevent a sacrifice? Or if a wife religiously believed it were her duty to burn herself upon

the funeral pile of her dead husband, would it be beyond the power of government to prevent her carrying her belief into practice? So here, as a law of the organization of society under the exclusive dominion of the United States, it is provided that plural marriages shall not be allowed.

The Chief Justice concluded:

Can a man excuse his practices to the contrary because of his religious belief? To permit this would be to make the professed doctrines of religious belief superior to the law of the land, and in effect to permit every citizen to become a law unto himself.

The sub-text was clear. Freedom of belief had its limits, with the boundaries defined by social convention.

The Mormon Church outlawed polygamy in 1890, excommunicating these who practised it in a deal with the federal government that brought statehood for Utah. Polygamy, however, is still practised in separatist sects such as the Fundamentalist Church of Jesus Christ of Latter Day Saints, which is based in the secretive community of Colorado City (population 5,000), straddling the Utah–Arizona border. The township has a distinctive demography, skewed towards older men and young girls with long braided hair and ankle-length dresses. Many liberties have been suppressed in order to defend the rights of the polygamist. Women are taught from infancy to be subservient or to suffer eternal damnation. Makeup, jewellery, newspapers and television are banned. In behaviour that seems better fitted to the deer-rutting fields of the Scottish island of Rum, the Church – which owns most of the property in Colorado City through the 'United Effort Plan' – is said to drive young men from their homes to thin out the male population, forcing teenage girls to marry elders as rewards for loyalty.

The law tries, periodically, to strike back: in 2002, a sect member who lived with five wives and twenty-nine children in a trailer-home camp, was convicted of child rape after impregnating his thirteen-year-old 'spiritual wife' – the first such prosecution in Utah in half a century. Four years later, in 2006, the leader of the sect, Warren Jeffs, husband to some seventy wives, was arrested. His trial, which began early in September 2007, lasted less than a month and the jury found him guilty of two counts of rape as an accomplice. He was sentenced to imprisonment for ten years to life and is now lodging in Utah State Prison. But there can be no certainty that the law will prevail: the FBI first raided Colorado City in 1944, and troops and police mounted an assault in 1953, in bids to suppress polygamy. Despite these efforts, the practice – judged 'always odious' over 120 years ago – continues.

The Reynolds ruling – with its principle that an individual's religious beliefs cannot excuse him from compliance with a law prohibiting conduct that the state is free to regulate – has been a point of reference for other Supreme Court judgments. In *Employment Division v. Smith* (1990), for instance, the court endorsed the punishment of two American Indians who lost their job and the right to unemployment compensation after ingesting peyote – a hallucinogen used for sacramental purposes at a ceremony of their Native American church. The majority opinion was delivered by Justice Scalia, who recognized that religious belief frequently entailed the performance of physical acts such as assembling for worship, or consuming bread and wine. Government could no more ban the performance of these religious acts than it could ban the beliefs that compel those actions. He wrote: 'It would doubtless be unconstitutional to ban the casting of statues that are to be used for worship purposes or to prohibit bowing down before a golden calf.' But, Oregon's ban on the possession of peyote was a 'neutral law of general applicability', and the court held that the First Amendment's protection of the 'free exercise' of religion did not allow a person to violate such generally applicable laws.

However, sixteen years later, in February 2006, the Supreme Court ruled unanimously that a small congregation in New Mexico <u>could</u> use hallucinogenic tea as part of a four-hour ritual intended to connect with God. Federal drug agents were reprimanded for confiscating a consignment of hoasca tea –

which contains an illegal drug known as DMT; it is considered sacred to members of O Centro Espirita Beneficiente Uniao do Vegetal, who believe they can only comprehend God by drinking the tea twice a month.

This apparent inconsistency reminds us that the Supreme Court can behave like a frail oyster-boat zigzagging across the Chesapeake – first in one direction, then another – as it tacks in the wind of public (or ideological) opinion. For some, this transient quality represents the ultimate proof that American society is free. For others, it illustrates the elusive condition of liberty and the illusory nature of judicial authority: the law is an exercise in power, not justice. Another example of flip-flop emerges from the long-running debate about that most mundane feature of American schooldays: the Pledge.

In 1892, a children's magazine, the *Youth's Companion*, published a pledge to celebrate the 400th anniversary of Columbus's arrival in the New World. This caught on, becoming part of school routine. However, in 1940 two children from a community of Jehovah's Witnesses were expelled from their Pennsylvania academy for refusing to participate in the daily salute to the Flag (following parental guidance that this was prohibited by their religion). The Supreme Court upheld the expulsions as reasonable, since 'the ultimate foundation of a free society is the binding tie of cohesive sentiment'. Three years later, the court performed a complete about-turn in the case of another group of Jehovah's Witnesses, when Justice Robert H. Jackson concluded:

If there is any fixed star in our constitutional constellation, it is that no official, high or petty, can prescribe what shall be orthodox in politics, nationalism, religion, or other matters of opinion or force citizens to confess by word or act their faith therein. If there are any circumstances which permit an exception, they do not now occur to us.

The controversy is alive today. The original Pledge has been expanded to accommodate references to the nation and the words 'under God' (distinguishing the country, at the time, from the godless Soviet Union): 'I pledge allegiance to the flag of the United States of America, and to the republic for which it stands, one nation indivisible under God, with liberty and justice for all.' The last amendment bothers Michael Newdow, an atheist and an attorney. He wants the deity out of the Pledge, objecting to his daughter reciting the words 'under God' at school. His case – *Elk Grove Unified School District v. Newdow* – went before a federal court in San Francisco where the judge ruled in his favour, believing that the phrase breached the wall that Jefferson built between church and state. Those who hoped that the subsequent Supreme Court judgment, published in June 2004, would amend the Pledge were disappointed: the case was thrown out on a procedural technicality. However, three justices went on to consider the constitutional question, concluding that the use of the Pledge did not offend the Charters of Freedom: in the words of Chief Justice William Rehnquist, the term 'under God' merely acknowledges the nation's religious heritage, in particular the role of religion for the Founding Fathers; the pledge is a secular act rather than an act of indoctrination in religion or expression of religious devotion.

In 2005, Newdow filed a new federal case in the Ninth Circuit Court of Appeals, representing two families against the Elk Grove School District. Judge Lawrence Karlton said it was an unconstitutional violation of a child's right to be free from a coercive requirement to affirm God. Newdow told the Associated Press:

> Imagine every morning if the teachers had the children stand up, place their hands over their hearts, and say, 'We are one nation that denies God exists.' I think that everybody would not be sitting here saying, 'Oh, what harm is that.' They'd be furious. And that's exactly what goes on against atheists. And it shouldn't.

America might appear truly utopian if the most pressing questions of personal liberty and individual rights revolve around the number of wives a Mormon can take or the number of phonemes a schoolchild must enunciate. However, the Supreme Court has made decisions of the greatest significance, affecting the liberty and wellbeing of millions of US citizens over many years. The judgment about abortion (described above) is one case in point. Colour prejudice is another. It is ironic that the new nation, forged with such humanist fervour by the Founding Fathers, accommodated institutions of slavery in the South. Thomas Jefferson himself travelled to the Continental Congress of 1775 in a phaeton accompanied by three slaves, Richard, Jesse and Jupiter. As we have seen, the Constitution regarded a slave as three-fifths of a person, and what was striking about the 'peculiar institution' (a popular nineteenth-century euphemism for slavery) was the absence of any law on enslavement apart from some codes inherited as French legacy with the Louisiana Purchase. In *Dred Scott v. Sandford* (1857) the Supreme Court ruled that a slave was neither a citizen of any American state nor of the United States.

The amendments that followed the Civil War should have transformed the position of the African-American. In 1865, the Thirteenth Amendment abolished slavery and involuntary servitude; in 1868, the Fourteenth Amendment gave national and state citizenship to all those born in the US; in 1870, the Fifteenth Amendment tackled discrimination in the right to vote on grounds of race, colour or 'previous condition of servitude'. However, in an 1883 ruling (that high-school children still learn about today), the Supreme Court concluded that Congress had exceeded its authority in a new Civil Rights Act that prevented railroad carriers, innkeepers and theatre owners from discriminating on the basis of race or colour. The Fourteenth Amendment was aimed at states not individuals, the court argued: 'Private persons may violate the rights of others, but only the government, its officers and agents can deprive them of their rights.' Matters got worse for the African-American in 1896, when in *Plessy v. Ferguson* the court upheld the power of a state to require common carriers to segregate their passengers on a racial basis – a reasonable exercise of police power, in the court's opinion, designed to preserve the public peace and promote harmony between races.

These two judgments sapped the spirit and vitality of the three amendments to the Constitution that had followed the Civil War. The Supreme Court appears to have taken liberties with freedom in order to appease a South that was demoralized after the humiliation of defeat. It took sixty years for the court to adjust its stance. This omission must have had profound and long-term effects on American culture, although there are commentators who would argue that this demonstrates the fact that judges cannot rise above public opinion and political realities.

Today, it could be argued that the clapper in America's Liberty Bell has swung in the opposite direction. The judicial canvas in the first decade of the twenty-first century has regularly featured cases linked to Equal Employment Opportunities (EEO) legislation stemming from Title VII of the Civil Rights Act (1964). An EEO Commission was established in 1965 to protect individuals from discrimination in the workplace on grounds of race, colour, gender, national origin, religion, age or disability. 'Affinity Groups' now operate in many large organizations to promote and safeguard minority interests. Michael, a senior executive in one government agency, says, 'We've got an Affinity Group for everyone – Jews, Asians, Arabs, African-Americans, Catholics, Hispanics, Witches!'

The number of new complaints handled by the EEO Commission has grown (rising to 95,400 in 2008) and it carries a backlog of some 35,000 additional complaints. EEO generates heated debate in the workplace and a challenging case-load for the Supreme Court: in 2004–05, for instance, it addressed ten cases linked to EEO. The lawsuit of *Ricci v. DeStefano* (argued before the court in April 2009) exemplifies the challenge. 'The New Haven 20' – described in the media as one Hispanic and nineteen white fire-fighters – claimed to be victims of reverse discrimination because they were thrown over for promotion within the Fire Department despite passing the test. None of the twenty-seven black candidates in the exam had scored enough marks to qualify for consideration and the city's Civil Service Board voted to abandon the exercise in order to avoid violating the Civil Rights Act. Tensions mounted, with battle-lines drawn up between the 'Firebirds' (the local branch of the International Association of Black Fire-fighters) and the New Haven Hispanic Fire-fighters Association (supporting the New Haven 20).

This inevitably, became a *cause célèbre* for those engaged in America's clash of cultures who regard themselves as non-liberal freedom-lovers. Take 'JMK', a (white) member of the Fire Department of New York, who complained in his 'Workingclass Conservative' blog about the perversity of EEO: 'In a free society, based on individualism and private property rights (as America IS), there is only one answer – Meritocratic standards.' In June 2009, the Supreme Court grudgingly agreed with him: it ruled by a narrow majority (five to four, split along conservative versus liberal lines) that the white fire-fighters' rights had been violated by the city's actions.

Over the centuries, millions of people in the Old World have heard the message of freedom advanced in the Declaration of Independence and committed themselves to a new life in the United States. They and their descendants have responded to something intrinsically noble, elevating and transcendent about the American experiment. The enduring appeal of America is that it promises individuals the chance to optimize whatever small percentage of destiny lies within their gift.

Most Americans would assert with confidence that they are free. They are free from the three-taloned claw of want, hunger and tyranny that has gripped and shredded unnumbered lives through the course of human history. They are also free to pursue happiness in all manner of different ways. Twenty-first-century America is, superficially at least, a permissive society where anything can be believed, said, achieved and acquired.

It is surprising, then, that American citizens demonstrate such a strong – if erratic – commitment to the values of the group.

In the 'Land of the Free' liberty is negotiable. Strict controls apply to behaviour. There is an orthodoxy that is enduring and inviolate. Social regulation – ranging from simple conformity to rules, to muttered disapproval of otherness, through to outright bigotry and violence – is applied like a bridle. Louis Hartz, the American political scientist, recognized that there is something distinctive and paradoxical about the concept of freedom in the US: he spoke of a 'fixed dogmatic liberalism' where the American Way contains a compulsive power that threatens liberty itself. He wrote:

> A sense of community based on a sense of uniformity is a deceptive thing. It looks individualistic, and in part it actually is ... but in another sense it is profoundly anti-individualistic, because the common standard is its very essence, and deviations from that standard inspire it with an irrational fright.

This is an imperfect world and troubling contradictions stem from any society that places 'freedom' at its fountainhead. Family, faith and community can provide some comfort, but society must operate instruments that control envy and disappointment in the face of forces, out of our control, that dispense tricks and treats with indifference. It has fallen to justice to perform that role. Lawyers learn at the start of their professional training that they are gatekeepers to liberty in American society. 'Justice' is not an antonym to 'Freedom', but there is a tension between the two, exacerbated by the fact that so much public rhetoric extols freedom, while so much public practice imposes law. Intolerance endures as a feature of the American way of life, shadowing the principle of liberty.

But to what extent is this American Way, with all its crash-spots and crossroads, a unique and exceptional phenomenon? After all, when the British jurist James Bryce wrote *The American Commonwealth* (1888), he concluded that there were fundamental dogmas about man's inalienable rights, popular sovereignty and the distrust of centralized political power that made the United States more English than England.

It is, then, worth gaining some perspective on the land of the Cracked Bell by asking if its conflicted, paradoxical nature reflects a deeper, Anglo-Saxon phenomenon.

CHAPTER EIGHT

Angles and Equations – On the Anglosphere

'I admire Britain so much!' The lawyer, dressed in the WASP style that imitates a bygone English era, was walking his miniature schnauzer through the leafy streets of northwest Washington, DC, before going to the Kennedy Center to hear Ralph Vaughan Williams' *A Sea Symphony*. 'You gave us Anglo-Saxon law and Anglicanism. If the Muslims had that, there wouldn't be the trouble we have today.'

The reference to Islam betrays the fact that this sentiment was expressed after 9/11, but the underlying thesis about Anglo-Saxon values has held currency for over a century. It lies behind the mantra of the 'Special Relationship' invoked in the UK Foreign Office and (to a lesser degree) the US State Department. It is found in the concept of 'Anglo-American' law and the enduring notion of 'Anglo-Saxon' finance (that served as a butt for Franco-German arrows in 2008 and 2009). Ralph Waldo Emerson observed, in *English Traits* (1856), that 'the American is only the continuation of the English genius into new conditions, more or less propitious', and in 1903 *The Anglo-Saxon Century* by John Randolph Dos Passos Sr called for the two nations to reunite as a benign world power.

Winston Churchill wrote in his *A History of the English-Speaking Peoples* (1956–58) of the 'formidable virtues' of the Anglophone nations coming together to preserve peace and freedom; and his theme was given a twenty-first-century makeover by the British historian Andrew Roberts with *A*

History of the English-Speaking Peoples Since 1900 (2006). An Anglosphere Foundation has even been established in Virginia in recent years promoting a 'new concept in geopolitics' – that nations of the English-speaking world represent an emerging branch of civilization characterized by the justice of common law, freedom guaranteed by traditions of individual liberty, representative constitutional government and strong civil society. In *The Anglosphere Challenge* (2004), James Bennett has argued that a 'network commonwealth' of English-speaking nations could make this the Anglosphere century, following the British nineteenth century and the American twentieth century.

There is, however, a contrary position to those who see the United States' destiny, values and distinguishing features intertwined with those of the United Kingdom. This dates back at least to Thomas Paine, the English radical who travelled to America in time to participate in the Revolution. In *Common Sense* (1776) he aired the view that America was a new country that had outgrown the British mother country. These sentiments chimed with the separatist ethos of the first Puritan migrants and underpinned the American Revolution. Tocqueville coined the term 'American exceptionalism' in 1831, and it has retained currency ever since. Twentieth-century commentators such as the political scientist Seymour Martin Lipset see the United States as qualitatively different from any advanced industrial nation.

There is, of course, no doubt about the bond between the two nations. Over many decades, British ambassadors in Washington, DC, have quoted the successful Foreign Office candidate who, when asked what matters most in the world, replied: 'God, Love and Anglo-American relations'. Meanwhile, when Americans are invited to assess other countries as a 'close ally', Great Britain comes ahead of the rest of the pack. Seventy per cent of respondents rated the UK a close ally in 2004; Canada came second with only 51 per cent.

Common language provides a bedrock to the relationship. For over eighty years the quarterly *American Speech* has been delving into the vocabulary, accents and grammar of the English dialects found in North America, and comparison with the British Isles has been a constant theme. This is exemplified by the publication of a 1988 lecture given by Allen Walker Read (leading scholar of American-English in the twentieth century) entitled 'Words Crisscrossing the Sea: How Words Have Been Borrowed Between England and America'.

In 2001, the *Cambridge History of the English Language* produced a volume dedicated to *English in North America*. In his preface, John Algeo explains how language systems undergo fluctuations and adjustments over time. Linguists have adopted terms-of-art to describe the process: 'drift' and 'analogy', 'assimilation' and 'dissimulation', 'pull-chain' and 'push-chain'. With limited contact between the mother-country and her colonies, the grammar and vocabulary used in Britain and America began to drift apart, and dialects evolved over time. However, Dr Algeo argues that after 300 years of differentiation, the process seems to have been arrested or even reversed by improved transportation and communication. 'OK' is a notable example of a word travelling eastwards; it is the linguistic equivalent to the spread of branded products like Coca-Cola. Indeed, there is something truly innovative about this Americanism, with its eccentric use of abbreviation (a craze among Boston's literati in the late 1830s) and playful use of misspelling (the letters allegedly stand for 'oll korrect': 'all correct').

There is another word in the English language whose usage – on both sides of the Atlantic – is possibly even more prolific than 'OK'. Professor Read dealt with this in another classic article (entitled 'An Obscenity Symbol') that appeared in *American Speech* in 1934. A sense of propriety prevented him from using the word, referring to it instead as 'the most disreputable of all English words – the colloquial verb and noun, universally known by speakers of English, designating the sex act'. It is, of course, the profanity 'fuck' – the most common of American expletives, and an old Anglo-Saxon word meaning 'to plough'. In the same vein, the most common surname in the US – representing almost one out of every hundred people in the country – is Smith, which describes the craft of the blacksmith, deriving from the Anglo-Saxon word *smitan* (to smite, or strike). It seems fitting that these monosyllables from the Old World should remain so vital in the New. The antiquarian can take comfort from the thought that whenever the curse 'Fuck Smith!' rings out in the trading-rooms of Wall Street or the 'hoods of Chicago, citizens of the most modern nation in the world salute two of the greatest achievements of the Old World – agriculture and metallurgy.

The proportion of 'Smiths' in the US population is almost identical to that in the UK (where it is also the most common surname). In fact, up until the start of the new millennium records showed that all top ten family names in America – representing over 5.5 per cent of all US citizens – derived from the British Isles. But the 2000 census revealed that Moore and Taylor had been thrown out by Garcia and Rodriguez – an early indication of how America is going to change over the next few decades. The 2000 chart looked like this:

1. Smith (0.88 per cent)
2. Johnson (0.69 per cent)
3. Williams (0.57 per cent)
4. Brown (0.51 per cent)
5. Jones (0.50 per cent)
6. Miller (0.42 per cent)
7. Davis (0.40 per cent)
8. Garcia (0.32 per cent)
9. Rodriguez (0.30 per cent)
10. Wilson (0.29 per cent)

Beyond language and nomenclature, and the sense of real or imagined kinship that goes with both, there are shared values and habits. It has been said that the cultural gap is wider across the English Channel than it is across the Atlantic, and a joking relationship has become established around the small differences that exist between Britain and the US. However, as every anthropologist knows, there are hidden and uncomfortable truths lurking behind every joking relationship. At the very opening of the twenty-first century, an email mocking the presidential election crisis of 2000 spawned a flurry of internet exchanges that highlighted the variables between the two cultures while acknowledging a common destiny. It started with a 'Notice of Revocation of Independence', purportedly issued by the Supreme Court of Florida:

> To the citizens of the USA: in the light of your failure to elect anybody as President and thus to govern yourselves and, by extension, the free world, we hereby give notice of the revocation of your independence, effective today. Her Sovereign Majesty Queen Elizabeth II will resume monarchical duties over all states, commonwealths and other territories. Tax collectors from Her Majesty's Government will be with you shortly to ensure the acquisition of all revenues due (backdated to 1776).

To help the transition to a British crown dependency, the citizens of the former republic were urged to reconnect with British culture and learn to enjoy steak and kidney pudding and warm flat beer; replace 4 July with 5 November as a public holiday; drive on the left and pay British prices for fuel ($6 a gallon); stop referring to a baseball competition involving the US, Cuba and Japan as a *World* Series; and resolve personal issues without the use of guns, lawyers or therapists. The authors of the 'Revocation' concluded: 'There is no such thing as "US English". We will contact Microsoft and inform them.'

A retaliatory strike arrived almost immediately, with a declaration annexing the British Isles to the US:

> In the light of your indecision over joining a common European Currency, your dissatisfaction with the European Union, your bickering with European Governments and the fact that you already almost speak our language and refuse to speak any other European languages, you are to be annexed as a State of America. Your state code will be GB. Zip codes will be assigned to replace your old postal

districts. The state capital will be Stratford-upon-Avon which is a lot prettier than London.

The new citizens of the 51st State had assimilated so much American culture that they would hardly notice, but the following rules were to be introduced (in addition to daily singing of 'The Star-Spangled Banner'):

- learn to cook: 'there's a reason why the best food in your country is Indian or Chinese; your contributions to the culinary arts are soggy beans, warm beer, and spotted dick';
- stop playing soccer and rugby: 'there is no need to have two games, one confusingly like Football and one called football which isn't; if you insist on cricket, introduce a simplified scoring system, timeouts, colored strips and cheerleaders to make it more interesting';
- 4 July replaces 5 November as Fireworks Day: 'If you want a fireworks party on November 5th, we will help you to blow up your Houses of Parliament; you won't be needing them any longer: Disneyland London will be situated there';
- all inter-personal communications between family members, even if resident in the same house, must be through a lawyer; it is compulsory to sue somebody at least once per year and to have therapy three times each week; you will be given compulsory courses on how to become dysfunctional;
- the British must name children after interesting medical conditions, stop using the word *fortnight*, and accept that *caravanning* is *camping* while the thing Scouts do with tents and bedrolls is *tenting*.

These spoof declarations focus on seemingly superficial features – sport, food and drink, highway codes, public holidays and the variations in spelling, pronunciation and usage of English words. It is only in the field of personal relationships that the repartee becomes less jocular, moving beneath the surface to touch on areas of conflict and turmoil that we have seen in *The Cracked Bell*.

But how substantive are the differences between British and American culture? In the algebra of political economics, is the relationship best defined as an angle (where lines diverge from a single point) or an equation (the expression of fundamental equality)? In this chapter these questions are posed with reference to the seven varieties of American paradox revealed in *The Cracked Bell*. Do the confusion and complexity around identity, consumerism, belief, innovation, wilderness, war and peace, freedom and conformity amount to a distinctive American riddle of the twenty-first century, or are they part of a bigger, Anglo-Saxon, conundrum?

In the opening chapter, 'The Many and the One', we saw Americans living – sometimes painfully – with multiple identities and ethnicities.

There are some who argue that the 'British' are experiencing a long-running identity crisis of their own. This descriptor always has been an inadequate word for the people of the United Kingdom of Great Britain and Northern Ireland, and it is occasionally a source of confusion and embarrassment. Self-definition was stress-tested in the second half of the twentieth century by a collapsed empire, an expanding European Union and a fragmented kingdom, with power devolved 'up' to Brussels and 'down' to assemblies in Scotland, Wales and Northern Ireland. Some commentators would argue that any remaining certainties have been challenged by an influx of migrants from the former empire and the European Community.

The electoral success of the openly racist British National Party in the European elections of June 2009 appears to lend weight to this argument, with the BNP winning two out of Britain's sixty-nine seats in the European Parliament with 6.2 per cent of the vote. There are reasons to discount the apparent significance of this result – a disenchanted, Eurosceptic electorate used 'votes that don't matter' to punish the nation's mainstream parties following exposure of a lax expenses system in the House of Commons. However, this did signal a gnawing concern – in the opening years of the twenty-first century – about migrants who resist integration and threaten to impose their own values on British society. The multiple suicide attacks on the London Underground on 7 July 2005 were especially troubling because they were perpetrated by 'homegrown' Muslim terrorists, of Pakistani origin, who had been born and raised in Britain.

The cultural inscape of towns like Leeds, Bradford, Barnsley and Oldham has been transformed over recent years, as migrants have been drawn – by employment, cheap housing stock and an expatriate vanguard – to 'zones of transition'. Substantial ghettoes are forming, where the physical segregation of housing estates and inner-city wards is compounded by social exclusion zones: ethnic communities can operate within a bubble, with separate schools, language, temples or mosques, social networks and voluntary organizations. Birmingham – Britain's second largest city – exemplifies this: Handsworth, in the northwest quadrant of the city, was a centre for West Indians; now Iraqi Kurds, Somalis, Pakistanis and Bangladeshis have settled there. Kashmiris are in Saltley to the northeast. Small Heath and Bordesley, to the east of the city centre, was a poor Irish area which is becoming a mosaic of communities from the Indian subcontinent and North Africa (with inter-ethnic tensions between these groups). The 'Balti Belt' of Sparkhill in the southeast is home to Pakistanis from the Mirpur region – many of them from 250 villages destroyed when the Mangla Dam was built in the 1960s.

There is a perception among ethnic minorities that populist media have pandered to deep-seated fears of cultural and linguistic fragmentation. Unfavourable images of non-white migrants deepen the chasm between 'us' (the UK's white indigenous population) and 'them' (the newcomers). By February 2008, surveys showed that the British public believed 20 per cent of the population to be immigrants (the correct figure was 4 per cent); another poll found that the average Briton believed the country took 25 per cent of the world's asylum-seekers – the true figure was 2 per cent. The bureaucratic response to all of this has been to adopt protocols informed by the American system. For instance, the UK Nationality, Immigration and Asylum Act of 2002 includes a citizenship oath and pledge.

It would be a travesty to deny both the travails of Britain's inner-city ghettoes and the strain of intolerance that runs through a small portion of the indigenous British society. However, some perspective is required here. The overwhelming public call – in May 2009 – for Nepalese soldiers of the Gurkha Regiment of the British army and their families to be given the rights of British citizenship represents a very different attitude to non-whites (swayed by the passionate advocacy of a British TV star, and by the argument that men prepared to die for our country should be allowed to live here).

There is recognition, more broadly, that British culture has been enriched by the influx of migrants over recent decades, and there is evidence of American-style 'double consciousness' flourishing within hyphenated communities – Anglo-Jewish, British-Caribbean, British-Pakistani. Daljit Nagra has captured the experience of Indian migration in his Punjabi-English poem 'Look we have coming to Dover!' – regarded as a masterpiece of English literature in the opening decade of the twenty-first century – and a number of films in recent years have explored the phenomenon to powerful effect: *My Beautiful Laundrette* (1985), *Bhaji on the Beach* (1993), *East is East* (1999), *Bend It Like Beckham* (2002) and *Brick Lane* (2007).

Those in need of quantitative data should scrutinize the government's annual Citizenship Survey (based on polling in England and Wales), where the results from 2007–08 show a similar picture to responses from earlier years: 82 per cent of people see their community as 'cohesive', where people from different backgrounds get on well together; and 84 per cent of people feel strongly they belong to Britain. It is interesting to note that citizens originating from the 'New Commonwealth' (or 'Old Empire') – Africans, Black Caribbeans, Indians and Pakistanis – share that sense of belonging as emphatically as their white counterparts (the figure rises to 89 per cent for those originating from the Indian subcontinent).

This reference to the British Empire leads us to the first of three points that need to be understood in any analysis of the differences between the crisis in British and American identity. Firstly, our heritage is clearly one of emigration – of outward engagement with the world – rather than of immigration. Readers will recall the OECD statistic cited earlier that showed over 9 per cent of British nationals living permanently abroad (compared with less than 0.5 per cent of Americans). The British settlements of America, Australia, Canada and New Zealand represent an extraordinary testament to a spirit of adventure.

Secondly, Britain, like America, has developed a narrative around the concept of *e pluribus unum*. This is exemplified by a poster on display in the London Underground and on the buses in 2005: 'The English: Just a Bunch of Foreigners'. It has been said there are at least seven different ways to define the indigenous peoples of the UK – and this does not even include the category 'Yorkshireman' that stirs the doughty ardour of those living in the largest county in the country. But time has been a powerful agent here, almost operating within the geological or glacial range to smooth out and mix up the ethnic ingredients.

The English, in particular, subscribe to a myth of cultural assimilation. English identity has evolved over 2,000 years with the absorption of waves of immigrants – invaders, colonists, traders and seekers of sanctuary. The illuminations of the *Lindisfarne Gospels* exemplify this, with the artist incorporating the iconography of different ethnic traditions – native Celtic and Anglo-Saxon elements blend with Roman, Coptic and Eastern. In the ninth century, King Alfred instigated a project to translate great works (by Boethius, Gregory and Augustine) into the English language, and pursued the political objective of the idea of a unified England as he translated and distributed a version of Bede's *Ecclesiastical History of the English People*: this gave a sense of ethnic unity to the diverse tribes and provinces of the country. Today, a small number of media channels has informed a sense of identity for the whole nation: generations have grown up together watching *Top of the Pops, Match of the Day, Dr Who, Steptoe and Son, Porridge, Dad's Army, Eastenders* and *Little Britain*. A shared treasury of catch-phrases ('Exterminate!', 'You dirty old man!', 'Don't tell him, Pike!', 'You silly moo!', 'I'm the only gay in the village!') has a powerful unifying effect.

Thirdly, however, it should be recognized that variegation in the British character is as rich as the topography of the island. There is, for instance, a strong sense of affiliation to place: one is associated with country (Ireland, Wales, Scotland); county – Yorkshire, Lancashire, Somerset, Dorset, Sussex; city, and even district or village. This is reflected in a British obsession with dialect and accent such as Cockney, Brummie, Scouse, Mancunian, Geordie, Morningside and Kelvinside. This may explain why the impressionist represents an especially British form of entertainment: many of them are household names: Mike Yarwood, Lenny Henry, Rory Bremner, Alistair McGowan, John Culshaw and Ronni Ancona.

Accent also plays its part in the taxonomy of the class system, that most British of institutions. The accent known variously as 'Received Pronunciation', 'Home Counties', 'BBC English' or 'Queen's English' is associated with a ruling class. Many of the values that underpin style and manners in British society continue to be informed by the class system. The experience of two world wars has created a commitment to wealth redistribution and to equality of opportunity, and class today is rarely a barrier to choice of occupation or progression in the way that it was in the past. However, the English class system continues to operate as an extraordinary and elaborate social construct that has sliced, diced and packaged the population into subtly defined categories. There is no simple formula for establishing an individual's class; the phenomenon is far more complex than the three- or six-tier systems favoured by market researchers. The anthropologist, Kate Fox, has illustrated the point in *Watching the English* (2004):

> A schoolteacher and an estate agent would both technically be 'middle class'. They might even both live in a terraced

house, drive a Volvo, drink in the same pub and earn roughly the same annual income. However, we judge social class in much more subtle and complex ways such as precisely how you arrange, furnish and decorate your terraced house; you are not judged just by the make of car you drive, but whether you wash it yourself on Sundays, take it to a car wash or rely on the English climate to sluice off the worst of the dirt for you. Similar fine distinctions are applied to what, where, when, how and with whom you eat and drink; the words you use and how you pronounce them; where and how you shop; the clothes you wear; the pets you keep; how you spend your free time; the chat-up lines you use, and so on.

For at least 2,000 years, different cultural and ethnic traditions have interacted within ever wider circles around the globe – like some experiment in combinatorial chemistry. Unpleasant strains of racism and jingoism have emerged from the mix, but ultimately the end-product is chaotic, confusing but not conflicted. This has created a distinctive British paradox that is best described as the 'equality of difference' (not to be confused with the 'equality of opportunity' – a value that the British struggle to realize).

Taken at face value, one might conclude that Britain – that 'nation of shop-keepers' as Napoleon sneered – is as much a Temple of Trade as America. There are, after all, the symbols of an entrenched free-market economy: billboards, fliers, TV ads and promotions; credit cards and flexible repayment schemes; boutiques and shopping centres. In September 2009, the British government even announced that 'American-style' product placement would be allowed on commercial TV (but not, of course, on the BBC). Psychologist Oliver James has argued that an obsession with possessions (a concern with having, not being) is a feature of all English-speaking cultures; this is portrayed as a fixation with status and acquisition that leads to high levels of mental illness. His name for the condition is 'affluenza', which also formed the title of an anti-consumerist book published in 2001: *Affluenza: The All-Consuming Epidemic*.

In the last twenty years the UK has seen a growth in something akin to America's lifestyle shopping, especially among the younger, more socially mobile middle class (emblemized in the popular imagination by highly-paid professional footballers and their WAGs – wives and girlfriends). However, this should not distract us from the bigger picture. Britain has a tenth of the shelf-space per head of population, and also has oases of calm from the relentless sales-pitch through commercial-free television and radio stations delivered by the BBC. There is, ultimately, none of the intense, all-embracing, spiritualized commercialism of the United States. There is more conservation, restoration and preservation in Britain: 'Make do and mend' is a familiar refrain. The idea of taking a broken toaster to be repaired appears risible to the American mind, but it happens in Britain, sustaining a service sector, and a type of handyman that hardly exists in the US.

The British shopping experience is inevitably affected by the subtleties of the class system. Many Britons, especially the upper middle and upper classes, place a premium on hand-me-down clothes, inherited chattels and other second-hand items that are imbued with a value that Americans find eccentric if not unconscionable; this has an inevitable impact on commerce and markets.

The British shopping experience more generally is focused on 'essentials'; it is primarily about provisioning; the cost of living is a major concern. This approach is reflected in media programmes such as *Checkpoint, How to Spend It, Choice* and *Watchdog*. The very word 'consumption' grates in an English ear (as a colloquialism for tuberculosis, it reminds us of a disease that killed hundreds of thousands); and organizations like the Consumer Council and Consumers' Association (CA) are associated with the application of prudence in the process of 'shopping around'. The latter – established in 1958 – publishes the popular *Which?* magazine, and has shifted from being a research-based organization to an activist campaigning group: in September 1999, for instance, it urged motorists to stop buying new cars in the UK until prices fell; it then launched 'carbusters.com' (complete with a vehicle painted in the Union Jack and featuring the licence plate 'GB RIP OFF'), and entered the market itself to help people obtain the cheaper prices available to the rest of Europe. There may be frequent talk about UK customers becoming more 'consumer-savvy' and active – but there remain strong expectations that they will be protected by government agencies and by firms themselves.

Research by social psychologists Peter Lunt and Sonia Livingstone suggests that there is only limited preoccupation with the sort of shopping experience that is the norm in America's Temple of Trade. No more than 24 per cent of British shoppers conform to the American stereotype of Leisure Shopper ('I shop therefore I am') – defined as enjoying a range of shopping experiences including window shopping and using consumer goods in their social relationships as rewards, promises and bribes. The rest were far more cautious:

31 per cent: Routine – they shop on the high street when they need something, but seem disengaged from consumer culture; they rarely buy on impulse and do not use the alternative market: shopping is a routine, not a pleasure.
18 per cent: Thrifty – find some pleasure in shopping, especially for clothes, food and presents; but they look for the best buy and wait for the sales for expensive items.
15 per cent: Careful – enjoyment is in the use rather than the acquisition of products;
12 per cent: Alternative – avoid the pleasures and pressures of modern consumer culture, buying second-hand books and clothes and attending jumble sales.

The reading of a society's cultural topography is, of course, informed by the relative position and experience of the viewer. (The rolling hills of East Anglia that appear vertiginous to a

Fenman are decumbent to an Alpine goat-herd.) Peter Lunt captured the 'in-betweeny' sensation that many Britons experience when he wrote (in an e-mail to the author in August 2009):

> The trend in the UK is towards the US – or perhaps a better way of putting it is that the UK is halfway between Europe and America! When Sonia and I did the work in the late 1980s we were struck by this being a point of transition – marked by intergenerational differences – the older people were grounded in the welfare contract and the younger people were adapting to a world of credit and debt and more instrumental consumption.

There is little doubt that the shopping experience in Britain is radically different from that across the Atlantic. Ask any American expatriate who has moved to Britain what they miss about home, and the topic of customer service will almost certainly arise: 'You English are so rude. It's like the shop-girl is doing you a favour serving you, and that is given grudgingly'; 'I've stopped going to my bank in London. I won't be treated that way!'; 'When I appeared with an armful of dresses I wanted to try on, I was told – *They're expensive, you know* – in a tone of voice that implied I was wasting everyone's time because I couldn't afford it.'

The explanation given, by those who are willing to reflect on these issues, is that in some way the consumer is underrated. Advocates of the free market will claim that the prices charged by British retailers demonstrate the difference between a society where the producer has the upper hand and one where the consumer reigns supreme. Hugh, a senior American diplomat in London, takes a historical viewpoint:

> I think it goes back to the days of rationing in the Second World War, when the fate of your table was in the hands of the butcher and the fishmonger and the grocer. They had the power. You had to ingratiate yourself to them.

In reality, the reasons are more complex than that. Beyond a subdued British style of interaction that is far removed from the folksy manner of shop assistants and waitresses in the US, there is the added dimension of a proletarian reaction against the notion of service as Britons have attempted to overturn the more sclerotic vestiges of the old class system. British society continues to carry demarcation lines formed by class and race, and there is relative poverty in the land. However, partially in keeping with that English fixation with 'fair play', a social democratic tradition has ensured that safety-nets exist, providing security to millions who suffered in the *laissez-faire* era of Britain's nineteenth century in a similar fashion to the underclass seen in the US today. These safety-nets have helped ensure that non-deference is very much *de rigueur* in Britain today.

In the first year of Obama's presidency, Americans were gripped in impassioned argument over the question of a national health service, and inevitably comparisons were made with the UK. There was talk – fed by lobbyist groups and political advocacy groups like 'Conservatives for Patients' Rights' – of British state-run 'death panels' deciding whether old people should live or die. In town hall meetings, women were seen in tears begging their Congressmen to stop America being turned into a communist state. The United States' customer-centric, service-centric, free-market approach to healthcare was contrasted with a system where care is delivered not bought. Barack Obama's voice could be heard in the background pleading on behalf of the 47 million people without health insurance; and British voices were heard pointing out that child mortality rates in the US are worse than those of Cuba and life expectancy in the UK exceeds that of the US. This became a powerful demonstration of the cultural and political differences between the two countries in a sphere – the delivery of service to customers – where 'Anglo-Saxon' values are allegedly aligned.

It is fitting that one of the first English sounds voiced by the natives of the North American continent would appear to be

'Gnaah' – in imitation – according to Francis Drake's chaplain, of the way that Englishmen sang their psalms. Britain provided the root-stock for many of the faiths that have flourished in the US – Episcopalian, Quaker, Shaker, Presbyterian, Methodist and Baptist. British visitors to the National Cathedral in Washington, DC, will be amazed at the extent to which the shape, structure and symbology of a medieval English church has been re-created. The pulpit is carved from stone taken from the tower of Canterbury Cathedral and bears images of Magna Carta; the first bishop was buried, in the English manner, in the Bethlehem Chapel and the kneelers there were hand-stitched by British women (including the Queen) as a gesture of thanks to the American people after the Second World War.

Here however, the equation ends. There is, in fact, an oblique angle between the vigorous person-centred, fundamentalist Christianity flourishing in the US and the weak religious engagement in twenty-first-century Britain where traditional religion is more parson-centred. The American viewpoint is illustrated by this extract from an article (supporting youth ministry in Britain) by Rick Lawrence – editor of the Colorado-based Christian magazine *Group* – in 2000:

> What started as a tiny pagan campfire a few decades ago has whipped up into a monster wildfire that's raced through the dry tinder of the UK church. When I was in England nine years ago, the cavernous old churches were lucky to have a smattering of elderly folks show up on Sundays. Forget youth friendly; these churches looked like nuclear test zones – desolate, decimated and sad.

British society has indeed become markedly secular in recent years. Church-going is low (now less than 7 per cent of the population, according to a 2005 census by Christian Research), and a poll conducted in December 2006 revealed that non-believers outnumber believers in Britain by almost two to one. Britain is a sceptical nation: most people have no personal faith – only 33 per cent of those questioned describe themselves as 'a religious person', while 63 per cent say that they are not religious, including more than half of those who describe themselves as Christian.

The style of religious worship in Britain is backward-looking; it sustains the continuity of society and the status quo. Churches are the centre of medieval parish boundaries and help to articulate the landscape (even if they are now redundant, or only used for occasional worship). They also help to articulate our lives: millions of people who otherwise will not bother with worship and would not count themselves as 'believers' go to church to baptize their children, exchange marriage vows and perform funeral rites for their dead.

Christianity in Britain, then, is in many ways more of a cultural force than a spiritual one. Religious buildings have become part of something called 'British heritage', with a number of great cathedrals – such as Chester, York, Winchester, Durham and Ely – marketed as centres of both Christianity and tourism. Where religion is practised, the emphasis is predominantly on liturgy, heritage and ritual. The shared experience of sanctity is important and a distinctive Anglo-Catholic tradition of architecture, ritual, choral music and nuanced sermons has created a rich aesthetic and cultural heritage. However, God – and any explicit interest in personal salvation – is often incidental to the process. Benign indifference is the rule. In contrast with the US, politicians and other prominent public figures avoid demonstrating their devoutness and are rarely to be found invoking their deity. This was exemplified by the comments of Prime Minister Tony Blair in an interview screened after his retirement from the premiership in 2007: 'If I talked, as Prime Minister, about my faith I would have been thought to be a nutter!'

It comes as no surprise, then, that the archetypal Anglican vicar tends to skirt over contentious issues such as good and evil, heaven and hell, eternal damnation and even (it seems) the existence of God. This sense of compromise and accommodation has become a feature of English religious practice (different from Non-Conformist traditions in Scotland and Wales, or the sectarian traditions of Northern Ireland where 82 per cent of the population involve themselves in religious worship as if their lives depended upon it). One milestone was marked – in the mid-nineteenth century – by the publication of 'Dover Beach' by Matthew Arnold, acknowledging the loss of religious faith in the modern world. This poem, which ends with its vision of a warring world stripped of all certitude and charity, includes the lines:

> The Sea of Faith
> Was once, too, at the full, and round earth's shore
> Lay like the folds of a bright girdle furl'd.
> But now I only hear
> Its melancholy, long, withdrawing roar,
> Retreating, to the breath
> Of the night-wind, down the vast edges drear
> And naked shingles of the world.

An overwhelming majority (82 per cent) see religion as a cause of division and tension – greatly outnumbering the smaller majority who also believe that it can be a force for good. Religion is the violent politics of Northern Ireland, suicide bombers exploding their devices on the London Underground and death threats against authors who offend Iranian mullahs. In a society that values freedom and individuality, religion is becoming – to use a theological term – anathema. These reservations extend to a disinclination to rush to moral judgments: 'live and let live' is a well-worn British aphorism that carries its own moral hazard (when respect for another's privacy can turn into neglect of suffering).

In the chapter called 'The Lattice Constant', we saw an American society that has turned innovation into a tradition. There may be a gap between the political realities of power-blocs and interest-groups and the ideal of 'entrepreneurial heaven', but there is no doubting that 'new' carries almost as much weight as 'freedom' in American public discourse.

Nothing could be further from the truth in British culture. If America imagines itself into existence by believing in a future destiny, Britain imagines itself into existence by remembering a past glory. The motto chosen by the Party in George Orwell's *Nineteen Eighty-four* is a very English construct: 'He who controls the present controls the past. He who controls the past controls the future.' Orwell published his work in 1949, five years after Winston Churchill had told the House of Commons: 'I confess to be a great admirer of tradition. The longer you can look back, the further you can look forward.' Retrospection is all.

This is at odds with the views of some in the political, business and intellectual elite who picture themselves in the engine-room of a modern nation. The British are swift to congratulate themselves for their inventiveness. They enjoy an outstanding record in the creative arts (literature, music, stage and screen) and there is a small but vital sector of Britain's 'knowledge economy' where venture capitalists fund start-up enterprises. An Oxbridge tradition underpins a world-class university system that has contributed to an impressive British roll-call of Nobel Prizes. Between 1900 and 2008, 114 Britons (or British institutions) were awarded prizes and in national league tables the country comes second only to the US (with 304). Interestingly, the UK and US have the same number of Literature laureates (11) and Britain has 14 Peace Prize-winners compared with the US's 21. In other fields (notably relating to discoveries and inventions) the UK's 88 winners is outstripped by 272 American laureates – but let us not forget the substantial difference in the size of respective populations!

This does not, however, change the backward-looking stance of British culture. The weight of history and tradition bears down on every walk of life; the nation is infused with a nostalgia for a lost past and a passion for the recovered past. Patrick Wright has written, in a collection of occasional essays *On Living in an Old Country* (1985), of his return to Britain in 1979 after five years in North America: 'I felt as if I had stumbled inadvertently into some sort of anthropological museum.'

In Britain, words like 'ancient' and 'medieval' are charged

with emotional meaning and energy in the way that words like 'new' and 'modern' operate in the US. Draconian planning regulations – that would be regarded as communist in the US – reflect a passion for heritage and the past. 'Preservation' and 'conservation' are powerful words – as inured into the fabric of society as the jams and pickles ('preserves' and 'conserves') that feature in the British diet. The word 'conversion' in Britain refers first and foremost to a building project, not a religious experience: barns are converted into homes, churches into mosques, malt houses into concert halls.

The antiquarian tradition in Britain is inspired by the ancient henges and grave-mounds that cover the country. The Anglo-Saxons' word for 'most excellent' or 'very best' was *aergod*, literally meaning 'as good as the beginning'. Enthusiasts in Wiltshire claim that 'local history is the new rock 'n' roll' and the hobby of 'metal-detecting' (a sort of land-based angling) was given a boost in September 2009 with the discovery of a hoard of Anglo-Saxon gold in Staffordshire. In Britain, government agencies like English Heritage and independent charities like the National Trust spends tens of millions of pounds restoring old buildings and maintaining ancient landscapes – even maintaining the disrepair of artificial ruins that featured in the eighteenth and nineteenth centuries grandees. The National Trust dates back to 1895 and aims to acquire and protect threatened coastline, countryside and buildings: it cares for 600,000 acres of countryside, over 700 miles of coastline and more than 200 buildings and gardens. It has 3.5 million members and 50 million people visited its properties in 2007; for them, the name of the organization seems to have become synonymous with National Security.

Dr Who is a more recent phenomenon, but a no less powerful emblem of British culture. This enigmatic 'Time Lord' travels the space–time continuum in an outdated police telephone-box which is far larger inside than it appears from outside. Like 'The Doctor', the British Isles themselves seem to distort space and time: 12,000 miles of coastline (including the Scottish islands) surround an area described in the CIA's *World Fact Book* as 'slightly smaller than Oregon'; and the proliferation of accents, the complex geology (demonstrating remarkable variegation in a few square miles), overlaid with a thick patina of local and ancient heritage can make Britain feel far bigger than the US.

There is little opportunity for a paradox to develop between the spirit of innovation and the enervating clay of institutions, since there is so little of the former – relatively speaking – in relation to the latter. Indeed, even British institutions have a gravity that makes them appear immobile when compared with the turbulent cut-and-thrust of American power-politics and the dynamic nature of voluntary associations in the US. The British version is, however, more about spectacle, theatre, ritual and mystification than about meeting the material needs of competing interests.

The monarchy occupies the apex of a pyramid of institutions that are engaged in the manipulation of symbolic – rather than material – capital. The British map out their past in relation to their monarchs – for instance, the dating of architecture, music, poetry, furniture, silver and art is more often than not defined in terms like Tudor, Elizabethan, Jacobean, Georgian, Victorian. In the wider world of what philosopher Roger Scruton has called 'rituals, uniforms, precedents and offices', a clubbable instinct is at work everywhere from guilds to trade unions, cathedral chapters to colliery brass bands, and public schools to learned societies. Each village will have its cricket team, darts club and Women's Institute, typically protected in law by a trust, with appointed president, chairman, secretary and treasurer, and an annual general meeting at which the accounts are approved and minutes are taken.

However, there are consequences for this institutionalized existence, best illustrated in the dependency culture that seems deeply engrained in the UK. Social welfare provides a safety-net for the poor, with the government performing a role once played by the more philanthropic gentry. For American observers, this has created a population disinclined to take risks and initiatives. Dan is a New York commercial lawyer who has lived in London for ten years. He has two words to describe the character of the British people: 'passive' and 'envious'. In contrast with an energized American culture of enterprise, the British population sits back and assumes others will do the work for them. Dan says, 'The British are great at complaining, but this doesn't often turn into doing something about it and making a difference.' Then, in contrast with American admiration for wealth and achievement, the British resent those who are successful and want to tear them down; press, comedians and commentators play their part in this, but envy is a general British trait.

The nation is dogged by mediocre performance in innovation, poor investment in infrastructure and a low skill-base. Even the legendary prowess of the Industrial Revolution is deceptive: Geir Lundestad has demonstrated that at its height – in 1750–75 – Britain was behind only 47 per cent of the world's major inventions, discoveries and innovations. This compares with a record performance for the US – in 1940–50 – of 82 per cent. Today, American submissions to the US Patent Office are made at a rate of 275 per million of the population; the equivalent figure for British submissions is 52. British patriots may cry 'foul' at this point, suggesting this is explained by home advantage . . . but even American submissions to the European Patent Office outpace the UK, using the same metric: 168 for the US, 121 for the UK.

Novelty is not where British values seem to lie. The coronation ceremony derives from a rite designed by Dunstan, Archbishop of Canterbury, to anoint Edgar King of England in Bath in 973. When the Sword of State was passed to Queen Elizabeth II by Dunstan's twentieth-century successor, the accompanying instructions are clear: 'Restore the things that are gone to decay, maintain the things that are restored, punish and reform what is amiss, and confirm what is in good order.'

'The Wood-Cut and the Wilderness' chapter revealed an America gripped by the myth of enduring frontier. Americans journey, in their minds, through limitless solitude in pursuit of the pipedream of self-expression and self-discovery. America is built through the conquest of wilderness; the citizen finds his moral compass recalibrated through an encounter with the wild. There is an almost predatory aspect to this asymmetrical relationship: Man needs Nature for fulfilment; Nature is destroyed in the process.

As in the United States, Britain has developed a powerful national myth about the natural world, but the dynamic is very different. Instead of the opportunity and challenge of the wild frontier, Britain has the certainties and comfort of a rural landscape (where the emphasis is on cultivation rather than exploitation) and village society; and the surrounding landscape is as much about mythical time as it is about space – a recent past and a distant archaeological past. Of course, those members of this island race in need of some deeper engagement with Nature can always turn to the sea – it is never far away. Our 'frontier' is the coast.

This is a country where – without a hint of irony – archaeologists will argue that their work is in the national interest, and teams of these hardy practitioners appear on the *Time Team* on Channel 4, digging into the nation's anatomy in a TV slot traditionally dedicated to religious broadcasting. Bill Bryson has observed wryly that the British have more heritage than is good for them and it is easy to look on it as a kind of inexhaustible resource:

> Do you know that in my Yorkshire village alone there are more seventeenth-century buildings than in the whole of North America? And that's just one obscure hamlet with a population comfortably under one hundred.

At the heart of the British myth of the countryside is a lost rustic idyll – a simpler but ordered life. This is surprising given the realities. In 1998, the proportion of the population defined as urban dwellers stood at over 90 per cent, agriculture contributed no more than 2 per cent to GDP and employed less than 2 per cent of the labour force. However, in city pubs across the nation, 'Country Ales' wash down 'Ploughman's Lunch' and 'Shepherd's Pie', and in urban homes the British indulge in the fantasy of a bucolic social order through engaging with television and radio dramas about the countryside. One British fantasy sees the rural order threatened by murder – normally in a domestic setting, ideally involving a country house. This is the world of *Cluedo, Midsomer Murders* and series featuring the sleuths Miss Marple, Lord Peter Wimsey and Adam Dalgliesh. There are also a disproportionate number of dramas about farms, vets and market towns: *All Creatures Great and Small, Lark Rise to Candleford, The Darling Buds of May, Emmerdale* and *The Archers*. The last of these is a daily radio soap (running since 1 January 1950) that is set in and around the mythical village of Ambridge. Its theme tune, based on a maypole dance called 'Barwick Green', summons some 4.5 million 'Archers addicts' to listen to the show each day (with an omnibus edition broadcast on a Sunday). *Gardeners' Question Time*, meanwhile, has featured a panel of three experts answering questions in village halls since 1947; the triumvirate remained the same for much of that time, and when – in 1994 – the panel was given a makeover, the social fabric of the nation was briefly shaken.

Escape to the countryside is a key feature of British life, both in reality and also in fantasy: Britons drive out of their cities in their millions for weekends, bank holidays and longer holidays – 'a natural anti-depressant', the Campaign for the Protection of Rural England has called it. Yet they flee to a farmed landscape – even the most remote vectors are the product of human activity: vast tracts of marshy fenland, that had briefly protected Hereward the Wake from the Normans, were drained and cultivated by the Adventurers' Company in the seventeenth century, and the moors of Yorkshire, Cumbria and Scotland are maintained for grouse shooting.

For American author William Least Heat-Moon, 'the difference between them and us' is ultimately about British distance from the wild. Robert Macfarlane tried to find *The Wild Places* (2007) when he journeyed to remote locations in the British and Irish landscape – the summit of Ben Hope in Sutherland, the secluded valley of Loch Coruisk beneath the Cuillin of Skye, the sunken lanes of Dorset, the salt marshes of Essex. In doing so, he nursed a vision of wildness similar to the one that inspires Americans: 'somewhere boreal, wintry, vast, isolated, elemental, demanding of the traveller in its asperities. To reach a wild place was, for me, to step outside human history.' But ultimately he concedes this is a fruitless mission. No such chaste land exists in Britain or Ireland and no such myths of purity can hold.

In 1995, the British government published a White Paper entitled 'Rural England: A Nation Committed to a Living Countryside'. It lends weight to Robert Macfarlane's thesis, opening emphatically with the claim that the enduring character of England is most clearly to be found in the countryside:

> Much of what we most value in the natural scene is the product of farming – hillsides whose beauty is dependent upon grazing, water meadows which need to be used for cattle if they are to be preserved, dry stone wall, hedges and traditional buildings.

One of the surprises for Americans visiting the country is the extent to which this landscape is accessible to all, through the network of public footpaths. The reaction is nicely captured on the world wide web by Mona Sims on her Travel is Awesome website:

> The first time I saw a sign that seemed to tell me I could climb over a farmer's fence and tread through his fields, along with his cows, I was so sure I was misunderstanding things I could not bring myself to try it! Only after seeing several more of these signs, and other people taking them at face value, did I get up the nerve to try for myself. I spent the first few hours convinced someone would 'catch' me and put me in jail (or gaol) for trespass. Then I met the landowner in one place, the kind gentleman stepping quickly out of 'the way' and waiting for me to snap a few photos before hauling his load further along the path. He

didn't arrest me, didn't accost me, didn't even ask me what the blazes I thought I was doing skirting the edge of his orchard. Could this be for real?

Ms Sims is right to extol the virtues of Britain's network of public footpaths – it is a jewel in the nation's crown, and contrasts with the trespassing protocols of the US. The footpath also provides a unique way of discovering and understanding the layers of meaning that thousands of years of occupation have applied to the countryside. Britain's natural contours are drawn over, as novelist Ronald Blythe has observed, with religious symbols and references (both Christian and pre-Christian): in an old country, where everything from a hut to the kingdom itself was once placed under divine protection, there is a hidden 'holy land'.

In 'The Cicada's Wing' chapter, we saw an America speaking the language of peace while deploying massive military might overseas to protect national security and promote the key principle of the American Way – liberty. This has generated a sense of paradox, and much discussion about whether the country is or is not an imperial nation.

There are clear parallels with the military history of the UK. The English were serial empire-builders for more than 500 years: first in the British Isles, then across tracts of North America and the Caribbean, India and southeast Asia, Africa and the Pacific. At its height, just after the First World War, this empire covered a fifth of the world's surface and accommodated a quarter of its population.

England had its own 'Chosen People Syndrome', influencing – if not driving – the development of these global empires. Edward Elgar put A.C. Benson's words to music in an anthem that seems to sum up a particular pious jingoism: 'Land of Hope and Glory, mother of the Free,/How shall we extol thee, who are born of thee?/Wider still and wider shall thy bounds be set;/God who made thee mighty, make thee mightier yet.'

But the experience of the First World War had a profound impact on this worldview. It was as if a machine had been engineered to reduce the crop of several generations to compost, feeding blood and bone to the battlefields of Belgium and France. The horror of this experience largely erased the ideal of military glory for Britain: '*Dulce et Decorum est (pro patria mori)*' – the Latin phrase meaning 'It is sweet, and meet, to die for one's country' – became 'the old Lie' for poet Wilfred Owen.

The baton of world leadership is said to have passed from the British Empire to the American Republic in the middle of the Second World War. Britain has certainly travelled a long distance from the super-power that sent an expeditionary force to burn down Washington, DC, in 1814, defeated Napoleon at Waterloo in 1815 and commanded the oceans with the largest navy in the world at the end of the First World War. The United Kingdom came to define itself in the second half of the twentieth century as 'postwar' and 'post-imperial'. There were, nevertheless, some military deployments overseas in the closing decades of the last century – most notably to fight an unexpected war in the South Atlantic, countering an Argentinian invasion of the Falkland Islands in 1982; this introduced a brief revival of flag-waving patriotism.

However, the tempo changed after 9/11, when Britain embarked on military commitments in both Afghanistan and Iraq in support of multinational forces (dominated by the United States) in the ensuing 'Global War on Terror'. Prime Minister Tony Blair justified military action in Iraq by reference to those terrorist attacks on American soil:

> what galvanised me was that it was a declaration of war by religious fanatics who were prepared to wage that war without limit. They killed 3,000. But if they could have killed 30,000 or 300,000 they would have rejoiced in it.

The extent of the nation's commitment to military engage-ment is reflected in 'boots on the ground', lost lives and expenditure. Britain sent 45,000 troops to invade Iraq in 2003 (all withdrawn by August 2009) and over 8,000 troops were operating in Afghanistan in 2009. The fighting in Afghanistan has, however, been more costly, killing over 220 British soldiers (by October 2009) compared to the 179 killed in Iraq. The UK's defence budget of approximately 2.4 per cent of GDP may seem small compared with a US defence budget that was over 4 per cent (£37.5 billion compared to over $662 billion or £414 billion); but Britain is described by the Ministry of Defence as the second highest spender (in cash terms) in the world after the US, reflecting – politicians will claim – the importance and significance of Britain's international role.

There remains an honourable tradition that sees the first priority of Britain's armed services as defence of the realm. Buoyed by the refrain 'Rule Britannia, Britannia rules the waves. Britons never never never shall be slaves', the nation recognizes a military tradition that has protected its shores from invasion since 1066. The relative inaccessibility of the British Isles, and the relative inhospitality of the surrounding seas, provided the British with a sense of invulnerability which – like America – precluded the need for a standing army. There is an established narrative about a 'time-worn tradition dating back to medieval times' of young men summoned from city and countryside to fight only when a pressing need arises; then they return – as broadcasters regularly remind the nation when they cover solemn military ceremonies – to their ordinary lives as postman, milkman, ploughman or factory-hand.

As a consequence, the British public appears all too often disengaged from the fray and their cultural fabric carries little of the uplifting iconography of war that seems to inspire so many Americans. Britannia's global obligations and imperial ambitions are long past, and there does not appear to be much fire in her belly. This can lead American critics to complain about the lack of British commitment. In July 2009, for instance, Irwin Stelzer, the economist and conservative commentator, expressed views that seem to emblemize the distance between the two societies:

America has an important self-interest in a reversal of Britain's current policy of starving its military in order to fund a continued expansion of its welfare state. We are not disinterested observers . . . If Britain does not shore up its military so that it is capable of holding up its end of the bargain implicit in the special relationship, that relationship will be under severe threat. Fortunately, it is deep – culturally, socially, politically and militarily – and can endure temporary strains. But not a permanent decision by Britain to become still another free-rider on US military outlays. Both of our nations will be the poorer if the Special Relationship is no more, and the world will be a more dangerous place.

If there is any constant in the arguments advanced by champions of the Anglosphere it centres on the principles of an individual liberty and common law.

On the eve of the revolution, Edmund Burke – the great Anglo-Irish political theorist and orator – delivered an impassioned plea for reconciliation when addressing the House of Commons, focusing on a shared commitment to liberty:

England, sir, is a nation, which I still hope respects, and formerly adored her freedom. The colonists emigrated from you when this part of your character was most predominant; and they took this bias and direction the moment they parted from your hands. They are therefore not only devoted to liberty, but to liberty according to English ideas, and on English principles.

One of these principles, of course, was embedding the protection of individual's freedom in the law, and it is fitting that an early do-it-yourself book in America – published on the cusp of the revolution – was William Blackstone's *Commentaries on the Laws of England*. Some fifty years later (in 1829) a Supreme Court Justice, Joseph Story, became the first professor at Harvard Law School; he is still remembered for his genius in trawling the legacy of English casework to find usable principles to be applied to the New World. For Daniel Boorstin, American law schools like Harvard came to exert a nationalizing influence 'comparable to that which Eton and Harrow, Oxford and Cambridge long exerted on the English ruling class'. To this day, law students in these establishments use text-books like *The Anglo-American Legal Heritage*, which teach them about the Anglo-Saxon and Norman-Angevin periods of English law and the birth of the English legal profession.

However, a comparative analysis by scholars P.S. Atiyah and Robert S. Summers in 1987 revealed profound differences in the style, culture and reasoning of the American and English legal systems. American society – as we saw in 'Liberty under the Law' – regards the law as an outward expression of the community's sense of right or justice. The system is in thrall to the currents of public opinion, stemming from the grass-roots concern of the citizen: moral, economic and political factors are all taken into careful consideration. Juries are a common feature and judges are frequently chosen by a local electorate (so their judgments closely attuned, consequently to public sentiment).

In contrast, the English rules are authoritative, with the underlying notion that the law has been laid down by ancient 'sovereign' institutions. The English system is more centralized and homogeneous. Judicial independence is the cornerstone of Britain's unwritten constitution – the judge does not have to compete for the favours of an electorate and is prepared to act as a counterweight to executive authority; he (as it normally is) is disinclined to trust the people, preferring to place faith in a legal-political establishment.

Atiyah and Summers were the first to warn against reducing this analysis to caricature: we are, after all, dealing in each case with a system of common law underpinning a just society. However, the differences revealed here are incontrovertible, and the description of the English regime reflects the retrospective, hierarchical, class-based nation that has emerged earlier in this chapter. It also chimes with a chronic American complaint directed against the British approach to freedom. Britain is regularly portrayed by American libertarians as a dystopia, when compared with the Land of the Free: they rail against Britain's 'socialist' democracy and look askance at the level of taxation in the country required to pay for social security and a national health service. Others fulminate against a 'nanny state' (with fox-hunting banned, for instance, and restrictions imposed on smoking in public places) or – worse – a 'surveillance society' filled with security cameras and automatic number-plate readers. Periodically, these lines of attack merge, as in August 2009 when novelist Jeff Perren (from Sandpoint, Idaho) mourned the arrival of 'Nanny State Fascism', writing in his 'Shaving Leviathan' blog:

> It's a commonplace – and well-founded – truth that social/political trends in the UK often become mainstream in the US a generation later. It's with great trepidation, even horror, therefore that I feel obligated to highlight a recent news story in the Daily Express. It outlines a not-entirely-new program for the government to place cameras inside private homes to monitor the inhabitants. These are not criminals, but parents who may or may not, according to the government, be treating their children properly. . . . The pols are concerned that the children are not eating right, going to bed on time, not being given the proper lessons in values, and so forth.

In the same month, Americans across the political spectrum expressed views ranging from disbelief to outrage at the release – on compassionate grounds – of the 'Lockerbie Bomber' by Scotland's justice minister. This emblemized the gulf in attitudes towards crime and punishment in the two societies. For instance, the conservative blog 'Red Maryland' contained a reflection by Professor Richard E. Vatz (a teacher of political rhetoric at Towson University) that opened as follows:

> It is the second most horrible nightmare – just after the obscenity of mass murder itself – of everyone who distrusts

weak and flabby criminal justice systems: the unqualified releasing of a mass murderer. That murderer was Abdel Baset al-Megrahi, the only man convicted of the 1988 bombing and murder of 259 airplane passengers, whose provocation was to be flying on Pan Am Flight 103, and 11 innocents on the ground, whose provocation was equally absent.

This prompted the following response on the website from Bruce: 'I have no problem with the return of this man to Libya. None whatsoever. My problem is that the Scottish government lacked the power to execute him and allow the corpse to assume ambient room temperature before the shipment out.'

However, an alternative American account reveals a very different British society. This view is more often than not rehearsed by that inconstant breed of American who has chosen to settle in Britain. There are approximately 150,000 of these, and it could be argued we are veering off from the mainstream American viewpoint to address the views of heretics who grasp at any argument to justify the betrayal of their homeland. But their message is quite clear: liberty has a distinctive quality in Britain; specifically, 'difference' is better tolerated than in the United States.

Tracy Abrusci, for instance, a nurse and single mother from Chicago who has settled in Birmingham, and who aired the following views in an article by journalist Richard Tomkins in the *Financial Times* in April 2006:

Where I lived in the States I was often made to feel uncomfortable about being divorced with children. Here I feel it's much more acceptable. And gay issues are really bad in the States. The other thing people don't understand is that there's a very clear line between black and white. For instance, my sister is married to a black man and there's only certain places they can live because they would fear for violence against them. I can't see that happening here in such a violent manner.

In the same article, Sean Aaron, an IT consultant who moved from California to Stirling in Scotland with his wife Michelle, says one thing he likes about Britain is the way diverse views are tolerated. If anyone revealed communist leanings in the US, he says, people would call them insane:

But here it is like, hey, you can have the Scottish Socialist party calling for Scotland to become a socialist republic and they have six seats in the Scottish parliament. Regardless of what you might think about the Scottish Socialist party I think that says a great deal about tolerance and diversity of viewpoint. I find it very reassuring.

The individual experiences of Tracy and Sean chime with the findings of Louis Hartz, the American political scientist. In a number of works published in the mid-twentieth century, he compared the fixed dogmatic liberalism of the US with the British variety, which exhibits 'a marvellous organic cohesion [that] has held together the feudal, liberal and socialist ideas':

Freedom in the fullest sense implies both variety and equality; but history, for reasons of its own, chose to separate these two principles, leaving the one with the old society of Burke and giving the other to the new society of Paine ... A society like England, in the very midst of its ramshackle class-ridden atmosphere, seems to contain an indefinable germ of liberty, a respect for the privacies of life, that America cannot duplicate. At the bottom of the American experience of freedom ... there has always lain the inarticulate premise of conformity.

We are dealing with matters of degree, here, but the people occupying a crowded archipelago on the edge of Europe have – through centuries of interaction between competing cultures and ideologies – established the conditions to accommodate what the American philosopher, John Rawls, called an 'overlapping consensus'. Liberty has inevitably evolved under different conditions in the US, where the open skies of a seemingly boundless land encouraged the idea that the independent spirit is sovereign: if the community accepts your lifestyle, that's fine; if not, move on and create a community of your own.

The British brand of liberty has also had to cope with the iniquities of a deeply entrenched property class. Compared, at least, to the American blueprint, there is far less equality of opportunity in Britain; so the impulse to create a fairer, more just society has focused on redistributing wealth and opening up opportunities. This has developed a reflex in the British 'body politic' that has never taken root in the US. It is found in the tenets of Chartism, the Cooperative Movement, the Fabians and the Labour Movement. The American challenge has been to achieve equality of difference – hence the strong Civil Rights tradition and the EEO machine.

In seeking some philosophical reference point to anchor our understanding, we can turn to John Rawls' teacher, Isaiah Berlin. In 1958, he gave his inaugural lecture as professor of social and political theory at Oxford University. His paper, entitled 'Two Concepts of Liberty', drew a distinction between a 'negative' liberty that seeks to curb authority and provide the individual with freedom from the coercion of other men; and a 'positive' view that is self-directive, giving an individual the freedom to be his own master and to participate in a chosen way of life.

It is tempting to argue that the positive ideal is in the ascendancy in the US; whereas in Britain, the vision of negative liberty seems to predominate. Each society cherishes its form of freedom, but in each case liberty has its limitations: Britain may have incorporated equality of difference into its national narrative, but it sustains a social structure that struggles to offer opportunities to all. Americans may speak of equality of opportunity, but we have seen that the spirit of individualized liberty brings unfortunate, unintended consequences of its own. Each society, in its own way and according to its own unique circumstances, seeks to reconcile liberty, equality and justice. Each fails, but the consequences – the afflictions of liberty –

seem especially acute in a society like America which gives liberty such a dominant status in its national narrative.

It would be irrational to deny the existence of an Anglo-Saxon consciousness, shared between the United Kingdom and the United States. The lineaments are present in a common language and the common law; in long-cherished values of freedom and independence that bring an aversion to authority; and in folk traditions carried westwards by thousands of migrants in America's formative years and embedded into the practices of everyday life.

However, just as language is transformed over time under the influence of 'pull-chain' or 'push-chain' effects, 'drift' and 'analogy', so cultures also shift and change. The UK can appear to be in transition – an American 'mini-me' – with the statistical data showing it to mediate between the US and Continental Europe in such diverse metrics as prison population, fiscal measures, teenage pregnancies, shelf-space, charitable giving, Nobel Prizes and levels of innovation. Yet our analysis has shown there to be little commonality between the set of American paradoxes examined in this book and Britain's contemporary culture. It has become apparent that *The Cracked Bell* is not addressing an Anglo-Saxon syndrome: the features described here are further evidence for the exceptionalism of the American Way.

Countless effects, many imperceptible, cause a culture to adapt and adjust. Analysts can point, for instance, to the mix of racial, ethnic and cultural traits that have shaped the American Way; also to environmental features such as geography, climate and the availability of natural resources; and to the political economy. However, the suite of paradoxes examined in these pages has exposed a particular grain of grit in the American oyster: the inflated, extravagant, nationalistic ideal of the independent, liberated individual.

It is this ideal of the liberated individual within an atomistic social order – this hyper-individualism – that distinguishes the US from its Anglo-Saxon cousin across the Atlantic. This ideal may derive from the British Isles – a cultural seed blown across the Atlantic to lodge in American soil – but it has acquired distinctive characteristics of its own. This was, for Louis Hartz, 'the secret root from which have sprung many of the most puzzling of American cultural phenomena'.

It is certain that cultural exchanges across the Atlantic will continue, in both directions. It can also be assumed that voices will be heard, in both the Old World and the New, bemoaning the consequences. This is, nevertheless, a creative tension full of potential and promise, and it is even possible to imagine a reconfiguration of American and British ways, with two different traditions of liberty synthesized to create conditions – in each nation – for a more just and equitable society.

In this spirit, it seems fitting to follow the path taken by our Anglophile lawyer to that recital of *A Sea Symphony* in May 2004. This work matches the visionary verses of Walt Whitman with the music of Ralph Vaughan Williams – a great Anglo-American production, a transcendent, universal work, which ranges across such varied themes as exploration and innovation, the movement of ships across the surging sea, the meaning of progress and the Second Coming. The symphony also includes words, sung that night by the black baritone Gordon Hawkins, that express an equation – a unity of being – that extends far beyond the narrow confines of any Anglosphere:

On the beach at night alone,
As the old mother sways to and fro singing her husky song,
As I watch the bright stars shining, I think a thought of the
     clef of the universes and of the future.
A vast similitude interlocks all,
All distances of place however wide, all distances of time,
All souls, all living bodies though they be ever so different,
All nations, all identities that have existed or may exist,
All lives and deaths, all of the past, present, future,
This vast similitude spans them, and always has spanned,
And shall forever span them and compactly hold and
     enclose them.

Beyond Hobbes and Hobbits

The bell from Liberty Hall is cracked, and chimes with a hollow dissonance.

We have someone to blame for the fracture in the Liberty Bell. In 1911, Emmanuel Joseph Rauch admitted to the *New York Times* that he, as a boy, had been tugging at the rope attached to the clapper on that day in 1846 when the bell cracked.

It is not so simple, however, to ascribe blame for the afflictions of liberty described in this book. In all likelihood, the fault was there from the very beginning, when the germ of freedom crossed the Atlantic, embedded within the aspirations and dreams of countless millions fleeing the oppression of the Old World. The flaw, indeed, is probably a feature of our humanity, with the United States – that great experiment in political science – providing the conditions to amplify and expose it.

I find it instructive – even ironic – that a century before the Liberty Bell arrived in Pennsylvania, the English philosopher Thomas Hobbes had chosen America to emblemize the state of what he termed natural liberty. The title-page of his masterpiece – *De Cive* – contains an allegorical image of 'Libertas' depicted as an Indian squaw with longbow and arrow. (The picture was adapted from a 1580s drawing, by John White, of an Algonquian chieftain.) Behind this frowning Liberty – so different to the benign, solemn gaze of New York Harbor's beloved statue – three near-naked men chase two others, while a fourth predator stands in ambush, with club poised to strike. Nearby, two figures squat by a trestle-larder that looks to be stocked with a dismembered limb. This is a dystopian vision where every man upholds the right to everything: liberation is a synonym for lawlessness, and for Hobbes the only logical outcome was war – a condition of unending hostility in which, ultimately, 'nature itself is destroyed'.

In my darker moments, I envisage an America under the sway of Hobbes' Libertas. Hobbesville USA is a frontier town, or an urban jungle like Liberty City in *Grand Theft Auto*. The radical spirit of the liberated individual is in the vanguard, with the emphasis on licence rather than liberty. There is intolerance and violence: conflict between and within ethnic groups; tension between classes of have-mores and have-nots. Hobbesville is radioactive with the fallout from rampant consumerism: debt, obesity, instant gratification, egoism and mindless disregard for finite natural resources. There is 'culture war' between religious and secular seekers after personal salvation, with charges of sinfulness exchanged between those who argue over the competing merits of the Second Coming and the Second Helping. Political grafters and corrupt lawyers are in the ascendant, and a strong police arm is available to the highest payer.

This is, I realize, a bad dream. Hobbes himself advocated the need for a social contract where the worst excesses of Libertas were contained by justice and good government; and the Founding Fathers were convinced that a society could be established in the New World that achieved the perfect balance between freedom and order, liberation and regulation. There are, indeed, moments of optimism when America appears to me as the idealized community of Hobbiton rather than Hobbesville. This archetype derives from the fantastical vision of J.R.R. Tolkien, who wrote of the Hobbits of Middle Earth:

In that pleasant corner of the world they plied their well-ordered business of living and they heeded less and less the world outside where dark things moved, until they came to think that peace and plenty were the rule in Middle-Earth and the right of all sensible folk.

Tolkien's inspiration came from the same utopian portrayal of early Saxon tribes that had sparked Jefferson's imagination. His creatures maintain a voluntary, ordered society where the sense of fellowship is strong and where government is small. They have an elected mayor who presides over a postal service and a small police force whose principal function is to round up stray livestock. There are rules, but all Hobbits obey them because they are just, and the few lawyers in the land are there to ensure that wills and contracts are drawn up in good order. There is also an underlying sense of destiny about this community – a feeling that the fruits of the land are evidence of a God-given Providence.

There is a piece of Hobbiton meshed into all but the most dysfunctional communities of the US, not least in the suburbs that harbour the bulk of the nation's population. The inhabitants of Hobbiton USA wrap themselves in a reassuring quilt of custom and ritual, material possessions and voluntary associations. Comfort and contentment come from a sense of consensus in common observances: the give and take of commerce in the mall; the uplifting quality of church rites; shared moments before the flickering flames of the television; the spectacular theatricality of myths narrated in the cinema or played out in computer games; the ritualized battles of baseball stadium, football field and NASCAR track; the drama and humour of parochial news; the cycle of the years marked out with Labor Day and Memorial Day, Thanksgiving and Halloween. A sense of solidarity comes from family and congregation, college fraternity and labour union, and just from being in the PTA or on the company's team. The residents of Hobbiton USA have little doubt that they are a chosen people and presume that the rest of the world wants to become like them.

However, in the opening decade of the twenty-first century the social cohesiveness of Hobbiton is undercut by the hyper-individualism of Hobbesville, creating a deep sense of insecurity about personal and national identity. Myth must inevitably crash against reality; aspiration fails to conform to expectation. This is the cultural equivalent to geological compression and contraction, creating a social topography that is confusing, threatening, even dangerous, for those who live on the slopes of the volcano.

If the spirit of freedom inspires the American Dream, the ghost of freedom infects the American Crisis, threatening to turn the dream into a nightmare. It may be simplistic to describe this syndrome as pathological, but Louis Hartz spoke of a 'psychic inflation' in describing how a fragment of English liberalism became isolated and subjected to metamorphosis in the decades after the revolution. There is resonance, here, with the Jungian concept of the 'inflated' neurotic who believes that an idealized image is the real self. This condition may not be contagious, but its damaging consequences extend beyond the borders of the fifty American states.

A fixation with consumption threatens to upset the ecological wellbeing of the whole planet as well as creating social, physiological and psychological problems at home. Many of the difficulties that the world is facing could be addressed by the bountiful marvels of American innovation but the pernicious presence of power-blocs in the country must inevitably suppress that spirit of invention. American ideas of liberty and 'chosen-ness' – reinforced by mythical notions of salvation and the frontier – underpin a subliminal logic of imperialism: if Everyman can enjoy the bounty of American individualism, Anyman who obstructs this pursuit of happiness stands in the path of progress and deserves to be thrown down.

I learnt from one wise old American – still operating at the heart of government after taking up his appointment thirty-five years ago – that it is best to focus on diagnosis and leave the therapy to others. For his part, the Swiss psychiatrist Carl Jung recommended that psychic inflation could be overcome only through patience, humility and self-analysis, and the reality is that legions of American citizens worry about the state of their nation, practising the very qualities that Jung espoused.

President Barack Obama is uniquely placed to apply balm to

the afflictions of liberty. He came to power on a tidal surge of good will and high hopes. Turnout in the 2008 election – at just under 63 per cent – has been bettered in the last fifty years only by the figure of 64 per cent in 1960, when John F. Kennedy beat Richard Nixon. He received multiracial support, with 95 per cent of blacks, 66 per cent of Hispanics and 43 per cent of whites supporting his ticket; and 66 per cent of all voters aged under thirty opted for Obama. The atmosphere that Obama conjured up during his campaign is evoked by the following commentary from one of those voices encountered earlier in *The Cracked Bell*. In the chapter called 'The Many and the One', David Giles described his experience of segregation in 1940s Virginia; and in 'The Lattice Constant' he extolled the entrepreneurial opportunities of America today. Now aged over seventy, he attended an Obama rally at Prince William County Fairground in Virginia, two days before the 2008 election:

What a spectacle! A boundless sea of arc-lit faces, amplifiers blasting out Soul Choirs and Bruce Springsteen – something between a rock concert and a Pentecostal-revivalist meeting. A huge American flag and illuminated signs proclaiming VOTE FOR CHANGE; a barrage balloon floating overhead advertising 'Boilermakers for Change', large yellow signs saying 'Fire-fighters for Obama'; everywhere the name and logo of Obama – on babies' caps and Dads' caps, on every coat and hat and T-shirt. And what a crowd: patient, cheerful, expectant, young and multiracial. The average age was 25–30; 60% black, 20% Hispanic, and 20% white. Young people were lending coats to old – it was a clear chilly night – everyone was swapping stories and Obama anecdotes. There was a huge cheer as Barack arrived. I've never felt such a surge of emotion, enthusiasm and hope. He spoke with ringing, almost religious conviction and confidence. As his slim figure reached the podium and he saw the huge crowd, a youthful sonorous voice rang out over the field: 'Wow . . . and this is Virginia . . . where the Union truly started: here at the first battle of

the Civil War, at Manassas.' And that was his main theme
– that the people before him were not black, nor white, nor
Hispanic; nor 'real-American' nor 'part-American', nor
Muslim nor Christian nor Hindu nor Jewish, nor 'red', nor
'blue' – but *American*. His soaring eloquence is extraordinary – a voice that cannot be connected with any race or
state or territory. It seems to represent the voice and hopes
of thinking Americans.

As an anthropologist, I am sceptical about the ability of one
individual to change culture. Memetic engineering (the process
of controlling social and cultural beliefs) is no easier than the
genetic variety. Obama's battle-cry in his 2008 campaign may
have been 'Change We Need', but we have seen in 'The Lattice
Constant' chapter how the language of innovation and transformation can carry a symbolic power in American society that
does not accord with reality. There is a risk that his aspirations
come to be seen as the Audacity of Hype: this word-play
was deployed by Obama's opponents during the election, and
The Audacity of Hype became the title of an album by the former
punk-rocker Jello Biafra, who was already expressing unease by
August 2009 that Obama would renege on his promises.
Meanwhile, conservative authors like Mark R. Levin and
Bernard Goldberg have gone to print attacking Obama's 'Statist'
tendencies. The lesson that a pessimist would draw from history
is that economic depression at home and political turmoil
abroad tend to reinforce rather than resolve anti-social,
protectionist and xenophobic traits within society.
     Nevertheless, Obama is well suited to the role of one striving
to 'perfect an imperfect union'. His mixed-race parentage gives
substance to his faith in America's ability to forge a national
identity from disparate tribes and races. He acquired a political
philosophy from his mother that was grounded in notions of
community and justice; and it was in search of a practical
application of her values that he worked as a community
organizer in Chicago, operating in deprived communities where
unemployment, drugs and a sense of hopelessness prevailed. He

combines years of teaching US constitutional law with the practical experience of seeking votes from low-income neighbourhoods. He recognizes a cynicism in the country about politics but his agenda is based on the idea that fellow citizens have a stake in one another, and that what binds them together is greater than what drives them apart.

This has led the Forty-Fourth President to understand the potentially unstable balance between freedom and the common good, between Hobbesville and Hobbiton. He has written:

> In every society (and in every individual) these twin strands – the individualistic and the communal, autonomy and solidarity – are in tension . . . At times these values collide because in the hands of men each one is subject to distortion and excess. Self-reliance and independence can transform into selfishness and license, ambition into greed and a frantic desire to succeed at any cost.

Finding the right balance between competing values is difficult in a free society like the United States, he argues, because we live inherently in a complex and contradictory world.

People once spoke of President John F. Kennedy as King Arthur in Camelot. If Obama succeeds in rebooting the American Dream, future generations could come to regard him as a latter-day Alfred the Great, forging a true commonwealth from the fragments. As with King Alfred, philosophy, art and literature can provide Obama with a touchstone to express the alchemy of re-evaluation and self-renewal. He could turn, for instance, to the work of the American whose words closed the last chapter: Walt Whitman voiced a humanistic synthesis of liberty and justice that is closer to the moral code of the Enlightenment than to the rugged individualism that has dominated the narrative for the past hundred years. Or he could celebrate the musical genres of jazz and blues that represent a fused, syncretized, American identity; or champion the work of a living poet like Maya Angelou, who recited 'Still I Rise' so beautifully on national television the day after the 2008 election.

President Obama could also profit from the profound insights of an American philosopher who died at the beginning of the new millennium. In works like *A Theory of Justice*, *Political Liberalism* and *The Law of Peoples*, John Rawls constructed the foundations of a 'realistic utopia', seeking a better balance between liberty and justice. For Rawls, 'Justice is the first virtue of social institutions, as truth is of systems of thought.'

There already exist then, in America, sources of illumination that can light the way to a world beyond that of Hobbes and Hobbits. The nation can overcome the American Crisis and reclaim the American Dream.

The cracked bell can be re-cast.

BIBLIOGRAPHY

Suggestions for Further Reading

Introduction: The American Crisis and the American Dream

Alsop, George (1666) *A Character of the Province of Maryland*, London

Crèvecoeur, J. Hector St John (1908) *Letters from an American Farmer*, London: Chatto & Windus; New York, NY: Duffield & Co.

Enriquez, Juan (2005) *The Untied States of America: Polarization Fracturing and Our Future*, New York, NY: Crown Publishers

Geuss, Raymond, and Hollis, Martin (1995) 'Freedom as an Ideal', in *Proceedings of the Aristotelian Society, Supplementary Volumes*, vol. 69, pp. 87–112

Gorer, Geoffrey (1948) *The Americans: A Study in National Character*, London: Cresset Press

Harriot, Thomas (1588) *A Brief and True Report of the New Found Land of Virginia*, London

Hartz, Louis (1955) *The Liberal Tradition in America: An Interpretation of American Political Thought since the Revolution*, New York, NY: Harcourt, Brace

Hartz, Louis (1964) *The Founding of New Societies*, New York, NY: Harcourt, Brace and World

Hook, Sidney (1962) *The Paradoxes of Freedom*, Berkeley, CA: University of California Press

Kammen, Michael (1972) *People of Paradox: An Inquiry Concerning the Origins of American Civilization*, New York, NY: Alfred A. Knopf

Leach, Edmund (1982) *Social Anthropology*, Oxford: Oxford University Press

Maritain, Jacques (1958) *Reflections on America*, New York, NY: Charles Scribner's Sons

National Commission on Terrorist Attacks upon the United States (2004) *The 9/11 Commission Report*, New York, NY, & London: W.W. Norton & Co.

Niebuhr, Reinhold (1952) *The Irony of American History*, New York, NY: Charles Scribner's Sons

Obama, Barack (2008) *The Audacity of Hope: Thoughts on Reclaiming the American Dream*, Edinburgh: Canongate Books

Paine, Thomas (1999) *The American Crisis, Number 1*, Philadelphia, PA: Independence Historical National Park

Patterson, James T. (1996) *Grand Expectations: The United States 1945–1974*, Oxford: Oxford University Press

Patterson, James T. (2005) *Restless Giant: The United States from Watergate to Bush v Gore*, Oxford: Oxford University Press

Pynchon, Thomas (1973) *Gravity's Rainbow*, New York, NY: Viking Press

Smith, John (1608) *True Relation of Occurrences and Accidents in Virginia*, London

Smith, John (1624) *The Generall Historie of Virginia, New England & The Summer Isles*, London

Tocqueville, Alexis de (1994) *Democracy in America*, London: David Campbell

Wills, Garry (1978) *Inventing America: Jefferson's Declaration of Independence*, Garden City, NY: Doubleday

Zinn, Howard (2003) *A People's History of the United States: 1492–Present*, London: HarperCollins

Chapter 1: The Many and the One – On Identity

Barth, Fredrik (1969) *Ethnic Groups and Boundaries: The Social Organization of Cultural Difference*, London: Allen & Unwin

Blair, Jayson (2004) *Burning Down My Masters' House*, New York, NY: New Millennium Press

Confederation of American Indians (1986) *Indian Reservations. A State and Federal Handbook*, Jefferson, NC: McFarland

Cruz, José E. (1998) *Identity and Power: Puerto Rican Politics and the Challenge of Ethnicity*, Philadelphia, PA: Temple University Press

Dawson, Michael (2001) *Black Visions: The Roots of Contemporary African-American Political Ideologies*, Chicago, IL: University of Chicago Press

De Beaumont, Gustave (1835) *Marie, ou l'Esclavage aux États-Unis*, Paris: Charles Gosselin

Dickerson, Debra (2004) *The End of Blackness: Returning the Souls of Black Folks to Their Rightful Owners*, New York, NY: Pantheon

Du Bois, W.E.B. (1905) *The Souls of Black Folk*, London: Archibald Constable & Co.

Frantz, Klaus (1993) *Indian Reservations in the US*, Chicago, IL: University of Chicago Press

Garcia, Alma M. (2002) *The Mexican Americans*, London: Greenwood Press

Goldberg, Myla (2001) *Bee Season*, New York, NY: Anchor Books

Gordon, Dexter B. (2003) *Black Identity: Rhetoric, Ideology and 19th Century Black Nationalism*, Carbondale, IL: Southern Illinois University Press

Huntington, Samuel (2004) *Who Are We?*, London: Simon & Schuster

Loury, Glenn C. (2002) *The Anatomy of Racial Inequality*, Cambridge, MA: Harvard University Press

Melville, Herman (1971) *The Confidence-Man: His Masquerade*, London & New York, NY: W.W. Norton

O'Brien, Sharon (1989) *American Indian Tribal Governments*, Norman, OK: University of Oklahoma Press

Porter, Harry (1979) *The Inconstant Savage: England and the North American Indian 1500–1660*, London: Duckworth

Roosevelt, Theodore (1889–96) *The Winning of the West*, vols 1–4, New York, NY: G.P. Putnam's Sons

Schlesinger, Arthur (1998) *The Disuniting of America: Reflections on a Multicultural Society*, London & New York, NY: W.W. Norton

Sen, Amartya (2006) *Identity and Violence: The Illusion of Destiny*, London: Allen Lane

Smith, Claire (2005) 'Decolonising the Museum: The National Museum of the American Indian in Washington DC', in *Antiquity*, vol. 79, no. 304, June, pp. 424–39

Somkin, Fred (1967) *Unquiet Eagle. Memory and Desire in the Idea of American Freedom. 1815–1860*, Ithaca, NY: Cornell University Press

Tolzmann, Don Heinrich (1975) *German-Americana: A Bibliography*, Metuchen, NJ: Scarecrow Press

Tolzmann, Don Heinrich (2000) *The German-American Experience*, Amherst, MA, & New York, NY: Prometheus Books

Turner, Frederick Jackson (1893) 'The Significance of the Frontier in American History', in *Report of the American Historical Association for 1893*, Washington, DC: American Historical Association, pp. 199–227

Utter, Jack (2001) *American Indians. Answers to Today's Questions* (2nd edition), Norman, OK: University of Oklahoma Press

Vigil, James Diego (2002) *A Rainbow of Gangs: Street Cultures in the Mega-City*, Austin, TX: University of Texas Press

Zangwill, Israel (1915) *The Melting Pot*, New York, NY: Macmillan

Chapter 2: The Temple of Trade – On Consumerism

Bryson, Bill (1996) *Made in America: An Informal History of the English Language in the United States*, New York, NY: HarperCollins

Butterfield, Steve (1985) *Amway: The Cult of Free Enterprise*, Boston, MA: South End Press

Castronova, Edward (2004) 'The Price of Bodies: A Hedonic Pricing Model of Avatar Attributes in a Synthetic World', in *Kyklos*, vol. 57, no. 2, pp. 173–96

Cross, Gary S. (2000) *An All-Consuming Century: Why Commercialism Won in Modern America*, New York, NY: Columbia University Press

De Grazia, Victoria (2005) *Irresistible Empire: America's Advance through 20th Century Europe*, Cambridge, MA: Belknap Press of Harvard University Press

Douglas, Mary and Isherwood, Baron (1979) *The World of Goods. Towards an Anthropology of Consumption*, London: Allen Lane

Farrell, James J. (2003) *One Nation Under Goods: Malls and the Seductions of American Shopping*, Washington, DC, & London: Smithsonian Books

Friedman, Walter A. (2005) *Birth of a Salesman: The Transformation of Selling in America*, Cambridge, MA: Harvard University Press

Galbraith, J.K. (1958) *The Affluent Society*, London: Hamish Hamilton

Greider, William (2004) *The Soul of Capitalism: Opening Paths to a Moral Economy*, New York, NY: Schuster

Heinze, Andrew R. (1990) *Adapting to Abundance; Jewish Immigrants, Mass Consumption, and the Search for American Identity*, New York, NY: Columbia University Press

Hertslet, Evelyn (1886) *Ranch Life in California: Extracted from the Home Correspondence of E.M.H.*, London: W.H. Allen

Houthakker, H.S. and Taylor, Lester D. (1970) *Consumer Demand in the United States: Analyses & Projections* (2nd edition), Cambridge, MA: Harvard University Press

Kenny, Michael G. (1994) *The Perfect Law of Liberty: Elias Smith and the Providential History of America*, Washington, DC: Smithsonian Institution Press

Klein, Naomi (2001) *No Logo: No Space, No Choice, No Jobs*, London: Flamingo

Moseley, James G. (1992) *John Winthrop's World*, Madison, WI: University of Wisconsin Press

Noll, Mark A. (ed.) (2002) *God and Mammon: Protestants, Money and the Market 1790–1860*, New York, NY: Oxford University Press

Norton, Edgar (1987) 'Is Capitalism Christian?', in *Liberty Report*, Oct.

Piper, John Stephen (1986) *Desiring God: Meditations of a Christian Hedonist*, Sisters, OR: Multnomah Publishers, Inc.

Potter, David M. (1954) *People of Plenty: Economic Abundance and the American Character*, Chicago, IL: University of Chicago Press

Sellers, Charles (1991) *The Market Revolution: Jacksonian America 1815–1846*, New York, NY: Oxford University Press

Weber, Max (1976) *The Protestant Ethic and the Spirit of Capitalism*, London: Allen & Unwin

Woods, Thomas E. (2005) *The Church and the Market: A Catholic Defense of the Free Economy*, Lanham, MD: Lexington Books

Chapter 3: Trick or Treat – On Belief

Ahlstrom, Sydney (1974) *A Religious History of the American People*, New Haven, CT: Yale University Press

Berger, Peter L. (1967) *Sacred Canopy: Elements of a Sociological Theory of Religion*, New York, NY: Anchor

Berger, Peter L. (1970) *A Rumour of Angels: Modern Society and the Rediscovery of the Supernatural*, Harmondsworth: Penguin

Berger, Peter L. (1977) *Facing Up to Modernity*, New York, NY: Basic Books

Berger, Peter L. (ed.) (1999) *The Desecularization of the World: Resurgent Religion and World Politics*, Washington, DC: Ethics and Public Policy Center

Brewer, Priscilla J. (1986) *Shaker Communities, Shaker Lives*, Lebanon, NH: University Press of New England

Chapman, Matthew (2000) *Trials of the Monkey*, London: Duckworth

Cleaver, Eldridge (1979) *Soul on Fire*, London: Hodder & Stoughton

Conrad, Mark T. (2003) 'Pulp Fiction: The Sign of the Empty Symbol: The Death of God and the Royale with Cheese', www.metaphilm.com (posted 29 August 2003)

Cooke, George Willis (1903) *Unitarianism in America*, Boston, MA: American Unitarian Association

Dallimore, Arnold (1970) *George Whitefield*, Edinburgh: Banner of Truth Trust

Demos, John Putnam (ed.) (1972) *Remarkable Providences: 1600–1760*, New York, NY: George Braziller

Demos, John Putnam (1982) *Entertaining Satan. Witchcraft and the Culture of Early New England*, Oxford: Oxford University Press

France, David (2004) *Our Father: The Secret Life of the Catholic Church in an Age of Scandal*, New York, NY: Broadway Books

Gaustad, Edwin S. and Schmidt, Leigh E. (1996) *The Religious History of America*, San Francisco, CA: Harpers

Gilbert, James (1997) *Redeeming Culture: American Religion in an Age of Science*, Chicago, IL: University of Chicago Press

Hudson, Winthrop S. (1965) *Religion in America*, New York, NY: Charles Scribner's Sons

Israel, Charles A. (2004) *Before Scopes. Evangelicalism, Education and Evolution in Tennessee 1870–1925*, Athens, GA: University of Georgia Press

Jenkins, Jerry B. and LaHaye, Tim (1996–2007) *Left Behind Series* (13 vols), Carol Stream, IL: Tyndale House Publishers

Jorstad, Erling (1993) *Popular Religion in America: The Evangelical Voice*, Westport, CT: Greenwood Press

Kahn, Herman and Wiener, Anthony (1967) *The Year 2000 – A Framework for Speculation on the Next Thirty-Three Years*, New York, NY: Macmillan

Kennedy, D. James and Black, Jim Nelson (1994) *Character and Destiny: A Nation in Search of Its Soul*, Grand Rapids, MI: Zondervan

Lindsey, Hal (1973) *The Late Great Planet Earth*, New York, NY: Bantam Books

Marsden, George M. (1991) *Understanding Fundamentalism and Evangelicalism*, Grand Rapids, MI: W.B. Eerdmans

Marsden, George M. (2006) *Fundamentalism and American Culture*, Oxford: Oxford University Press

Mather, Cotton (1693) *Wonders of the Invisible World: Observations as well Historical as Theological, upon the Nature, the Number and the Operations of the Devils*, Boston, MA: Benjamin Harris

McCarthy, Cormac (2006) *The Road*, New York, NY: Alfred A. Knopf

McDannell, Colleen (ed.) (2001) *Religions of the United States in Practice*, Princeton, NJ: Princeton University Press

Miller, Perry (1953) *The New England Mind: From Colony to Province*, Cambridge, MA: Harvard University Press

Peretti, Frank (1989) *This Present Darkness*, Eastbourne: Minstrel

Pew Research Centre Pollwatch (2005) 'Reading the Polls on Evolution and Creationism', Pew Research Centre Press Release, 28 September

Pollock, John Charles (1966) *Billy Graham. The Authorised Biography*, London: Hodder & Stoughton

Schaeffer, Francis A. (1982) *A Christian Manifesto*, Basingstoke: Pickering & Inglis

Stowell, Daniel W. (1988) *Rebuilding Zion: The Religious Reconstruction of the South 1863–1877*, Oxford: Oxford University Press

Tipton, Steven M. (1982) *Getting Saved from the Sixties: Moral Meaning in Conversion and Cultural Change*, Berkeley, CA: University of California Press

Van Allen, Rodger (ed.) (1978) *American Religious Values and the Future of America*, Philadelphia, PA: Fortress Press

Warren, Rick (1995) *The Purpose Driven Church*, Grand Rapids, MI: Zondervan

Warren, Rick (2002) *The Purpose Driven Life*, Grand Rapids, MI: Zondervan

Williams, Sally (2007) 'The God Curriculum', in *Daily Telegraph* magazine, 7 April

Wilson, Charles Reagan (1980) *Baptized in Blood: The Religion of the Lost Cause*, Athens, GA: University of Georgia Press

Wuthnow, Robert (1988) 'Divided We Fall: America's Two Civil Religions', in *Christian Century*, 20 April

Yurica, Katherine (2004) 'The Despoiling of America: How George W. Bush Became the Head of the New American Dominionist Church/State', published on www.yuricareport.com on 11 Feb. 2004

Chapter 4: The Lattice Constant – On Innovation and Enervation

Allison, Kevin (2007) 'Man in the News: Mark Zuckerberg', in *Financial Times*, 29 September

Angel, David P. (1994) *Restructuring for Innovation: The Remaking of the U.S. Semiconductor Industry*, New York, NY: Guilford Press

Arendt, Hannah (1969) *On Violence*, New York, NY: Harcourt, Brace and World

Barnett, H.G. (1953) *Innovation: The Basis of Cultural Change*, New York, NY: McGraw-Hill

Boorstin, Daniel (1974) *The Americans: The Democratic Experience* (Part Nine 'Search for Novelty'), New York, NY: Vintage

Brzezinski, Zbigniew, and Huntington, Samuel (1963) *Political Power: USA/USSR*, New York, NY: Viking

Chubb, John E. and Peterson, Paul E. (eds) (1989) *Can the Government Govern?*, Washington, DC: Brookings

De Graaf, John, Wann, David and Naylor, Thomas H. (2002) *Affluenza: The All-Consuming Epidemic*, San Francisco, CA: Berrett-Koehler Publishers

DeSantis, Alan D. (2007) *Inside Greek U.: Fraternities, Sororities and the Pursuit of Pleasure, Power and Prestige*, Lexington, KY: University Press of Kentucky

Erikson, Erik (1963) *Childhood and Society*, New York, NY: W.W. Norton

Evangelista, Matthew (1988) *Innovation and the Arms Race: How the United States and the Soviet Union Develop New Military Technology*, Ithaca, NY: Cornell University Press

Evans, Harold (2004) *They Made America. From the Steam Engine to the Search Engine: Two Centuries of Innovators*, New York, NY: Little, Brown

Ewing Marion Kauffman Foundation (2006) *Kauffman Index of Entrepreneurial Activity 1996–2005*, Kansas City, MO: Ewing Marion Kauffman Foundation

Gardner, John W. (1963) *Self-Renewal*, New York, NY: W.W. Norton

Gilfillan, S. Colum (1952) 'The Prediction of Change', in *The Review of Economics and Statistics*, Nov., pp. 368–85

Guerrera, Francesco, Reed, John, and Simon, Bernard (2007) 'Drama in Dearborn', in *Financial Times*, 29 October

Hawthorne, Nathaniel (1981) *The House of the Seven Gables*, New York, NY: Bantam

Hughes, Thomas P. (2004) *Human-Built World: How to Think about Technology and Culture*, Chicago, IL: University of Chicago Press

James, Oliver (2008) *Affluenza*, London: Vermilion

Kelley, Tom (2006) *The Ten Faces of Innovation: Strategies for Heightening Creativity*, London: Profile

La Fontaine, Jean S. (1986) *Initiation*, Manchester: Manchester University Press

Lukes, Steven (1974) *Power: A Radical View*, London & New York, NY: Macmillan

Makinson, Larry and Goldstein, Joshua (1994) *Open Secrets: The Encyclopedia of Congressional Money and Politics*, Washington, DC: Washington Congressional Quarterly Press

Mills, C. Wright (1956) *The Power Elite*, New York, NY: Oxford University Press

Mintzberg, Henry (2004) *Managers Not MBAs: A Hard Look at the Soft Practice of Managing and Management Development*, San Francisco, CA: Berrett-Koehler Publishers Inc.

Moe, Terry (1989) 'The Politics of Bureaucratic Structure', in Chubb and Peterson (q.v.)

Mueller, Robert Kirk (1971) *The Innovation Ethic*, Herndon, VA: American Management Association

Nuwer, Hank (1999) *Wrongs of Passage: Fraternities, Sororities, Hazing and Binge Drinking*, Bloomington, IN: Indiana University Press

Phillips, Kevin (2006) *American Theocracy*, New York, NY: Viking

Rockwell, Llewellyn H. (2005) 'Working Around Leviathan', Ludwig von Mises Institute website www.mises.org (posted 23 June 2005)

Rogers, Everett M. (1983) *Diffusions of Innovations*, New York, NY: Free Press

Schumpeter, Joseph Alois (1989) *Essays on Entrepreneurs, Innovations, Business Cycles, and the Evolution of Capitalism* (ed. Richard V. Clemence), New Brunswick, NJ: Transaction Publishers

Stelzer, Irwin (2002) *From Grave to Cradle: Building a Meritocracy*, London, Social Market Foundation

Stern, Marcus, et al. (2007) *The Wrong Stuff: The Extraordinary Saga of Randy 'Duke' Cunningham, the Most Corrupt Congressman Ever Caught*, New York, NY: Public Affairs

Sullivan, George (2001) *Thomas Edison*, New York, NY: Scholastic Reference

Sutton, Antony C. (1983) *America's Secret Establishment: An Introduction to the Order of Skull and Bones*, Billings, MT: Liberty House

Thompson, Victor A. (1976) *Bureaucracy and Innovation*, Tuscaloosa, AL: University of Alabama Press

United Nations (2005) *Trust in Institutions 2005*, New York, NY: United Nations

Vilcek, Jan and Cronstein, Bruce N. (2006) 'A prize for the foreign-born', in *FASEB Journal 2006*, no. 20, pp. 1281–3

Watts, Steven (2005) *Henry Ford: The People's Tycoon: Henry Ford and the American Century*, New York, NY: Alfred A. Knopf

Zegart, Amy B. (1999) *Flawed by Design: The Evolution of the CIA, JCS, and NSC*, Palo Alto, CA: Stanford University Press

Chapter 5: The Wood-Cut and the Wilderness – On Frontier

Advisory Committee on the Future of the U.S. Space Program (1990) *Report of the Advisory Committee on the Future of the U.S. Space Program*, Washington, DC: US Government Printing Office

Auch, Roger, Taylor, Janis and Acevedo, William (2004) *Urban Growth in American Cities: Glimpses of U.S. Urbanization*, Sioux Falls, SD: US Geological Survey

Beston, Henry (1992) *The Outermost House: A Year of Life on the Great Beach of Cape Cod*, New York, NY: Owl Books

Engel, Matthew (2007) 'Forty Acres and a Pool', in *Financial Times* magazine, 25–6 August

Grund, Francis J. (1837) *The Americans in Their Moral, Social and Political Relations*, 2 vols, London: Longman, Rees, Orme, Brown and Longman

Harding, Benjamin (1819) *Tour through the Western Country*, New London, CT: Samuel Green

Heat-Moon, William Least (1991) *PrairyErth (A Deep Map)*, London: André Deutsch

Horigan, Stephen (1988) *Nature and Culture in Western Discourses*, London: Routledge

Hughes, Robert (1997) *American Visions*, London: Harvill

Italie, Hillel (2007) ' "On the Road," and Jack Kerouac, still inspire young and old', Associated Press, 1 September

Jackson, John Brinckerhoff (1980) *The Necessity of Ruins*, Amhurst: University of Massachusetts Press

Jackson, John Brinckerhoff (1984) *Discovering the Vernacular Landscape*, New Haven and London: Yale University Press

Jackson, William Henry (1970) *Time Exposure*, New York, NY: Cooper Square

Johnson, Michael K. (2002) *Black Masculinity and the Frontier Myth in American Literature*, Norman, OK: University of Oklahoma

Kerouac, Jack (1950) *The Town and the City*, New York, NY: Harcourt Brace

Kerouac, Jack (1991) *On the Road*, New York, NY: Viking Press

Kerouac, Jack (1999) *Atop an Underwood: Early Stories and Other Writings* (ed. Paul Marion), New York, NY: Viking Press

Marsh, George Perkins (1965) *Man and Nature*, Cambridge MA: Harvard University Press

Morgan, Ted (1993) *Wilderness at Dawn: The Settling of the North American Continent*, New York, NY: Simon & Schuster

Moulton, Gary E. (ed.) (2003) *The Lewis and Clark Journals: An American Epic of Discovery* (abridged version), London: University of Nebraska Press

Murray, William H.H. (1869) *Adventures in the Wilderness: or, Camp-Life in the Adirondacks*, Boston, MA: Fields, Osgood

Nash, Roderick Frazier (2001) *Wilderness and the American Mind* (4th edition), London: Yale University Press

Public Lands Information Center (2002) *Lands That We Love: Americans Talk About America's Public Lands*, Albuquerque, NM: Public Lands Information Center

Regal, Brian (2002) *Henry Fairfield Osborn: Race and the Search for the Origins of Man*, Burlington, VT: Ashgate

Reps, John W. (1965) *The Making of Urban America*, Princeton, NJ: Princeton University Press

Reps, John W. (1980) *Town Planning in Frontier America*, Columbia, MO: University of Missouri Press

Roosevelt, Theodore (1889–96) *The Winning of the West*, vols 1–4, New York, NY: G.P. Putnam's Sons

Simpson, John Warfield (2002) *Yearning for the Land*, New York, NY: Pantheon Books

Stynes, Daniel J. and Sun, Ya-Yen (2003) *Economic Impacts of National Park Visitor Spending on Gateway Communities: Systemwide Estimates for 2001*, Washington, DC: NPS Social Science Program

Terkel, Studs (1980) *American Dreams: Lost and Found*, New York, NY: New Press

Thimmesh, Catherine (2006) *Team Moon: How 400,000 People Landed Apollo 11 on the Moon*, Boston, MA: Houghton Mifflin

Thoreau, Henry David (1999) *Walden*, Oxford: Oxford University Press

Tichi, Cecilia (1979) *New World, New Earth: Environmental Reform in American Literature from the Puritans through Whitman*, New Haven, CT: Yale University Press

Tymn, Marshall B. (ed.) (1972) *Thomas Cole's Poetry*, York, PA: Liberty Cap

US Department of Transportation (2001) *The 2001 National Household Travel Survey: Household, Individual, and Vehicle Characteristics*, Washington, DC: US Department of Transportation

Weisman, Alan (2007) *The World Without Us*, New York, NY: Macmillan

Wennersten, John R. (2001) *The Chesapeake: An Environmental Biography*, Baltimore, MD: Maryland Historical Society

White, David A. (1996-2001) *News of the Plains and Rockies 1803–1865: Original narratives of overland travel and adventure selected from the Wagner-Camp and Becker bibliography of Western Americana*, 8 vols, Spokane, WA: Arthur H. Clark Co.

White, Lynn (1967) 'The Historical Roots of Our Ecological Crisis', in *Science*, vol. 155, no. 3767, pp. 1203–7

Whitman, Walt (1949) *Leaves of Grass*, London: J.M. Dent & Sons

Worster, Donald (1979) *Dust Bowl: The Southern Plains in the 1930s*, New York, NY: Oxford University Press

Worster, Donald (ed.) (1988) *The Ends of the Earth: Perspectives on Modern Environmental History*, Cambridge: Cambridge University Press

Zubrin, Robert (1997) *The Case for Mars: The Plan to Settle the Red Planet and Why We Must*, New York, NY: Touchstone

Chapter 6: The Cicada's Wing – On War, Peace and Empire

Bacevich, Andrew J. (2002) *American Empire: The Realities and Consequences of U.S. Diplomacy*, Cambridge, MA: Harvard University Press

Bacevich, Andrew J. (ed.) (2003) *The Imperial Tense: Prospects and Problems of American Empire*, Chicago, IL: Ivan R. Dee

Bellow, Walden (2005) *Dilemmas of Domination: The Unmaking of the American Empire*, New York, NY: Metropolitan Books

Dolman, Everett Carl (2004) *The Warrior State: How Military Organization Structures Politics*, New York, NY: Palgrave Macmillan

Ferguson, Niall (2004) *Colossus: The Price of America's Empire*, New York, NY: Penguin

Fisher, Louis (1995) *Presidential War Power*, Lawrence, KS: University Press of Kansas

Gardiner, Lloyd C. and Young, Marilyn B. (eds) (2005) *The New American Empire*, London: New Press

Haas, William (ed.) (1940) *The American Empire: A Study of the Out-lying Territories of the US*, Chicago, IL: University of Chicago Press

Hartung, William (1999) 'Military-Industrial Complex Revisited: How Weapons Makers Are Shaping US Foreign and Military Policies', in *Foreign Policy in Focus*, 8 June

Human Rights Watch (2008) 'Afghanistan: Civilian Deaths from Airstrikes', interactive feature on www.hrw.org website, 8 September

Johnson, Chalmers (2004) *The Sorrows of Empire: Militarism, Secrecy and the End of the Republic*, New York, NY: Holt

Kagan, Robert (2002) 'Power and Weakness' in *Policy Review*, June–July

Kaplan, Robert D. (2001) *Warrior Politics: Why Leadership Demands a Pagan Ethos*, New York, NY: Random House

Lieven, Anatol (2004) *America Right or Wrong: an Anatomy of American Nationalism*, London: HarperCollins

Maier, Charles S. (2006) *Among Empires: American Ascendancy and Its Predecessors*, Cambridge, MA: Harvard University Press

Mann, Michael (2003) *Incoherent Empire*, London: Verso

May, Earnest (1967) *American Imperialism*, New York, NY: Atheneum

McPherson, James M. (1988) *Battle Cry of Freedom: The Civil War Era*, New York, NY: Oxford University Press

Murphy, Cullen (2007) *Are We Rome? The Fall of an Empire and the Fate of America*, New York, NY: Houghton Mifflin

Ninkovich, Frank (2001) *The United States and Imperialism*, Malden, MA: Blackwell

Nye, Joseph (2002) *The Paradox of American Power*, New York, NY: Oxford University Press

Riencourt, Amaury de (1968) *The American Empire*, New York, NY: Dial Press

Schurmann, Franz (1974) *The Logic of World Power: An Inquiry into the Origins, Currents and Contradictions of World Politics*, New York, NY: Pantheon

White House (2002) *National Security Strategy of the United States of America*, Washington, DC: White House

Wills, Gary (1992) *Lincoln at Gettysburg: The Words that Remade America*, New York, NY: Simon & Schuster

Chapter 7: Liberty Under the Law – On Freedom and Conformity

Arieli, Yehoshua (1964) *Individualism and Nationalism in American Ideoloogy*, Cambridge, MA: Center for the Study of the History of Liberty in America, Harvard University Press

Becker, Carl (1956) *The Declaration of Independence: A Study in the History of Political Ideas*, New York, NY: Alfred A. Knopf

Bosworth, M. and Flavin, J. (eds) (2005) *Regulating Difference: Race, Gender and Punishment in America*, New Brunswick, NJ: Rutgers University Press

Brackenridge, H.H. (1815) *Modern Chivalry: Containing the adventures of a captain, and Teague O'Regan, his servant*, Wilmington, DE: George Metz

Brinkmann, Reinhold and Wolff, Christoph (eds) (1999) *Driven into Paradise: The Musical Migration from Nazi Germany to the US*, Berkeley, CA: University of California Press

Brown, Richard Maxwell (1975) *Strain of Violence: Historical Studies of American Violence and Vigilantism*, New York, NY: Oxford University Press

Chessman, Caryl (1956) *Cell 2455 Death Row*, New York, NY: Longman

Clayton, Bruce (1972) *The Savage Ideal: Intolerance and Intellectual Leadership in the South, 1890–1914*, Baltimore, MD: Johns Hopkins University Press

Cleaver, Eldridge (1969) *Soul on Ice*, London: Jonathan Cape

Cohen, Mark Nathan (1998) *Culture of Intolerance: Chauvinism, Class and Racism in the United States*, New Haven, CT: Yale University Press

Cook, Robert (1998) *Sweet Land of Liberty: The African-American Struggle for Civil Rights in the Twentieth Century*, London: Longman

Dray, P. (2002) *At the Hands of Persons Unknown: The Lynching of Black America*, New York, NY: Random House

Ellis, Joseph J. (1998) *American Sphinx: The Character of Thomas Jefferson*, New York, NY: Vintage Books

Fabian, Johannes (1998) *Moments of Freedom: Anthropology and Popular Culture*, Charlottesville, VI: University Press of Virginia

Feeley, Malcolm M. (1979) *The Process is the Punishment: Handling Cases in a Lower Criminal Court*, New York, NY: Russell Sage Foundation

Foner, Eric (1970) *Free Soil, Free Labor, Free Men: The Ideology of the Republican Party before the Civil War*, New York, NY: Oxford University Press

Foucault, Michel (1979) *Discipline & Punish: The Birth of the Prison*, Harmondsworth: Penguin

Ginzburg, R. (1988) *100 Years of Lynching*, Baltimore, MD: Black Classic

Gray, John (2003) *Straw Dogs: Thoughts on Humans and Other Animals*, London: Granta

Haskins, Jim (1990) *Voodoo & Hoodoo: Their Tradition and Craft as Revealed by Actual Practitioners*, Chelsea, MI: Scarborough House

Himes, Chester (1973) *The Quality of Hurt*, London: Michael Joseph

Himmelfarb, Gertrude (1999) *One Nation, Two Cultures*, New York, NY: Alfred A. Knopf

Hook, Sidney (1962) *The Paradoxes of Freedom*, Berkeley, CA: University of California

Jackson, George (1971) *Soledad Brother: The Prison Letters of George Jackson*, London: Jonathan Cape

Jennings, Al (1922) *Through the Shadows with O. Henry*, London: Duckworth & Co.

Kammen, Michael (1986) *Spheres of Liberty: Changing Perceptions of Liberty in American Culture*, Madison, WI: University of Wisconsin Press

Kauper, Paul G. (1956) *Frontiers of Constitutional Liberty*, Ann Arbor, MI: University of Michigan Law School

Knobel, Dale T. (1996) *America for the Americans: The Nativist Movement in the United States*, New York, NY: Twayne

Laidlaw, James (2002) 'For an Anthropology of Ethics and Freedom', in *Journal of Royal Anthropological Institute*, vol. 8, no. 2

Mandelbaum, Seymour J. (1964) *The Social Setting of Intolerance: The Know-Nothings, The Red Scare, and McCarthyism*, Chicago, IL: Scott, Foresman

Neubauer, David W. (1991) *Judicial Process: Law, Courts, and Politics in the United States*, Pacific Grove, CA: Wadsworth

Radin, Paul (1956) *The Trickster: A Study in American Indian Mythology*, New York, NY: Schocken

Rapson, Richard L. (ed.) (1967) *Individualism and Conformity in the American Character*, Boston, MA: D.C. Heath

Royce, Josiah (1900) *The World and the Individual: Series 1: The Four Historical Conceptions of Being*, New York, NY: Macmillan

Royce, Josiah (1901) *The World and the Individual: Series 2: Nature, Man and the Moral Order*, New York, NY: Macmillan

Ruether, Rosemary Radford (2007) *America, Amerikkka*, London & Oakville, CT: Equinox Publishers

Somkin, Fred (1967) *Unquiet Eagle. Memory and Desire in the Idea of American Freedom. 1815–1860*, Ithaca, NY: Cornell University Press

Twain, Mark (1983) *The Adventures of Tom Sawyer*, London: Scholastic

US Department of Justice (1983) *Report to the Nation on Crime & Justice*, Washington, DC: Bureau of Justice Statistics

Wallace, David Foster (1996) *Infinite Jest*, New York, NY: Little, Brown

Ward, Nathaniel (1647) *The Simple Cobbler of Aggawam*, London

Weinstein, Michael A. (1982) *The Wilderness and the City: American Classical Philosophy as a Moral Quest*, Amherst, MA: University of Massachusetts Press

Wolfe, Tom (1968) *The Electric Kool-Aid Acid Test*, New York, NY: Straus & Giroux

Chapter 8: Angles and Equations – On the Anglosphere

Ackroyd, Peter (2002) *Albion: The Origins of the English Imagination*, London: Chatto & Windus

Alexander, David, and Archer, Simon (2000) 'On the Myth of "Anglo-Saxon" Financial Accounting', in *International Journal of Accounting*, vol. 35, no. 4, October, pp. 539–57

Algeo, John (ed.) (2001) *Cambridge History of the English Language: English in North America*, Cambridge: Cambridge University Press

Atiyah, P.S. and Summers, Robert S. (1987) *Form and Substance in Anglo-American Law. A Comparative Study of Legal Reasoning, Legal Theory, and Legal Institutions*, Oxford: Oxford University Press

Beecher Stowe, Harriet (1854) *Sunny Memories of Foreign Lands*, 2 vols, Boston, MA: Phillips, Sampson

Bennett, James C. (2003) 'The Anglosphere Primer', www.anglosphereinstitute.org

Bennett, James C. (2004) *The Anglosphere Challenge: Why the English-Speaking Nations Will Lead the Way in the Twenty-First Century*, Lanham, MA: Rowman & Littlefield

Berlin, Isaiah (1969) *Four Essays on Liberty*, New York, NY: Oxford University Press

Blythe, Ronald (1998) *Divine Landscapes: A Pilgrimage through Britain's Sacred Places*, Norwich: Canterbury Press

Bruce, Steve (2001) 'Religious Culture in Contemporary Britain', in Morley and Robins (q.v.)

Bryson, Bill (1995) *Notes from a Small Island*, London: HarperCollins

Burk, Kathleen (2007) *Old World, New World: The Story of Britain and America*, London: Little, Brown

Churchill, Winston (1956–58) *A History of the English-Speaking Peoples*, London: Cassell

Colls, Robert (2002) *Identity of England*, New York, NY: Oxford University Press

Coquillette, Daniel R. (2004) *The Anglo-American Legal Heritage*, Durham, NC: Carolina Academic Press

Davies, Norman (1999) *The Isles: A History*, Oxford: Oxford University Press

Dos Passos Sr, John Randolph (1903) *The Anglo-Saxon Century*, New York, NY: Putnam's Sons

Emerson, Ralph Waldo (1856) *English Traits*, New York, NY: Phillips, Sampson

Eurostat (2007) *Statistics in Focus: National Patent Statistics*, Luxembourg: Office for Official Publications of the European Communities

Fischer, David Hackett (1989) *Albion's Seed: Four British Folkways in America*, New York, NY: Oxford University Press

Fox, Kate (2004) *Watching the English*, London: Hodder & Stoughton

Franklin, Benjamin (1784) *Two Tracts: Information to Those Who Would Remove to America. And, Remarks Concerning the Savages of North America*, London: J. Stockdale

Friedman, Lawrence M. (2002) *American Law in the 20th Century*, New Haven, CT: Yale University Press

Gowers, Andrew (2006) *Gowers Review of Intellectual Property*, London: HM Treasury

Hartz, Louis (1964) *The Founding of New Societies*, New York, NY: Harcourt, Brace & World

Hilton, Matthew (2003) *Consumerism in Twentieth Century Britain: The Search for a Historical Movement*, Cambridge: Cambridge University Press

Hitchens, Christopher (2004) *Blood, Class and Empire: The Enduring Anglo-American Relationship*, New York, NY: Nation

Julios, Christina (2008) *Contemporary British Identity: English Language, Migrants and Public Discourse*, Aldershot: Ashgate

Kagan, Robert (2003) *Of Paradise and Power: America and Europe in the New World Order*, New York, NY: Alfred A. Knopf

Kennedy, Duncan (1979) 'The Structure of Blackstone's Commentaries', in *Buffalo Law Review*, vol. 28, pp. 209–11, 381–2

Kumar, Krishan (2003) *The Making of English National Identity*, Cambridge: Cambridge University Press

Letwin, Dr Shirley Robin (1993) *The Anatomy of Thatcherism*, New Brunswick, NJ: Transaction

Lipset, Seymour Martin (1997) *American Exceptionalism: A Double-Edged Sword*, New York, NY: W.W. Norton

Longley, Clifford (2002) *Chosen People: The Big Idea That Shaped England and America*, London: Hodder & Stoughton

Lunt, Peter and Livingstone, Sonia (1992) *Mass Consumption and Personal Identity: Everyday Economic Experience*, Buckingham: Open University Press

Lury, Celia (1996) *Consumer Culture*, Cambridge: Polity Press

Macfarlane, Robert (2007) *The Wild Places*, London: Granta

Madsen, Deborah L. (1998) *American Exceptionalism*, Jackson, MS: University Press of Mississippi

Morgan, Kenneth O. (2001) *Britain Since 1945: The People's Peace* (3rd edition), Oxford: Oxford University Press

Morley, David and Robins, Kevin (eds) (2001) *British Cultural Identities: Geography, Nationality, and Identity*, Oxford: Oxford University Press

Organization for Economic Co-operation and Development (2001) *Knowledge and Skills for Life*, Paris: Organization for Economic Co-operation and Development

Orwell, George (1944) *The English People*, London: Collins

Paine, Thomas (2000) *Common Sense; and The Rights of Man*, London: Phoenix Press

Rawls, John (1993) *Political Liberalism*, New York, NY: Columbia University Press

Read, Allen Walker (1934) 'An Obscenity Symbol', in *American Speech*, December 1934

Read, Allen Walker (1963a) 'The First Stage in the History of O.K.', in *American Speech*, February 1963

Read, Allen Walker (1963b) 'The Second Stage in the History of O.K.', in *American Speech*, May 1963

Read, Allen Walker (1963c) 'Successive Revisions in the History of O.K.', in *American Speech*, in December 1963

Read, Allen Walker (1964a) 'The Folklore of O.K.', in *American Speech*, February 1964

Read, Allen Walker (1964b) 'Later Stages in the History of O.K.', in *American Speech*, May 1964

Roberts, Andrew (2006) *A History of the English-Speaking Peoples Since 1900*, London: HarperCollins

Roberts, Andrew and Sykes, Allen (2009) *A Compelling Necessity: The Case for Increasing the Defence Budget despite the Present Severe Economic Crisis* (with a foreword by Irwin Stelzer), London: UK National Defence Association

Rogers, David and McLeod, John (eds) (2004) *The Revision of Englishness*, Manchester: Manchester University Press

Sampson, Anthony (1962) *Anatomy of Britain*, London: Hodder & Stoughton

Scruton, Roger (2000) *England: An Elegy*, London: Chatto & Windus

Seitz, Raymond (1999) *Over Here*, London: Phoenix

Shanks, Michael (1972) *The Stagnant Society*, London: Penguin

Storry, Mike and Childs, Peter (1997) (ed.) *British Cultural Identities*

Sutton Trust (2003) *Nobel Prizes: The Changing Pattern of Awards*, London: Sutton Trust

Tomkins, Richard (2006) 'Transatlantic Drift', in *Financial Times*, 8 April

Van Wormer, Katherine (1999) 'Harm Induction vs Harm Reduction: A comparison of American and British Approaches to Drug Use', in *Journal of Offender Rehabilitation*, vol. 29, nos 1–2, pp. 35–48

War-Book-of-Facts, The (1914), London: A.W. Shaw

Whitman, Walt (1949) *Leaves of Grass*, London: J.M. Dent & Sons

Word, David L., Coleman, Charles D., Nunziata, Robert and Kominski, Robert (2008) *Demographic Aspects of Surnames from Census 2000*, Washington, DC: US Census Bureau

Wright, Patrick (1985) *On Living in an Old Country*, London: Verso

Afterword: Beyond Hobbes and Hobbits

Goldberg, Bernard (2009) *A Slobbering Love Affair: The True (and Pathetic) Story of the Torrid Romance Between Barack Obama and the Mainstream Media*, New York, NY: Regnery Publishing Inc

Hartz, Louis (1964) *The Founding of New Societies*, New York, NY: Harcourt, Brace and World

Levin, Mark R. (2009) *Liberty and Tyranny: A Conservative Manifesto*, New York, NY: Threshold Editions

Obama, Barack (1995) *Dreams from My Father*, New York, NY: Three Rivers Press

Obama, Barack (2008) *The Audacity of Hope: Thoughts on Reclaiming the American Dream*, Edinburgh: Canongate Books

Rawls, John (1991) *A Theory of Justice* (revised edition), Oxford: Oxford University Press

Rawls, John (1993) *Political Liberalism*, New York, NY: Columbia University Press

Rawls, John (2001) *The Law of Peoples*, Cambridge, MA: Harvard University Press

Skinner, Quentin (2008) *Hobbes and Republican Liberty*, Cambridge: Cambridge University Press

Index